JOHN HONDERICH

D1130364

Arctic Imperative:
Is Canada Losing the North?

UNIVERSITY OF TORONTO PRESS
Toronto Buffalo London

© University of Toronto Press 1987
Toronto Buffalo London
Printed in Canada

ISBN 0-8020-5763-2

Canadian Cataloguing in Publication Data

Honderich, John, 1946–
   Arctic imperative

   Includes bibliographical references and index.
   ISBN 0-8020-5763-2

   1. Arctic regions – Strategic aspects. 2. Canada –
   Military policy. I. Title.

   US601.A7H6 1987   355'.0330719   C87-094758-3

For Katherine

Contents

viii   Contents

Preface

The Arctic Imperative is a wedding of two of my fascinations: the Arctic and strategic affairs. My attachment to the Canadian Arctic began when I was a youth reading of the exploits of RCMP Sergeant Henry Larsen and his voyages through the Northwest Passage in the *St Roch*. My first trip to the North came in 1967 as part of my own centennial project to see my country. Later I was to return several times, on some occasions working as transportation director for Richard Rohmer's misunderstood but essentially noble Mid-Canada Corridor Development Plan in the early 1970s and several times just for fun, including one New Year's Eve spent in Frobisher Bay (now Iqaluit).

My interest in strategic affairs was first whetted as bureau chief with *The Toronto Star* in Ottawa and later grew into a fascination when, as the *Star*'s Washington correspondent, I watched Ronald Reagan begin his presidency. When Reagan proclaimed that there was a 'window of vulnerability' in which North America might be vulnerable to a nuclear attack, journalistic instinct and intense curiosity led me to study and enquire about the intricacies of strategic affairs. Once I'd started, I became fully 'hooked,' I suspect for ever. Since Canada had been relatively uninvolved in the superpower confrontation, my interest remained academic.

However, the Strategic Defense Initiative, known more commonly as Star Wars, was to change all that. Watching Reagan first announce the plan and later realizing that its development would in all likelihood involve Canada, particularly its Arctic, I became more fascinated and concerned. What did this plan mean for Canada? Was our Arctic to become fully militarized as an offshoot of the superpowers' vying for supremacy in the Arctic?

The later controversial passage of the *Polar Sea* through the Northwest Passage and the recent flurry of arms-control proposals reinforced my feeling that Canada is approaching a watershed over the use of its Arctic. Unfortunately, the debate on the future of our North, until very recently, had been taken up by very few.

With the subsequent generous assistance of the Canadian Institute for International Peace and Security in Ottawa, I set out to do more research. My travels took me to Ottawa, Calgary, Montreal, Washington, Norway, Denmark, West Germany, Belgium, London, and Cambridge to meet with that dedicated cadre of experts interested in both the Arctic and strategic affairs. I also interviewed five of Canada's former defence ministers along with the current minister, Perrin Beatty, as he surveyed Canadian troops in Norway as part of the process leading up to the White Paper on Defence. Nearly all the research and the writing of this book, however, preceded the publication of that White Paper.

I was particularly inspired by and am indebted to two individuals, William Arkin of the Washington-based Institute for Policy Studies and Dr Franklyn Griffiths of the University of Toronto. Their research, dedication, and clarity of thought on the subject-matter proved invaluable.

The work, largely academic, of those few other Canadians intrigued by the Arctic and its future was also of great help. It is partly through their collective insight that it became apparent to me that Canada had to rethink its policy in regard to its Arctic. If this book can successfully draw attention to the issue, then one hopes their work will be more appreciated.

Among others who provided encouragement and help at critical times were Ray Timson and Mary Deane Shears, who helped arrange a leave of absence from the *Star*, Nancy Gordon, Abe Rotstein, Dr George Govier, Trudy Govier, John Hutcheson, Steve Handelman, Richard Gwyn, Sandra Gwyn, Alan Brew, Christopher Walker, and Kevin McMahon.

A special acknowledgement is owed Virgil Duff, my publisher, who on the basis of a letter and a bare-bones outline, took a flyer on publishing this book. I would also like to acknowledge the generous and kind assistance of the Walter and Duncan Gordon Charitable Foundation.

Finally, I wish to thank most of all my wife, Katherine Govier, without whose patience, encouragement, critical eye, and superb editing skills this project would not have been possible. It is to her that I dedicate this book.

JOHN HONDERICH
London, May 1987

ARCTIC IMPERATIVE:
IS CANADA LOSING THE NORTH?

1

The age of the Arctic

The age of the Arctic is coming. After centuries of benign neglect, the once-forbidding Arctic is now the scene of developments that are increasingly drawing the world's attention. Evidence of this transformation appears across the spectrum. On the economic front, the exploitation of the region's untapped wealth has already begun. With it have come the risks of Arctic navigation and Arctic pollution. On the security front, the Arctic Ocean has been jolted into becoming the world's newest military frontier as the two superpowers confront each other, submarine to submarine. Meanwhile, research and testing continue on futuristic lasers and particle-beam weapons for the controversial Star Wars plan, which envisages explosive-missile interception in Arctic airspace. On the arms-control front, a sense of urgency over Arctic disarmament has evolved in response to this worrisome new strategic environment. Finally, on the technological front, man is channelling his energies to devising exotic if now utopian ways to open up the Arctic. One u.s. oilman even talked of constructing a new superhighway - World Route One - built of granular ice across the Arctic ice-cap, with branches leading to Russia, Europe, and Greenland. With it would come a city - Polestar - located right at the North Pole, whose residents would live mainly on food processed from Arctic fish and shrimp.[1]

No longer can Canada afford to ignore these developments. For too long this country has been an Arctic nation by default.[2] Despite our geography, most Canadians don't think of their country as an Arctic state. We're somehow schizophrenic about the Arctic. At one level, the North is part of us, part of our self-definition and occasionally the object of our passion. Most often, though, we simply forget about it, remain doggedly unaware of what is happening there, and are disinclined even

The *Polar Sea*, in the Passage, 1985 (Canapress Photo Service)

to visit. Then, once every decade or so, something happens that demands our attention. Interest peaks temporarily, but then subsides with predictable rapidity. In the late 1940s we responded to the cry to eradicate disease; in the late 1950s, to the threat of Soviet bombers over the Pole; in the late 1960s to a challenge to sovereignty over our waters; and now, to fears for both our sovereignty and our security.

The federal government, as if acting in concert with this ambivalence, has rarely shown more than marginal interest in the Arctic. Most initiatives have taken shape in response to these once-every-decade concerns, not in anticipation of them. For example, the two major pieces of legislation in the past two decades – the anti-pollution law[3] and the encompassing of the Arctic archipelago to ensure Canadian sovereignty[4] – were introduced directly on the heels of an unwanted foreign intrusion into the Northwest Passage. The first was the 1969 passage of the reinforced supertanker *Manhattan* and the second was the controversial 1985 transit of the u.s. Coast Guard cutter *Polar Sea*. In each case, the highly publicized intrusion cut sharply into the Canadian psyche. There was an outpouring of energy directed by a desire to 'do something' to reaffirm our northern heritage. In almost rhapsodic tones, the litany of the northern challenge or the northern vision was dusted off and replayed. Then, as before, interest waned and once again the Arctic was relegated to its usual low status.

In the past, Canada has been able to get away with this apathy, partly out of luck and partly because foreign interest in the Arctic was equally limited. But those times are gone. Canadians can no longer afford the luxury of simply reacting to events. This book is both a call and a plan for action. Its thesis is simple yet urgent: the time has come for a new national will and a new made-in-Canada manifesto to meet the Arctic imperative. If we want to ensure that *we* control how the Arctic is used and *we* determine how its security and peacefulness are preserved, then the time to act is now. But if we continue to fall prey to our collective Arctic apathy, events may soon overwhelm us. Make no mistake – the stakes are that high.

First, our political sovereignty is being threatened over the Northwest Passage. Canada considers this fabled water-way to be under its exclusive control. We feel we have the right to determine how, when, and under what conditions any vessel can travel through the passage. However, the United States does not agree. It argues that the passage is an international strait through which its vessels can move unannounced and unimpeded. Other countries may concur with that view, but only the United States, in the infamous cases of the *Manhattan* and *Polar Sea*, has directly challenged Canadian authority. In both instances, the United States made it a point not to seek prior Canadian permission to ply the passage. Controversy over this issue reached such a pitch that it jumped to the top of the Canada–United States bilateral agenda in early 1987. In a visit to Ottawa early in that year, u.s. president Ronald Reagan promised to 'inject new impetus' into resolving the dispute.[5] Despite this pledge and Prime Minister Mulroney's declaration that the passage is ours 'lock, stock and icebergs,' Canadian sovereignty over this water-way is far from secure.

Second, risks are being posed by the exploitation of the Arctic's resources, particularly its oil and gas. Some of the specialized technology has been put to the test, towering rigs have been built, and recent drilling has rekindled oilmen's hopes that predictions of Arctic gushers may be true. On their drawing-boards, the oil giants have plans for mammoth reinforced tankers the size of a football field to transport Arctic crude. With ongoing lower world prices for oil, the prospects of an Arctic oil boom are still down the road. However, one oil giant, GW Ltd, has announced it may not wait. If the necessary approvals can be secured, it could start part-time commercial delivery of Arctic crude in 1988.[7] Then will come the challenges of pollution and navigation control.

It has become a truism, but one worth repeating, that the fragile environment of the North is particularly susceptible to the ravages of an oil spill or a nuclear accident. The peculiarly cold conditions can trap pollutants, effectively 'deep freezing' and prolonging their harmful effects on both wildlife and the landscape. Anti-pollution laws are in place, but the means to fully enforce them are not. In fact, Canada does not possess a single vessel capable of patrolling its Arctic region year round.[8] Those few than can operate in moderately ice-clogged waters are already stretched to the limit with other tasks. Navigation in the North is already a reality; the prospect of greater traffic, a near certainty. Will Canada be ready to control it?

Third, our security is being threatened. Not since the heyday of Cold war tensions in the 1950s, with the Soviet bomber threat, has Arctic security been so topical. With leaps in both nuclear-submarine and cruise-missile technology, the Arctic Ocean has suddenly emerged as a new theatre for superpower confrontation. On the Soviet side of the ocean, the bulk of the Soviet giant ballistic-missile–carrying submarines are deployed. As part of a new strategy, U.S. attack submarines regularly probe northern Soviet seas. Closer to home, in Canada's own Arctic waters, U.S. subs routinely roam.[9] Canadian defence officials warn of the threat of Soviet subs armed with new long-range cruise missiles penetrating Canadian territory.[10] And, fears of new Soviet bombers carrying payloads of more accurately, longer-ranged cruise missiles have prompted Canada and the United States to develop a new warning system atop the edge of Canada's northern mainland. The days of a benign Arctic are over.

Then, we are facing the dilemma of Star Wars. The controversial U.S. missile defence system may produce the biggest crisis ever in Canada–United States security relations. Although still in the planning stages, the intricate multi-layered defence network envisaged by the Pentagon virtually demands Canada's involvement, particularly its northern territory and airspace. Although no formal request has yet been made to Ottawa, not-so-subtle hints that Canada's Arctic is essential to the plan have come from the U.S. defence secretary[11] and many below him. During his 1987 Ottawa visit, President Reagan repeated his resolve to carry through with Star Wars.[12] If Canada is to stay out of the program, the decision will be a tough one and may have enormous consequences. But if Canada is to have a choice, planning must begin now.

The Star Wars dilemma leads directly to the challenge of Arctic arms control. In the past, Canada has let the United States do its arms-control talking for it, out of both loyalty and necessity. Now, the possibility of Star Wars and a rapidly changing strategic environment in the Arctic may cause Canadian and U.S. interests to diverge in the North. Canada has specific concerns, particularly about weapons systems, such as the cruise missile, that directly threaten Canadian territory. Most Canadians are not eager to see an arms buildup in their North. Nor are they keen to have their backyard used as a new superpower war zone. The question is how to prevent both, peacefully.

Finally, there is the challenge of the Arctic itself, its secrets and its hidden treasures. Technology is unfolding on all fronts, from fish-spawning techniques to designing Arctic drilling bits and high-powered ice-breakers. Around the Arctic Ocean, the countries of the circumpolar world are pressing at their geographic limits to make Arctic life and exploration more of a reality. Canada has much to offer. It also has much to learn, particularly from the Soviets and the Scandinavians.

When considered together, these issues present Canada with an agenda for action. But it is an agenda that demands more than the piecemeal approach taken by governments in the past. The Arctic is more than a geographic region, more than a security problem, more than a sovereignty issue. The agenda for action demands an integrated approach, one that acknowledges the interrelatedness of issues. For example, full sovereignty over the Northwest Passage is intrinsically linked to oil and gas exploration, new ice-breaker technology, and clandestine U.S. submarine transits through the water-way. A secure Canadian Arctic requires not only a new air warning system but also satellite technology, submarines, arms control, and co-operation among our circumpolar neighbours. A decision to stay out of Star Wars could demand a complete redefinition of our defence priorities, both in North America and in Europe. In other words, an integrated approach is absolutely vital to dealing with any one of the problems.

For Canada, this approach will require fundamental changes in thinking and planning. The chapters that follow will analyse the issues – sovereignty, economic development, security, Star Wars, Canada's membership in NATO, arms control, and foreign policy – in greater detail. Proposals will be put forward with the goal of formulating a new integrated northern policy for Canada. It is time that Canada became aware of its Arctic and reached out to its circumpolar neighbours. The Arctic provides Canada with its final great challenge in the twentieth century. Are we up to it?

2

Canada: victim of a Mercator mind-set

As a populace, Canadians share an unfortunate misconception about our country's geography. We are victims of a 'Mercator mind-set.' When we picture Canada on a standard flat world map based on Mercator's projection, the true North, strong and free, is always at the upper left-hand side, tapering off to end abruptly at the top edge. Parts of the Arctic archipelago, particularly Ellesmere Island, are often cut off. The difference between land, sea, and island often blurs. But when the globe is viewed from the 'top down' with the North Pole at the centre – as shown in the accompanying map – Canada's geography is seen from an entirely different, more accurate, perspective. No longer, for example, is the Soviet Union a world away on the other side of the map. It is directly across the Arctic Ocean, much closer to Canada than any other part of Europe. Also, our 'forgotten' neighbour, Greenland, is virtually cheek to jowl with our eastern flank.

Furthermore, from this circumpolar perspective, Canada is a significant geographic power. If one were to stand right at the Pole, rotate and survey the horizon, one would discover Canada occupies almost 25 per cent of the territory. The Soviet Union would take up about 40 per cent, Alaska less than 10 per cent, and Norway about 6 per cent.[1] Despite our membership in this select group of eight circumpolar nations (the others being Finland, Sweden, Iceland, and Denmark (Greenland)[2], Canada has made precious few efforts to forge special ties with any of them, other than the United States. While we may feel a special affinity for and even have the same outlook as the Scandinavians, we haven't done much about it. Our external affairs department, unlike those in all Scandinavian countries, has no special division keeping track of relations in the

The circumpolar world

circumpolar world. We don't have a resident diplomat in either Iceland or Greenland[3], and in 1987 there was an attempt to shut down our embassy in Finland for economic reasons.[4] Only a storm of protest in both Canada and Finland changed Ottawa's mind.[5]

Probably the most revealing example of our 'Mercator mind-set' came with the government's 1986 green paper on foreign policy. In a dramatic flourish on the first page of the document, Canada is described as an Arctic nation and 'special because of it.' Yet on no subsequent page are the Arctic and the circumpolar region mentioned again. Virtually every other region of the world, no matter how far distant, receives some special attention in the document. The Arctic is simply ignored. It is little wonder that the green paper came under attack from those who questioned how long Canada would continue to neglect 'the only international regional system to which we really belong: the circumpolar system.'[7]

If Canada is ever to develop a truly integrated Arctic policy, this mind-set will have to change and with it Canada's traditional outlook on foreign and defence policy. Old patterns, prejudices, and allegiances will have to be held in abeyance while the country conducts a total reappraisal of its priorities, based on domestic need. This is precisely the area where the Arctic challenges facing Canada must be given precedence, not shunted aside as was done in the past. Once the priorities are set, then Canada should work out from there. There is no reason why Canada's new priorities must necessarily conflict with our commitments to our allies. However, if they do, Canada must be prepared to stand firm. Surely it is up to us to develop a made-in-Canada policy suited to our needs, cognizant of our geography and not tailored primarily to please our allies. As one of Canada's leading Arctic experts, University of Toronto professor Franklyn Griffiths, puts it:

I would say this country is long overdue to establish its own independent perspective, one that reflects Canadian security needs and one that is suited to the environment we live in today. As I've said before, we're driving into the future with a rear view mirror and attitudes that reflect more the world after World War ii rather than today's needs. In those times and shortly thereafter, the Arctic wasn't on anyone's strategic agenda. But times have changed. Unfortunately, Canadian policy hasn't.[8]

Before examining the principles on which a new northern policy should be based, one should understand some of the debates of the past, how the Arctic has been treated, and how our Mercator mind-set has permeated our thinking.

Experience shows that the Arctic traditionally gets the short end of the stick. Be it in terms of economics, defence, trade, technology, or arms control, our attention has been consistently focused elsewhere. Strung out laterally as we are, most of us within hailing distance of the u.s. frontier, our attention is unalterably transfixed southward. South is the direction in which we trade and the direction from which we receive much of our inspiration and frustration. There are so few of us living north of latitude 60 degrees, we can barely relate to the Arctic. Our weather maps don't show it much of the time. Our newscasts and newspapers rarely mention it, save for the occasional disaster, oil strike, or foreign intrusion. And, even the final report of the special joint Senate-Commons committee formed to study Canada's foreign policy – which specifically referred to the need for a new 'Arctic' dimension – has on its cover a map of the world with the northern half of Canada's Arctic archipelago left off.[9]

Nor has there ever been much of a national will to 'go north' and stake a firm claim to lands the fathers of confederation strove to incorporate. Canada, it is often said, is a nation of three oceans, but only two are used. We have the world's longest coastline, with the waters of the Arctic archipelago and the Northwest Passage alone accounting for some 6.3 million kilometres of shoreline.[10] Yet we have no independent means of knowing who is intruding into either our waters or our airspace. We have to rely on the United States to tell us. Our navy does not possess a single vessel capable of operating in Arctic waters except during the summer season. We don't have any submarines that can navigate under ice despite the fact one-third of our territorial waters is ice-covered most of the year.[11] And, only one of our current fleet of ice-breakers can manage in moderately ice-clogged waters.[12] Clearly, we have only the minimum ability to enforce our strict pollution laws and protect our exclusive Arctic Fishing Zone, both of which were heralded as signs of our commitment to preserve our North.

Despite this situation, there is little outcry or acknowledged sense of shame that we somehow have our priorities mixed up. In fact, often it is quite the opposite. When the government announced plans in 1985 for a powerful new ice-breaker, capable of giving Canada its first year-round presence in the Northwest Passage, there were snickers of derision in many quarters about the $450 million price-tag.[13] But not a whimper has been heard about the $1.1 billion being spent on a low-level air defence system in West Germany. Our Northern Region Headquarters based in Yellowknife, which is responsible for overseeing the defence of more than one-third of the total area of the country, has an annual operating budget of just $2 million.[14] That is just one-five-thousandth of the total defence budget. Yet we're going to spend double that amount, or $4 million, on a new hospital for our troops in West Germany in 1987.[15]

It is probably in the security area where the effects of our Mercator mind-set are most apparent. Our natural tendency, if not fixation, has been to look eastwards across the Atlantic to Europe. We dispatched troops there during two world wars and we still maintain almost seven thousand military personnel in West Germany. Since the last war, the prevailing view in Ottawa has been that the greatest threat to Canadian security lies in a war-torn Europe. So, through NATO, we have pledged to keep troops in West Germany, to send five thousand troops to Norway in a crisis (now under review),[16] to send forces to Denmark in similar periods of crisis, and to patrol the north-west quadrant of the Atlantic Ocean. Because the military threat to the Arctic has been viewed as marginal, the only real threat being that of a nuclear attack, we keep on average only one thousand military personnel in northern Canada at any one time. In fact, a Senate committee estimated that if Canada did send all the troops it has promised to dispatch to Europe, there would only be two thousand to three thousand front-line troops left to defend all of Canada.[17] While there has been little debate on the relative military threat to Europe as compared to that directed at the Arctic, at least until recently, there has been controversy on how Canada's military has been ordered to divide its energies in tending to both areas.

Keeping Canada secure is obviously one of the military's primary jobs. So is asserting control and sovereignty over our land. When the Trudeau government came to assign defence priorities in 1971, pride of place dictated that sovereignty protection be given top priority.[18] Defence of North America was second, and our commitment to Europe placed third. Yet, in the ongoing tug of war between the 'Atlanticists' who are wedded to our European commitments and the 'Northernists' who want the sovereignty role to be emphasized, the 'Atlanticists' have clearly won out.

While it is virtually impossible to break down defence figures on a Europe-vs-the-Arctic basis, the accompanying chart reveals startling differences in basic expenditure. For purposes of comparison, the current operating budget for maintaining Canada's Northern Region Headquarters was compared with the operating budget for keeping our forces in Europe. Over the last four years, the European budget has been roughly five hundred times greater! Some critics may argue that the Northern Region budget does not include monies spent on such Arctic-related matters as NORAD's air defence system, occasional Arctic military manoeuvres, and our regular sovereignty patrols by long-range Aurora

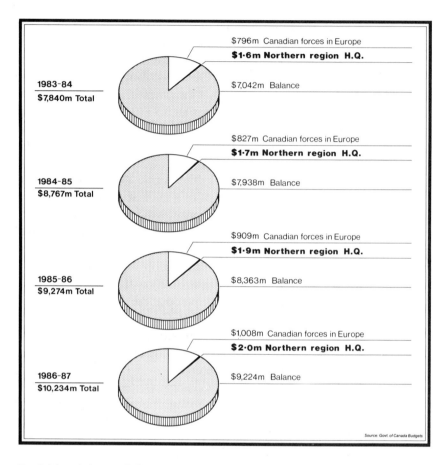

$796m Canadian forces in Europe
$1·6m Northern region H.Q.
1983-84
$7,840m Total
$7,042m Balance

$827m Canadian forces in Europe
$1·7m Northern region H.Q.
1984-85
$8,767m Total
$7,938m Balance

$909m Canadian forces in Europe
$1·9m Northern region H.Q.
1985-86
$9,274m Total
$8,363m Balance

$1,008m Canadian forces in Europe
$2·0m Northern region H.Q.
1986-87
$10,234m Total
$9,224m Balance

Source: Govt. of Canada Budgets

Partial breakdown of Canada's defence budget

patrol aircraft. By the same token, the European budget does not include such expenditures as the $1.1 billion low-level defence system slated for West Germany and the hundreds of millions being spent on buying CF-18s for use in Europe. The debate will rage on. However, the fact remains that despite its top billing, sovereignty protection, particularly in the Arctic, has suffered.

It is precisely this state of affairs that prompted the extraordinary spectacle in late 1986 of the town burghers of Inuvik voting to ask the United States to set up a 'military presence' in their region and to start drilling in waters of the Beaufort Sea claimed by Canada.[19] Smarting from the proposed shut down of the Canadian Forces base in Inuvik and the loss of seven hundred jobs, the town's politicians were obviously out to make a point. But the comments of John Hill, mayor of this community of 2,900, which is closer to the Soviet Union than it is to Edmonton, are illuminating: 'More than 90 per cent of the people here think the federal government ... has offered up the North to anyone who wants it. We feel completely undefended.'[20] Daniel Holman, operator of the town's newspaper and sponsor of the motion, expressed similar feelings. 'It's just another small mark of our frustration about living here. What we're saying basically is that we've lost faith in the federal government to represent Canadians living in the North.'[21]

Why is this attitude so prevalent? Why does Canada continue to govern its North in a manner once described by former prime minister Louis St Laurent as 'a state of absent mindedness'?[22] 'Mercator mind-set' may be part of it. But more likely this mind-set is a manifestation of a much larger collective schizophrenia about the Arctic. The reasons for this attitude have puzzled Arctic specialists who point out that other circumpolar countries, particularly the Soviet Union and the three Scandinavian countries, have all taken their Arctic heritage much more seriously.

One view is that Canadians have inherited a fundamentally 'British view' of the Arctic. 'This is a view that sees the Arctic as sublime, somehow absolutely sensationally beautiful, unsullied,' according to Franklyn Griffiths. 'It must be protected and yet, it is awesome and terrifying. It repels us and makes us fearful.'[23] This dual image, he adds, causes Canadians to be moved to act if the Arctic is any way threatened. But as soon as the threat dissipates, then uncertainty and ambivalence take over. This theory would certainly explain the once-every-decade phenomenon of Canadians rising up in protest over some potential danger to the Arctic, be it medical, political, environmental, or strategic. It also helps to put in perspective how any political call to come to the aid of the Arctic usually strikes a responsive, if unsustained, chord. With his exhortation of a new 'Northern vision' in the late 1950s, John Diefenbaker swept to one of the greatest electoral victories in Canadian political history. Sadly, the vision turned out to be little more than election rhetoric. Any special interest Diefenbaker had in the Arctic was soon submerged by other political woes. Canada's emotional links to the Arctic also surfaced in the mid-1970s during Mr Justice Tom Berger's one-man royal commission to study a possible gas pipeline down the Mackenzie River Valley. Confounding all prior expectations, this unique commission attracted nation-wide interest and helped focus attention on the environmental threat as well as posing the basic question: what do Canadians want to do with their North? However, then as before, interest soon subsided.

Although the peaks of interest are often fleeting, they seem to belie the arguments of some that Canadians simply don't care about the North. University of Toronto professor Jack Granatstein, for one, suggests that the increasing Americanization of Canada over the past two decades has meant Canadians have come to accept whatever the Americans want to do with our Arctic.[24] He argues, for example, that any u.s. military presence in our North doesn't particularly upset many Canadians 'because very few Canadians have ever been to the north, go to the north, know where it is. I don't think that matters very much to most Canadian people. It should, but it doesn't.' On one level, there appears to be some truth to this view. For example, it has been a basic assumption of Canadian defence policy that our country is just too big to defend by ourselves. Since the late 1950s, Canada has joined in a collective arrangement with the United States for defence of North America and, for the most part, the Americans have paid for and conducted the defence of our North. Our policy has been, in the words of former defence minister Paul Hellyer, 'to do everything the Americans will pay for.'[25] That is why the complaint is sometimes heard in u.s. circles that Canada is getting a 'free ride' in defence. It is a ride most Canadians take for granted and accept.

There is, however, another dimension to this supposed indifference. As a nation of pioneers, we opened up the country westwards, keeping basically within the confines of workable land and forests. With our geographical immensity and limited population, there has been no pressing need to push to our northern limits. However, our concerns about any foreign intrusion or threat to the Arctic suggest we haven't forgotten the North altogether. For most Canadians there has simply not been sufficient reason to focus our attention there on an ongoing basis. In short, we haven't had to care. In the defence area, for example, we have become accustomed to the Americans providing a protective umbrella. So long as u.s. and Canadian aims in the North were perceived to be identical, there has been no reason to be concerned. This passivity has been fostered, in turn, by successive federal governments.

If Canadians are shown that the Arctic is, indeed, threatened and that Canadian and u.s. interests in the region are no longer the same, then we will have reason to care and that sublimated passion will likely rise again. The furore over the *Polar Sea* and the subsequent determination to guarantee Canadian sovereignty over the Northwest Passage offer proof that that is the case. So do the many worries about the u.s. Star Wars program which surfaced when a parliamentary committee took a cross-country pulse of the nation in 1985. So does the rising tide of support for some arms-control measures, such as nuclear-weapons-free zone, to stem the growing militarization of the Arctic. We probably are schizophrenic about the Arctic, but our concern can still become predominant. In other words, the will is there to be tapped.

To reawaken this concern, however, Canadians will have to understand why the Arctic matters. For example, on the question of Arctic sovereignty, Judge Berger makes a good point when he says 'I think we have to ask ourselves: sovereignty for what? ... If Canada is going to assert its sovereignty over the Arctic archipelago and over the waters of the Northwest Passage, it ought to have a good reason.'[26] One might add: defence for what? It is hard to justify spending the hundreds of millions of dollars required for military hardware in the North solely on the basis of some hyped-up national pride. The series of Arctic challenges already mentioned does provide ample reason for Canadians to conclude that the Arctic matters. But on what philosophical foundation should an integrated policy for the North be based?

The bedrock of that foundation must necessarily be keeping the North peaceful and secure. There is certainly nothing to be gained from making Canada's Arctic a new arena for military tensions or a major staging area for weapons systems. Those who live there certainly don't want to see themselves as targets. Nor is there anything to be gained from the superpower confrontation taking place next door, in the Arctic Ocean. Canada must obviously take whatever steps are needed to defend itself; but security can be won in several ways. One way is through military might, another through effective arms control, and still another combines elements from both extremes. Surely the preferable stance for Canada is to adopt that third option: to take whatever limited military steps are required but ultimately to try to keep the Arctic as it is. For centuries the region has been peaceful. Canada should try to keep it that way.

As a necessary corollary, Canada has a vested interest in maintaining peace in the circumpolar world. There is little solace in keeping peace in your own backyard if the neighbourhood around you is engulfed in war. The circumpolar region is unique in that both superpowers are geographical members. They are also confronting each other in the region in an increasingly menacing fashion. Again, Canada has the choice of joining in the growing militarization, seeking arms-control solutions, or taking a blend of the two. Ever since 1978, Canada's adopted policy of not allowing the permanent stationing of nuclear weapons on its soil has won wide support. It is also the stated policy of all other non-superpower countries of the circumpolar world. While necessarily mindful of its military commitments and alliance preference, Canada still has much to gain if the nuclear activity in the circumpolar world is kept to a minimum. If that restriction can be formalized in some treaty or agreement, all the better.

A third level of the foundation should be a commitment to preserve the Arctic environment as it is. Here most Canadians can learn from their fellow Inuit who speak most passionately of their responsibility to pass on unpolluted what they have inherited. The peculiarly sensitive nature of the Arctic environment makes this task all the most important and difficult. Fortunately, Canada has already had the foresight to pass tough anti-pollution laws to protect the North. Unfortunately, the means aren't there to enforce them. It has also recently been argued that for the entire Arctic, environmental security is as important as military security.[27] Thus, it is critical that Canada seek agreements with other circumpolar countries to limit and control possible region-wide environmental hazards. Closer to home, Canada must also be conscious of the potential for pollution in the Northwest Passage and other Arctic waters as Arctic navigation steps up. In order to put such protection in place, we must first secure complete sovereignty over these waters.

The fourth level, related somewhat to the third, is the need for Canada to regulate the pace of economic development in the Arctic. It is only a question of time before full-scale exploitation of Arctic resources, particularly oil and gas, begins. That development will have wide-ranging ramifications for the Arctic, for its inhabitants and its environment. Unchecked and unregulated, development could easily get out of hand.

A fifth level, one that touches on all the others, is the need for Canada to know what is happening on, over, and under all its territory. Most sovereign states take such a principle for granted as a necessary ingredient of nationhood. They also accept without question that they must have the means to assert control if confronted by an intruder and the ability to deter any military adventurism. Yet Canadians have been content with far less. Not only do we not know all that happens in the Arctic and rely on others to tell us, we have pitifully few means to protect our northern borders. If we want to achieve peace and security, prevent pollution, and regulate development, then we will have to have both the intelligence *and* the means. No longer can we be satisfied with occasional sovereignty patrols and little else. In the past, it has suited our pocket-books and our purposes not to worry about these matters. The trade-offs seemed worthwhile. But it is foolish, if not dangerous, particularly in matters of national security, for us to presume we will never be called upon to act alone. Our size and strategic position dictate that we are to some extent reliant on our allies, particularly the United States. That reliance inevitably leads to a question of balancing interests, abilities, and resources. We must, however, keep in mind that every time we calve off a responsibility to others, there is a trade-off. By definition, that usually involves some loss of control and ultimately the possibility of putting ourselves at risk. If we want to take charge of the Arctic, then it is essential we know what is going on there. The time for too many trade-offs is past.

The final level of the foundation in an integrated policy must be that it is Canadian, that is, based on Canadian needs and adapted for Canada's benefit. Although that statement may smack of unbridled nationalism, it is intended to underline the point that the adoption of a made-in-Canada Arctic policy will not be easy. Difficult choices will have to be made, particularly when it comes to our relations with the United States. A conversation with a senior u.s. Pentagon official (off the record insofar as his remarks could not be directly attributed to him) illustrate the dilemma:

REPORTER:
There is more political will in Canada today to go to our North and make our presence felt. There is a feeling we should know what is happening on our borders.
PENTAGON:
What you're saying is you [Canada] want to do what's already being done. We [United States] already watch the Arctic and we're your best friends and allies.

Excuse me for being blunt, but what is the real motivation? Ego?
REPORTER:
Partly – but isn't that what nationhood is all about?[28]

From the Pentagon's point of view, it probably is preferable for Canada to stick to what it is doing in Europe and not meddle in Arctic security, which the United States is currently handling by itself. But from Canada's perspective, does this state of affairs suit our policy aims? Similar dilemmas will have to be resolved across the spectrum, for sovereignty over our waters, defence of our archipelago, participation in Star Wars, or adoption of an arms-control strategy. If we want to succeed, we must resolve to stick to our agenda. That means doing what *we* decide is best for the Arctic.

Success also means making some tough choices about where we allocate limited resources, particularly in the area of defence. There simply aren't enough troops, ships, planes, and dollars for Canada to live up to all its commitments both in Europe and at home. For the past decade, military specialists have pointed out that there is a 'commitment-capability gap'[29] between what Canada has said it will do and what it can do. If the Arctic receives the attention it deserves, then those resources will be stretched even farther. It certainly does nothing for Canadian self-esteem or our position abroad to make promises we can't fulfil. We aren't fooling anybody about our capabilities, only deluding ourselves. It is time for some backbone and commitment to put our security house in order.

In conclusion, a new Arctic policy will give Canada a valuable focus along with a sense of purpose for the next two decades. That policy could also be a source of great national pride. Preserving world peace, through peace-keeping forces and membership in international bodies, has been a long-standing Canadian tradition. The circumpolar world is an area where Canada is not only influential but where we have a direct stake. We could also find that we have a lot more in common with the citizens of the circumpolar world than we think. Recently, celebrated Canadian writer Robertson Davies commented: 'We are a northern people living in the northern reach of North America. Our writing is more like the writing of Scandinavian people than American or English.'[30] Astute writer and observer Sandra Gwyn, after living in Britain for a while, also came to the same conclusion. 'My theory is that we [Canadians] have more in common with the Scandinavians than with the Brits: the same northern-ness, the same introversion, the same topographical rawness, the same egalitarianism.'[31]

All of which brings us back to 'Mercator mind-set.' In the final analysis, Canadians will have to come to grips with our true geography and our true place in the world. The challenges in the Arctic are real, as is the need to deal with them urgently. All that is needed now is the resolve.

SOVEREIGNTY

3

Staking a human claim

In 1953, a small group of Mounties with an unusual proposition made their way to the northernmost reaches of Quebec, where the land suddenly plunges to Hudson Strait in breath-taking cliffs. They brought their proposal to the tiny Inuit camps strung out along the shore. The Mounties' purpose was to convince the Inuit of a better life farther north – better hunting, better money, and a better future.[1] About seventy-five Inuit, including John Amagoalik and his parents, were subsequently picked up in Inoucdjouac and relocated to Grise Fiord on Ellesmere Island and Qausuittuq, formerly known as Resolute, the airfield and weather station on Cornwallis Island. This is how John, who was five at the time, remembers the move:

We had been told that we would all be going to the same place, but once we got past Pond Inlet, the RCMP came to us and said okay, half of you have to get off here and half of you have to get off over there. I remember all the women started crying and all the dogs on the decks started howling. It was something I will always remember. This exercise has created quite a bit of bitterness because the Government of Canada was not honest with us. They did not tell us the real reasons. Instead they told us it was for better hunting and job opportunities. But the real reason was for Arctic sovereignty.[2]

The Mounties, as has now come to light, were acting on orders from Ottawa. The purpose of the move was exactly as John Amagoalik, now an active executive member of Canada's major Inuit association, Inuit Tapirisat, remembers it – to assert Canadian sovereignty. He says that had his family been told the truth 'we would have been happy to go up there and to tell anybody that this is Canadian territory.'[3] In fact, the families, who now call themselves 'Internal Exiles,'[4] found the going very tough. The climate, the fishing, and the hunting were markedly different than what they had been used to in northern Quebec. But they say that when they went back to the RCMP to remind them of the promise that they could return home after two years if they didn't like it, the RCMP turned a deaf ear.

The relocation of the Amagoaliks and others is a tragic chapter in Canada's century-long saga to assert sovereignty over its far-flung North. Most of the others weren't nearly as unusual or controversial. Yet this relocation is curiously symbolic of Canada's scattered and haphazard attempts to control its own domain. Admittedly, there was no compelling force, except for national pride, driving Canadians to show the flag in the North. Sovereignty incursions were restricted to the odd explorer, and oil drilling wasn't even imagined. None the less, there has been a curious reticence, broaching on the negligent, in the manner and determination with which Canadians have approached sovereignty over the North. It is one of the most poignant indications of our schizophrenic view of the Arctic. We have had occasional fits of passion about our North, but the record shows that when the time came to translate words into action, the spirit often faltered.

It is these 'falterings' which have laid the seeds of doubt to Canadian claims of Arctic sovereignty, specifically over the waters. Through a combination of luck, inadvertence, and some planning, Canada now has undisputed control over all lands in the North and in the Arctic archipelago. The same, however, cannot be said for the waters, specifically the Northwest Passage. The passages of the *Manhattan* and the *Polar Sea* testify to the fact that the current minimal sovereignty-vigil maintained by Canada is sadly lacking. There is no doubt Canada must dramatically step up its program of sovereignty patrol to successfully face any challenge, legal or otherwise. Equipment alone, however, is not enough.

There must also be some national resolve to break out of our 'Mercator mind-set' or Arctic schizophrenia. One need only look to Scandinavia and more particularly, to the Soviet Union, to see countries where there has been a sustained determination to settle even to the farthest extremes of their territories. In such countries, sovereignty and any encroachments on it cut right to the heart of national pride. Recent Soviet submarine incursions into Swedish territorial waters caused a national uproar in

Sweden. By contrast, revelations in 1986 that u.s. submarines routinely roam through our territorial waters raised a few questions in the House of Commons but nowhere near the same public upset.[5] The challenge for Canadians will be to reverse the pattern of the past. Today the Arctic is ours. Tomorrow sovereignty could be lost if a better vigil isn't established.

Bandied about freely, the term 'sovereignty' has come to mean many things. Canadian politicians, for example, have used the term in their justification of increased military spending, support of Canadian culture, building of an ice-breaker, and drawing of new boundary lines. The military, too, has had difficulty defining its mandate of 'sovereignty protection.' Until recently, it had interpreted this task only to mean providing essential police functions in the Arctic and performing a basic surveillance of Canadian territory – but little else. It hadn't attempted, for example, to perform military roles, such as being able to deny entry to outsiders to Canadian Arctic waters. With the 1987 White Paper on defence, the Canadian Forces' sovereignty role will be expanded to include more military roles in the Arctic.[6] For purposes of a new northern policy for Canada, this change is essential. Canada must be in a position where it can exercise exclusively all those rights and powers normally associated with a nation state over its territory. Knowing what is happening on, over and under Canadian territory, *and* being able to do something about it is one of those rights.

Whether Canada chooses to exercise this entry denial power, if acquired, poses a different dilemma. In the past, it is clear no Canadian government has been prepared to forcibly intervene to stop a u.s. ship passing through the Northwest Passage. Having the capacity to deny entry to intruders is one thing. Using it is another. The challenge is to find that right combination of steps, legal and military, to make such a decision unnecessary. Opening fire in the interests of protecting sovereignty would appeal to few Canadian politicians. It makes defining the military aspect of 'sovereignty' all that more difficult.

Then there is the legal aspect. International law is far from clear on the exact ways a state is judged to have acquired 'sovereignty' over land and water. However, certain litmus tests have evolved. A nation can acquire territory for example by occupation, discovery, subjugation, or cession from another state.[7] In the case of the Arctic, Canada could invoke any one of these tests. Individually, each one might not stand the rigours of legal scrutiny; but taken together they provide a solid basis for Canada's claims to general 'sovereignty' over the North.

In the case of the Arctic, another complication is the definition of what constitutes 'territory.' Pack ice along many parts of the Arctic basin makes it extremely difficult to delineate shoreline. General international legal practice has been to ignore 'temporary' ice coverage but to give some status to 'permanent' ice such as shelf ice and any projections of glaciers.[8] Ice floes and ice islands are considered like ships on the high seas.[9] The problem, of course, becomes one of fixing where the 'permanent' ice ends. Such a process has never been put to the test of international law and is never likely to be.

To trace Canada's quest for complete sovereignty over the Arctic regions, one has to go back more than a century, to 1870.[10] Then, just three years after the fragile confederation had been formed, Canada accepted all territories of the Hudson's Bay Company – comprising Rupert's Land and the North-Western Territory – from Great Britain. Rupert's Land was considered generally to comprise all territories through which waters drain into Hudson Bay and Strait. The North-Western Territory, meanwhile, comprised all remaining British continental territories north of the 49th parallel and east of the 141st meridian, with the exception of British Columbia. However, most of the Arctic archipelago was not demarcated. That wouldn't happen for sixty-seven years – an omission whose effects are still being felt.

In September 1880, Britain surrendered all rights to its other territories and waters in the high Arctic, although the geography was still not clearly defined. The question lingers whether these two transfers or 'cessions' were legally binding on other foreign states.[11] However, no untoward questions were asked and so the first Canadian claims were staked.

It is worth noting that most of the explorers of and expeditions to the area prior to these times were British. One or two foreigners did try to lay claim to certain areas – Jens Munk, a Dane, to Hudson Bay in 1619, and Charles Hall, an American, to Frobisher Bay in 1861 – but none of them stuck. Britain had been the only country to have acted in any concerted manner in the region, which in the absence of any competing claim, made Britain's far stronger. In reality, it was the Hudson's Bay Company that had asserted virtual uninterrupted authority over most of the North since the granting of its charter in 1670. When Canada became independent in 1867, a clause was inserted into the British North America Act (no. 146) anticipating the transfer of the trading company's territories. While settlers continued to trek to the West, the North remained largely unsettled and the government of the day decided 'no steps [shall] be taken with the view of legislation ... until some influx of population or other circumstances shall occur to make such provision more imperative.'[12] The voyage of the *Manhattan* was still a century away.

Not until fifteen years later, in 1895, was the first tentative step taken to extend legal jurisdiction over the North.[13] An order in council was passed creating four provisional districts – Yukon, Mackenzie, Ungava, and Franklin – the last extending north for an 'indefinite extent.' Foreign explorers, such as the American Robert Peary and two Norwegians, Roald Amundsen and Otto Sverdrup, passed through making random claims, but again there was no serious threat to Canadian supremacy. By 1912, the Yukon has been sliced off as a separate territory[14] and several Canadian-sponsored expeditions and RCMP patrols had visited many parts of the mid-Arctic.

The first real test came during the First World War when the Danish explorer Knud Rasmussen claimed Ellesmere Island for Denmark, a claim that was backed up by Copenhagen. Canada lodged a stiff protest and, in typical style, waited five years before sending up a patrol of a few Mounties. They even opened up a post office on the southern tip of Ellesmere. Whether this gesture impressed the Danes is not known but eventually Denmark let the whole matter drop.

A more concerted effort to police the North was begun in 1922 with the first Eastern Arctic Patrol. Small outposts of Mounties were set up in various communities and the Canadian presence became established and real.

This was also the time of the famous sledge patrols of one of Canada's unsung heroes, Staff Sergeant A.H. Joy. In 1929 he took his longest trip, 2,700 kilometres, starting from Dundas Harbour at the entrance to Lancaster Sound and ending at Winter Harbour on Melville Island. Staking out claims for Canada like a surveyor, Joy crossed over the Queen Elizabeth Islands to the ice-cap of Ellesmere Island ending up at Bache Peninsula where the RCMP had its small post. Eventually the Mounties made their presence felt throughout the archipelago. Certainly in this period those police posts were considered Canada's first staked claims to sovereignty.[15]

In 1925, three years after the first Arctic patrol, Canada took another bold step, laying claim to everything between the longitudinal lines of 61 degrees West and 141 degrees West, extending 'right up to the Pole.'[16] This dramatic claim for a giant slice of the Arctic pie was known as the 'sector claim.' Although such claims have not been formally recognized in international law, there were precedents for them in early treaties signed between the empires occupying Arctic territories. For example, two agreements between England and Imperial Russia in the early nineteenth century referred to the boundary between British North America and eastern Siberia extending 'in its prolongation as far as the Frozen Ocean.'[17] Australia, New Zealand, Argentina, Chile, and France have also made similar and sometimes conflicting sector claims to various slices of Antarctica. Interestingly, the United States has consistently refused to recognize any of these claims, be they in Antarctica or the Arctic. Needless to say, the Arctic countries who benefit most from 'sector claims' are those bordering on the Arctic Ocean. Thus, it is not surprising that such claims have been made by both Canada and the Soviet Union.

An interesting sidelight to the sector theory is ownership of the North Pole itself. The Soviets have considered this question and, as far as they are concerned, the Pole is just the intersection point at which all the sector lines converge. Legally, they say, the Pole belongs to no one although one Soviet scholar suggested a multi-sided post be planted with the colours of each sector nation painted on the appropriate side.[18]

In 1928, the Canadian government pre-empted any Norwegian claim to islands within Canada's sector, namely the Sverdrups, by paying $67,000 for the maps and charts of the explorer after whom they were named who had 'claimed' them for Norway. Norway then accepted Canada's claim to the islands but pointedly refused to recognize the sector concept. Various Canadian ministers reasserted the theory until 1956 when the first of several Soviet ice-floe stations drifted into the Canadian sector. Parliament was aflame with debate as to whether the Soviets had 'invaded' Canada and the then minister of northern affairs, Jean Lesage, declared 'we have never subscribed to the sector theory in application to the ice. We are content that our sovereignty exists over all the Arctic islands.'[19]

Since then there has been no serious attempt to resurrect the sector theory, and with good reason. While a limited number of legal scholars will argue its merits, the overwhelming majority reject it out of hand. As

Gordon Smith, a noted Canadian expert in this field, wrote: 'the most favourable thing that can be said is that it remains unsettled.'[20] Parliament has never been asked to codify the theory into Canadian law and the most recent moves in 1986 to establish straight baselines around the Arctic archipelago would imply a denial of the sector theory.[21]

International respect for Canada's claim to the Arctic archipelago, however, was given a substantial boost in 1933 following a decision of the Permanent Court of International Justice over the ownership of Greenland.[22] Norway had set up a small settlement on Greenland's eastern shores and had laid claim to parts of Greenland. Denmark, which still has ultimate responsibility for Greenland, objected and took the case to court. In its judgment, the court decided for the Danes, ruling that, in such a remote and uninhabited area, a country did not have to occupy *all* territory to retain sovereignty over it. This seemingly sensible ruling that, in such places as the far North, a nation need only have settlements in several locations adjacent or 'contiguous' to the area of dispute, had tremendous implications for Canada. While Greenland is one large island and the Canadian Arctic archipelago is a cluster of many, the general thrust and logic of this judgment could certainly be used by Canada in any foreign attempt to lay claim to individual islands.

Interestingly, even though the Danes won, they vowed never again to allow such an intrusion to occur. With a determination and vigour Canada would be well advised to emulate, Denmark initiated what has come to be known as the 'Sirius sledge patrols' to ensure no unwanted visitors land undetected. Using both husky-sled teams and motorboats, members of the patrol monitor ten thousand kilometres of eastern and northern Greenland every year. During the Second World War, the patrol put a stop to German weather stations which had been established in eastern Greenland. Today the patrols carry on as before, a tradition of sovereignty control most Greenlanders take for granted as essential.[23]

Canada, too, has its sovereignty patrols, both indigenous and military. Little-known and vastly under-used, the Canadian Rangers are a widely disparate group of 640 indigenous 'sovereignty soldiers' enlisted in thirty-seven communities across the North. The concept started with the Pacific Coast Militia Rangers, a group formed in the Second World war to warn British Columbia in case of a Japanese invasion. A lot has happened in the art of military defence since then, but not so with the Rangers. Sporting their official insignia – red baseball caps and arm-

Canadian Arctic Rangers en route to target-shooting practice at Lac Martre,
NWT (Canadian Forces photo, by Sgt Dennis Mah)

bands – and armed with bolt-action Lee-Enfield rifles (which date from
the Second World War), the Rangers have the official role of 'providing a
military presence in sparsely settled northern coastal and isolated areas
which cannot conveniently or economically be covered by other elements
of the regular or reserved force.'[24]

Experience has shown a tank can only move up to twenty kilometres a
day in the snow-encrusted terrain north of latitude 60 degrees. A Ranger
on a dog-sled or snowmobile can do two or three times that distance and
is much better equipped to survive. Usually the Rangers scout in groups,
patrolling the territory around their settlements. In the North, the
Rangers are selected from among local hunters and trappers and all but
three are Inuit or Dene. The prerequisites appear basic yet daunting to
the uninitiated: know the land, be able to survive, and be familiar with
native skills. The Rangers need little marksmanship training and are

usually given three days of basic training in their home settlements followed by four days out on the land. Map-reading and survival skills aren't on the course because the Rangers often know more in these areas than their instructors. Each Ranger draws $34 a day militia pay, plus expenses for his snowmobile and two hundred rounds of ammunition.

The total annual cost of the Rangers program to Canadian taxpayers is roughly $200,000[25] – one-fifty-thousandth of the defence budget – and a bargain. On land, the Rangers are probably one of the most visible and constant reminders of Canadian control and occupation of the North. One of their primary responsibilities is to spot intruders, submarines being the most common, and report back to the military. Sometimes a surveillance plane is sent up to check out a Ranger report.

The Rangers also operate as the 'eyes and ears' for regular Canadian troops who often rely on the Rangers to keep them out of trouble. Since Canada maintains no more than one thousand troops in the North at any one time, the Rangers would be in the first line of defence in the extremely unlikely event of a Soviet invasion over the top. Rangers can be called up in emergencies but are technically 'reservists.'

Much too little has been made of these 640 people but they, along with the roughly 24,000 other indigenous people who live in the far North are Canada's prime 'evidence' that the territory is occupied. One need only listen to any Inuit to hear how proud they are of the Ranger role.[26]

On the military side, the Canadian presence in the North has been kept to a minimum. While there is an occasional naval exercise in the summer months, the forbidding ice makes it impossible for *any* Canadian navy vessel to undertake winter patrol. In an Arctic country like Canada, with more than half its coastline in the North, it is a stunning example of our complacency that we can't even patrol the Arctic most of the year. The prime responsibility for sovereignty patrol is left to eighteen Aurora aircraft which do a fly-over of some region of the Arctic once every three weeks. These long-range patrol aircraft, CP-140s, with state-of-the-art surveillance equipment, represent Canada's principal weapon in its current sovereignty and anti-submarine arsenal. Starting from either Comox, B.C., or Greenwood, N.S., the Auroras traditionally spend three days patrolling the North to provide aerial photography for the armed forces. The patrols are limited to visual observation but over the course of a year, they cover the whole of the North, if only for a fraction of time. Designed specifically for Arctic patrol, these aircraft are highly valued by the military for what they can do. However, they have no ability (i.e., missiles) to either defend themselves or attack surface targets. Furthermore, bad weather and the three-month winter period when the North is in darkness twenty-four hours a day put a severe crimp in their effectiveness. Their reconnaissance capacity also has built-in limitations, as C.R. 'Buzz' Nixon, former deputy director of defence, points out:

One of the things that distressed me when I was deputy minister is that these repeated flights of the Aurora aircraft would go over and over and they would take pictures and more pictures and the pictures after three years were not any different than they were three years before. So you had to ask if that is the way

A cp-140 Aurora long-range patrol aircraft, at Canadian Forces Base, Greenwood, ns, flies an anti-submarine patrol off Canada's east coast (Canadian Forces photo)

to express surveillance and presence. When you talk about sovereignty in the present sense, I think you have the presence in other activities, in the non-military activities which are going in the Arctic. The only place where you need to have [military] surveillance and know what is there is in the air ... then maritime and practically nothing on land. There are also questions of penetration over or through the ice, and under the ice, particularly under the ice.[27]

Despite these shortcomings, which indirectly reflect the superiority of all-weather satellites, the Auroras do provide a necessary first line of sovereignty patrol. But for a country the size of Canada, it is generally agreed that the total complement of eighteen is woefully inadequate to do the mammoth job required. It is little wonder the Senate subcommittee studying the armed forces recommend that this number be doubled immediately.[28]

In the brouhaha following the passage of the *Polar Sea* through the Northwest Passage, the government chose to increase the Aurora patrols as part of its agenda for greater sovereignty protection. While the *Polar Sea* was plying the passage, it was an Aurora that monitored its course and took extensive photographs. For those aboard the Auroras, the boredom and similarity of terrain can be numbing, but for Canada surveillance is an important string in the bow of occupation of the North.

Another vital string is the constabulary service provided now by both the RCMP and the Coast Guard. The Mounties have come a long way since the days of Staff Sergeant Joy and his sledge patrols, although their numbers are still relatively small. For what is undoubtedly the world's largest precinct, the RCMP has a total staff of 250 and has 3 Twin Otters at its disposal. In addition to its police work, the force performs customs and excise duties throughout the Northwest Territories.

The Coast Guard, which has eight heavy ice-breakers and thirteen medium-sized and small ice-breakers, is principally concerned with safe and pollution-free shipping in the Arctic. Unfortunately, none of the ice-breakers can operate in winter in the far North, another startling example of Canada's inability to patrol the Arctic. But during the short shipping season, the Coast Guard does surveillance, ensures Canada's Arctic anti-pollution laws are observed, performs any needed search and rescue, and provides required escort service. Both forces are further examples of Canada's 'effective occupation' of the North and its assertion of total sovereignty.

While most of the government's legal moves in the past three decades have been to protect sovereignty over Arctic waters, one of the most recent steps has probably gone the farthest to cement sovereignty over the entire archipelago. In the aftermath of the voyage of the *Polar Sea*, the federal government finally established straight baselines around the archipelago to legally encompass all lands and waters within that area.[29] Legal experts had long been urging Ottawa to take such a step but it took the *Polar Sea* to force the issue. The baselines, similar to a border, follow all the outward-looking coastlines on the islands of the archipelago and link the islands by crossing channels. They came into effect 1 January 1986. Ottawa had considered making such a move after the passage of the *Manhattan* in 1969 but fears that it might provoke a court challenge deterred any action. However, Canada has already adopted the baseline approach on the west coast of Vancouver Island and along parts of Labrador and Newfoundland.

There is historical precedent for the baseline approach in the 1951 decision of the International Court of Justice in the Anglo-Norwegian Fisheries Case.[30] There Britain disputed Norway's right to draw baselines around the myriad islands that dot Norway's northern coast. The court ruled that the chain of islands could be considered a geological extension of the mainland and, therefore, all fjord waters, sometimes extending out almost sixty-five kilometres from the mainland, could be claimed as internal or national waters. Territorial water was considered to begin at the outer rocks or shoals of the island chain and to extend out to sea.

Whether the Arctic archipelago is exactly analogous to the Norwegian Islands is a matter of debate. However, the Soviets have recently chosen to draw baselines around two archipelagoes in the middle of the Northeast Passage across the top of the Soviet Union. Denmark has also used the straight-baseline approach. However, the United States has never used this system and in fact steadfastly opposes its application. None the less, the legal precedents would certainly give Canada an excellent dossier if a legal challenge were ever to be mounted.

Finally, but by no means lastly, Canada's best claim to the Arctic is undoubtedly is people who live there. Their daily lives, their hunting and fishing, and their social structures are arguably the best evidence of Canada's ongoing and real occupation of the area. In the words of John Amagoalik, one of the so-called Internal Exiles:

Inuit have an intense and personal interest in the sovereignty and security of the Arctic. We will not be made bystanders to the future of our homeland ... There have been Inuit living in the high Arctic perhaps a few hundred years now. There was evidence of stone-age Eskimos on the islands ... What we really object to when the Americans go through the Northwest Passage with the *Manhattan* and the *Polar Sea*, is that it is our backyard and we feel Canada should have the courage to tell Americans; look, if you are going to trample over our living room, at least have the courtesy of telling us ... Inuit have the most to gain and the most to lose in all such decisions. Therefore, it is essential that Canada's role in the Arctic be inextricably bound to that of the Canadian Inuit.[31]

Nor are they alone. The whites and Dene who live north of latitude 60 degrees are just as vehement. Michael Ballantyne, minister of justice and public services in the Northwest Territories, speaks to the same point: 'What the North is about is people. I think our greatest strength in ever defending Canadian sovereignty is pride in the people of the Northwest Territories.'[32]

One interesting sidelight of this argument is the whole question of aboriginal land claims, particularly to Arctic waters. Several Arctic specialists have put forward the thesis that Canada's claim to sovereignty is greatly enhanced by all land settlements which both recognize the traditional use and occupancy of the area by the Inuit and guarantee their right to continue to use it in a similar manner. As Peter Burnet, executive director of the Canadian Arctic Resources Committee, explains, 'it seems to me that it would strengthen Canada's case to say to the international community that we have bound ourselves domestically in law to protect the Inuit interest ... This is a national trust and responsibility and we are undertaking it.'[33]

The attractiveness of this argument is that as hunters and trappers the Inuit have always used the waters of the Arctic. The vast majority of their communities are on the coastline and the Inuit have been carrying on similar fishing and hunting activities for hundreds of years. By recognizing this historical continuity and committing itself to it, Canada may well enhance its legal entitlement to both the lands and waters of the archipelago. Some in Ottawa may argue that such agreements would create dangerous precedents for other land-claims settlements. However, the logic of the proposition is hard to dispute and would in all likelihood lend further support to the occupancy test so necessary for sovereignty.

In conclusion, the evidence is overwhelming that Canadian supremacy over the lands of the Arctic is clear. It also explains why during the last half of the twentieth century there has been no serious challenge to Canadian sovereignty over these lands. The only current dispute is over tiny, uninhabited Hans Island, exactly half way between Ellesmere Island and Greenland. Both Canada and Denmark claim the three-square-kilometre dot in the Kennedy Strait, mainly because of possible petrocarbon deposits. So far, they have agreed to disagree, leaving the status of Hans unsettled.[34] The rest of the Arctic land, though, is securely in Canada's control – unchallenged. The waters, however, present a different problem.

4

The Northwest Passage

Soon after the turn of the century, the fearless Norwegian explorer, Roald Amundsen set off in his forty-seven-ton herring boat, *Gjoa*, to do what no man had done before – conquer the Northwest Passage. The fabled highway to the Orient, which had lured the likes of Franklin, Frobisher, Hudson, and Parry and had fascinated Europeans and navigators for centuries, was about to be traversed. The voyage would take three years but it was the kind of endurance test Amundsen relished. After all, this Arctic explorer a few years later would take another ship as far north off Norway as he could, become locked in the ice, and 'set up camp' for five years to determine which way the current flowed.

The *Gjoa*, now on proud display overlooking Oslo's harbour, entered the eastern end of the Northwest Passage in 1904 at Lancaster Sound. For the next three years it would wend its way through Barrow Strait down the western shore of Boothia Peninsula, pass east of King William Island, then hug the mainland until it emerged at the gulf which now bears Amundsen's name. Altogether ship and crew would pass through sixteen different channels, sounds, and straits, later to carry such names as Peel, Franklin, Larsen, Rae, and St Roch, the last being the name of the first Canadian ship to match this feat. Of the possible routes Amundsen chose what was probably one of the most difficult ones from a navigational point of view. However, he had a choice; for, in fact, there are seven. When he finished, though, he was the toast of the navigators' world.

It would be an utterly different atmosphere eighty years later when a 122-metre long u.s. Coast Guard ship, with the seemingly innocuous name *Polar Sea*, set off from Thule in Greenland to conquer the passage.

Armed with two 40-millimetre guns, the *Polar Sea* would make the crossing in twelve days and save at least $100,000 in fuel costs.[1] Had the cutter taken the long route, via the Panama Canal to Alaska, it would have taken thirty days longer and thousands more litres of fuel. Unlike the *Gjoa*, the *Polar Sea* took the most direct and navigable route, starting in Lancaster Sound and then heading due west through Barrow Strait and Viscount Melville Sound, then down the Prince of Wales Strait to emerge at the western end. But it would be bricks not bouquets that greeted this voyage because for most Canadians the transit was a deliberate affront to Canadian sovereignty. Ottawa's tepid response was just as worrisome.

At the core of the dispute is the legal status of the Northwest Passage. The United States maintains it is an international passage through which ships of all nations can pass freely at any time. Canada, however, considers the passage to be part of its internal waters over which it has total control, including sole authority to regulate maritime traffic. The issue is by no means clear cut, but for Canada the stakes are enormous. If Canada's claim is secure, then it has the right to take whatever steps it deems appropriate to protect and maintain the water-way. If the Americans are right, then ships of any country would have a virtually unimpeded 'right of innocent passage' with little to restrict them.

The Canadian government has adopted primarily a legal approach to assert its sovereignty over the passage. Through historical use and a series of declarations and laws, Canada has come to the point where it says it has complete sovereignty over the waters. However, it has fallen woefully short on concrete measures to enforce its position. The passage may be ours, but it is also ours to lose.

Nothing could have driven home this point more forcefully than the *Polar Sea*'s recent voyage. Before the ship sailed, the United States took pains to notify Canada of its intentions but deliberately decided not to ask for permission.[2] The Americans also restated their refusal to recognize the Arctic Waters Pollution Prevention Act, Canada's stringent anti-pollution legislation, which demands extra precautions and construction standards for Arctic vessels to protect against ecologically damaging oil spills. However, as a slight sop to Canadian sensibilities, three Canadians – two Canadian Coast Guard ice-breaker captains and the Inuvik district manager of the Indian and northern affairs department – were invited aboard as 'observers and advisers.'

Three decades of legal manoeuvring to assure complete Canadian sovereignty over the passage tottered as Ottawa first expressed 'deep regret' over the voyage[3] and then, in an apparent face-saving gesture, granted the *Polar Sea* 'permission' to make the trip,[4] – despite the fact that the Americans had never asked for it. Then, almost comically, the government issued a statement saying that while Canada and the United States disagreed over the status of the waters, the purpose of the *Polar Sea*'s trip was 'merely to reduce its sailing time to Alaska,' where it was badly needed.[5] A rather more accurate description came from the usually blunt ex-u.s. ambassador to Canada, Paul Robinson, who snapped to reporters, 'we're saying it's international waters.'[6]

For the United States, the matter was more than a prod at the Canadian flank; it was yet another in a series of carefully calculated moves to show the flag and reassert the u.s. view that the right of innocent passage must be guaranteed through international waters. For example, the United States has forcefully and repeatedly denied Libya's claim that the Gulf of Sidra is entirely internal waters. Likewise, in early 1986, the United States sent the cruiser *Yorkton* and the destroyer *Caron* deep into the Black Sea on a route that deliberately passed through the Soviet Union's internationally accepted twelve-mile-territorial waters. Again, the Americans insisted the vessels were merely exercising the 'right of innocent passage.' In a time of crisis, the Pentagon desires the flexibility to dispatch its troops, carriers, and fighters wherever it wants, and often this means passing through narrow straits. If Canada were successful in closing off the passage, it might set a dangerous precedent for other nations to emulate, which could have unforeseen consequences for the United States. The Americans also have a growing strategic interest in the Canadian Arctic and are therefore anxious to retain all their options. That is why they hold so firmly to international law which generally guarantees the right of innocent passage through international straits, even where such straits pass through territorial waters. Canada, however, considers the Northwest Passage to be different. Today it claims complete sovereignty and insists the conditions are not present to make it an international strait. But before entering the forest of legalities, it is essential to define the passage itself.

In fact, there are seven routes, although only two can be considered navigable for today's supertankers or giant ice-breakers. To the Europeans, the passage was the quick route to the Orient. To later geographers, it was the route from Bering Strait in the west to Davis Strait in the

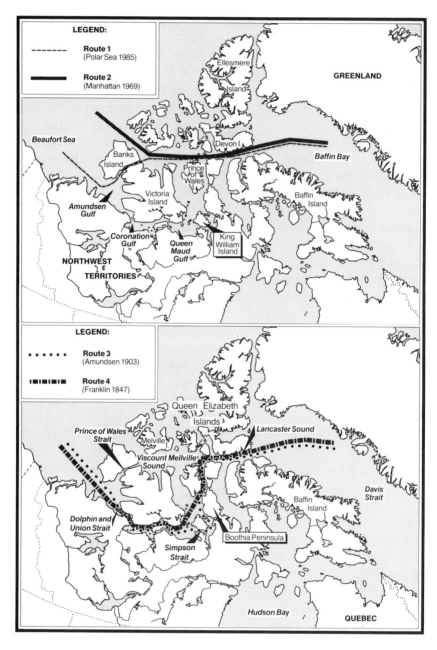

Routes 1, 2, 3, and 4 of the Northwest Passage

east. For sovereignty purposes, Canada defines the passage to be those waters within the Arctic archipelago, the most useful description for this discussion. Two other factors are essential to keep in mind: ice conditions and the relative depths of channels, otherwise known as bathymetry. Channel depth is particularly important because the type of specially reinforced ice-breaking vessel envisaged to carry oil or gas from the North requires a minimum draught of twenty metres.

The first and most navigable route, according to Canada's *Sailing Directions: Arctic Canada*,[7] the encyclopedic guide to all water-ways in the North, is the one taken by the *Polar Sea*. It is also the preferred route of the oil giants in their plans to transport hydrocarbons. The five sounds and straits that make up this passage can narrow to as little as nine kilometres and widen to as much as two hundred kilometres. What makes this route preferable are the navigable depths and the regular break-up of ice beginning in July that permits easier passage for two to three months. Its narrowest stretch is Prince of Wales Strait between Victoria and Banks Islands where, with shoals and islands, there is no more than a nine-kilometre gap.

The second route is the one chosen by the *Manhattan*, the reinforced U.S. supertanker whose controversial voyage in 1969 stirred many a nationalist's passion. The 155,000-ton tanker was dispatched into the Northwest Passage without permission from the Canadian government. However, in a sweet twist of fate, the Humble Oil giant got stuck in the massive ice jams of M'Clure Strait and was forced to call twice for help from a Canadian ice-breaker, appropriately named after our first prime minister. The route chosen by the *Manhattan* followed that taken by the *Polar Sea* until Banks Island, where instead of heading south through the narrow Prince of Wales channel, it headed due west into the ferocious ice packs of M'Clure Strait. Clogged with layers of old multi-year ice, M'Clure Strait is virtually ice-bound year round and impassable for surface navigation. The *Manhattan* was eventually forced to turn around and take the first route instead. Despite its limitations, this route is the oil companies' alternate choice.

The third route is the one made famous by Amundsen and his refitted herring boat. Its sixteen straits, channels, and gulfs comprise a much longer and more tortuous route than either of the first two, as it follows the twists and turns of the Canadian mainland. While ice conditions do not pose any special problems, the depths in at least two of the straits,

The *Manhattan* stuck in the ice (Canapress Photo Service)

most notably James Ross Strait and Simpson Strait, can shrink to only a couple of metres. This passage is for hardy Norwegian explorers and small craft only.

The fourth route is a variation of the third, somewhat shorter and less hazardous to navigation, although still unsuitable for larger ships. Discovery rights to it belong to the ill-fated Franklin expedition, whose leader perished at the entrance to Victoria Strait in 1847. The surviving members of the band straggled overland by foot. This route is identical to the third until King William Island, where this passage veers to the south-west down Victoria Strait instead of south-east alongside Boothia Peninsula. For routes three and four, the biggest obstacle is Queen Maud Gulf where islands, shallow waters, and shoals make it extremely difficult to traverse.

The fifth route, another variation of the third, was the one selected by the *St Roch*, Canada's first vessel to conquer the passage. Now on permanent display overlooking Vancouver harbour, it was built specifically for the Mounties in 1928 of extra-thick douglas fir. It has the distinction of

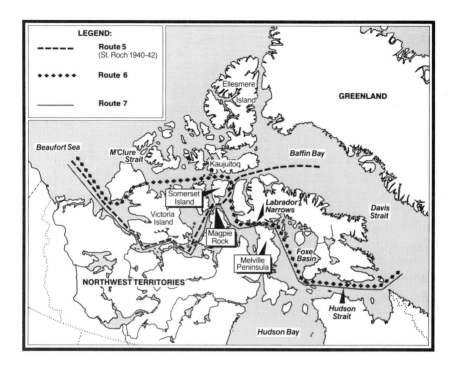

Routes 5, 6, and 7 of the Northwest Passage

being the first ship to navigate the passage in both directions and the first to make the voyage in a single season. On its maiden trip in 1940, under the command of Staff Sergeant Henry Larsen, it entered Lancaster Sound and opted to turn south just before Somerset Island and head for the narrow gap between that island and Boothia Peninsula. There in the middle of this gap is Magpie Rock, which *Sailing Directions* describes as a 'formidable danger.'[8] Although passable, it is not a route recommended for supertankers, and the other dangers accompanying routes three and four only compound the risks.

Routes six and seven are the only ones where the eastern entry to the passage is not made through Lancaster Sound. Instead, these routes begin south of Baffin Island and lead to a one-kilometre gap known as the Labrador Narrows, between Melville Peninsula and Baffin Island. From there, vessels have the options of heading to Magpie Rock to follow the fifth route to the end or veering north to Lancaster Sound, where the first route can be pursued. Several ice-breakers have forged the way but the shoals and restricted width of Labrador Narrows raise too many questions about its suitability, particularly for supertankers.

Donat Pharand, Canada's leading expert on the passage, concludes that of the seven routes 'only two are presently suitable for navigation by deep draft ships,' and of those two, the first, through the Prince of Wales Strait, 'is the better of the two ... because the prevailing ice conditions are less severe.'9

What then is the legal status of these passages? An answer to that question requires some discussion of international law.10 Three distinct types of water are recognized: a / *internal waters*, those found in freshwater lakes, rivers, harbours, waters surrounding coastal islands, and those waters lying inside boundary lines. In such waters, the coastal state has complete sovereignty and control. It can pass whatever laws it wishes to control traffic and, just as importantly, foreign ships do not have the automatic 'right of innocent passage.' To all intents and purposes, internal waters can be considered the same as land. To Canada, the waters of the Northwest Passage are *internal*; b / *territorial waters*, those coastal waters extending out to sea for a specified distance; for example, the old three-mile and now twelve-mile limits. In territorial waters, the coastal state can exercise some control but its legislative capacity is severely hampered. What cannot be forgotten is that foreign ships, with the exception of warships, have the recognized 'right of innocent passage' through these waters at any time without notice. In the case of warships, the coastal state has some residual control over traffic; c / *international waters*, often called high seas and including regularly used straits between larger seas or oceans. These waters are open to all traffic, and a coastal state has virtually no power to exercise any kind of control over them. The United States considers the Northwest Passage to be *international* waters.

For Canada the distinction is a dramatic one, particularly when it comes to traffic control and pollution standards, not to mention security and the transit of submarines. Canada has never attempted to close off the passage to outside traffic. As former prime minister Pierre Trudeau put it in 1969, 'to attempt to close off these Arctic waters and to deny passage to all foreign vessels in the name of Canadian sovereignty would be as senseless as placing a barrier across the entrances of Halifax and Vancouver harbours.'11 But the exercise of control has always been seen as vital to Canadian interests. Could the Northwest Passage be considered a strait? There are two fundamental tests: geography and usage.

Geographically, to be a strait, a water-way must join one area of high seas to another. Since all seven routes described earlier fundamentally link Davis Strait (a high sea) in the east to Beaufort Sea (a high sea) in the west, it would be very difficult to argue that they are not straits. Some legal scholars suggest that the presence of ice in the Beaufort may mean it is not a high sea; but this seems to be stretching the point. What is interesting is that each of the seven routes passes through Canadian territorial waters at some point. International law allows a country a twelve-mile or nineteen-kilometre zone of territorial waters off its mainland or islands. In the case of any waterway, that nineteen-kilometre zone can extend from both sides of the channel, making, in fact, a potential thirty-eight-kilometre band of territorial waters. As mentioned, each of the seven northwest passages narrows to less than thirty-eight kilometres at one or several points along the route. However, this does not alter the fact that, legally, they may still be considered international straits.

The other test is usage, which could become Canada's Achilles' heel. While both the 1958 and the 1982 Law of the Sea conventions laid down no specifics on usage, most scholars look to the one precedent in this area, the 1949 decision of the International Court of Justice on the North Corfu Channel.[12] Again it was Britain that took up the challenge on behalf of the sea powers of the world, arguing that the water-way between Corfu and the cost of Albania should be considered an international strait. Evidence was introduced that in a twenty-one-month period in the late 1930s, some 2,884 ships of seven different countries had put into port on the water way. The British navy said it had used the channel for eighty years; Britain also pointed out that many other vessels regularly used the channel but didn't stop in at its port. The court eventually ruled for the British, noting that the Corfu Channel 'had been used for international navigation.'[13] While there was no mention of the traffic required, Canadian expert Donat Pharand says it is now generally accepted that 'before a strait may be considered international, proof must be made that it has a history as a useful route for international maritime traffic similar to that shown to exist in the North Corfu case.'[14]

That situation just doesn't exist with general maritime traffic in the Northwest Passage. Figures compiled by the northern branch of the

Canadian Coast Guard Service reveal that there were only forty-four complete transits of the passage up to the end of 1986.[15] Of these, thirty were by Canadian ships, eleven by Americans, and one each by Norwegian, Dutch, and Japanese vessels. The vast majority of the completed transits have taken place since 1960 and the opening up of exploration for hydrocarbons in the North. Not surprisingly, most of the Canadian transits have been by ice-breakers, either doing surveys or aiding commercial tankers. But the list does include three yachts on adventure cruises and in fact, in 1985, the u.s. cruise ship *World Discoverer* offered 140 passengers, at prices ranging from $18,000 to $32,000, the chance to be on the first passenger ship travelling the passage west to east. While passengers were not enjoying the gourmet food, vintage wines, or use of the theatre, sauna, or sundeck, they were able to hear lectures by Canadian and American anthropologists on the Arctic. It should be added that the *World Discoverer* and two other cruise vessels, the Polish *Gdynia* and the Swedish *Lindblatt Explorer*, all asked Canada for permission in advance.

As evidence of increased economic activity in the area, Pharand points out that between 1977 and 1982, a total of 129 ships made partial use of the passage.[16] More than 80 per cent of them were Canadian – ice-breakers, survey ships, tankers, or tugs. Many of the tankers were carrying fuel for the various explorations, and several bulk carriers transported ore from the Nansivik Mine on Strathcona Sound. Interestingly, the overwhelming majority of ships making the complete voyage used the first route, suggested earlier as the most likely passage.

More worrisome in view of the usage test has been the unregulated foreign submarine traffic – mostly American – through Canadian Arctic waters. Since the first u.s. submarine *Nautilus* toured the Arctic Ocean in 1958, there have been constant and ongoing submarine operations in the North. In the brouhaha following the *Polar Sea* episode, some u.s. state department officials pointed out that several u.s. submarines had made transits of the passage in the past without Canadian consent being given.[17] They pointed specifically to the 1960 transit of the nuclear submarine *Seadragon*. Although there was a Canadian 'observer' aboard this purely military trip, *Seadragon* skipper Vice-Admiral George Steele recalls, 'neither government wanted to touch the status of the Northwest Passage.'[18] Recent statements by Prime Minister Mulroney and external affairs minister Joe Clark that they are 'aware' of American submarine traffic in Canadian waters only compounds these worries. Under repeated questioning in the House of Commons in late 1986, Clark would not specify where the government gets its information or whether Canada gives permission to such voyages. All he would say is 'there are provisions in place that allow us to know the information and to assert and protect our sovereignty, and those provisions are respected.'[19] What it seems to come down to is this: if we're told, we know; if we're not, we don't. That is hardly reassuring news for the Canadian sovereignty case.

Despite this situation, the total number of transits would not appear to come even close to constituting a historical record of regular international shipping. The numbers aren't high enough, particularly when compared with the traffic in the North Corfu Channel. However, the figures do contain a hidden warning: in addition to the submarine transits, the traffic is increasing and is bound to expand even more when exploration for oil and gas becomes viable again. It is little wonder then that the legal chorus to Canadians on what to do with the passage following the transit of the *Polar Sea* could be summarized in one phrase – either use it or lose it. The comments of University of Toronto professor Franklyn Griffiths were particularly poignant: 'We've got to put up or shut up about Arctic sovereignty. We've got to get up there. To put it simply: use it or lose it for those waters.'[20]

Canada has, none the less, an impressive argument to make, for there are several very persuasive pieces of evidence that suggest the passage is legally *internal* and, therefore, exclusively under Canadian control. The tracing of Canada's search for sovereignty over the waters must also begin a century ago. Many of the steps and practices outlined in the previous chapter – including the initial grants from Britain in 1870 and 1880, the gradual establishment of government authority, the police patrols, the Canadian Ranger patrols, the Aurora patrols, the hunting and fishing practices of the Inuit, and most recently, the establishment of straight baselines around the entire Arctic archipelago – can all be applied with equal vigour to the waters of the passage. So, too, can the fact that the vast majority of transits made through the passage have been by Canadian ships. With few notable exceptions – the *Polar Sea*, the *Manhattan*, and the *Seadragon* – most foreign ships entering the passage have also done so with Canadian approval. Such a pattern gives added weight to Canada's case that the waters are *internal*.

Canada's earliest legal moves to shore up sovereignty over Arctic waters came at the turn of the century, when it began to enforce its fishing and whaling regulations in the eastern Arctic. Later in the 1926 Arctic Islands Preserve Act, Ottawa moved to protect traditional hunting and fishing rights for the Inuit. However, most of legal moves have taken place in the last three decades as countries around the world have scrambled to increase their control over boundary waters. Until 1963, Canada only claimed a three-mile (five-kilometre) band of territorial waters, like most other countries in the world. As if to prove the adage that it is more difficult to pass laws about water than land, various international attempts to increase that limit had ended in stalemate.

About the only matter of significance for Canada was a 1956 international agreement on the use of a state's continental shelf. In essence, that Geneva Convention agreement gave to a coastal state the exclusive right to control and develop all exploration and exploitation of natural resources on its continental shelf. It also specified that this right did not require any occupation or proclamation by the coastal state and specifically excluded other states from doing anything without prior consent.

Unfortunately, the convention did not specify how the boundary between bordering coastal states was to be drawn on the continental shelf – an omission which was at the root of a 1986 flare-up between Canada and the United States over drilling rights in the Beaufort Sea.[21] The United States said it would offer in 1988 drilling rights for parcels on the shelf in areas claimed by Canada. Canada argues the border of the shelf between the Yukon and Alaska should follow the 141st meridian, while the United States says it should be drawn at a ninety-degree angle to the shore. The dispute in this region has simmered for years and will probably continue to do so until clarified by some international ruling. Despite this limitation and the fact the convention deals only with natural-resource extraction, it does by inference cement Canada's control over most of the immense shelf that lies off the Arctic archipelago. Since mineral and petrocarbon exploration is bound to be the principal activity in these areas for the next few decades, the convention virtually ensures Canada's authority. In the field of pollution control, this right is invaluable.

The next move came in 1963 when Prime Minister Lester Pearson fulfilled one of his election promises and declared a twelve-mile (nineteen-kilometre) exclusive fishing zone around all of Canada's coastline.[22] To eke out even more territory, Pearson also announced the application

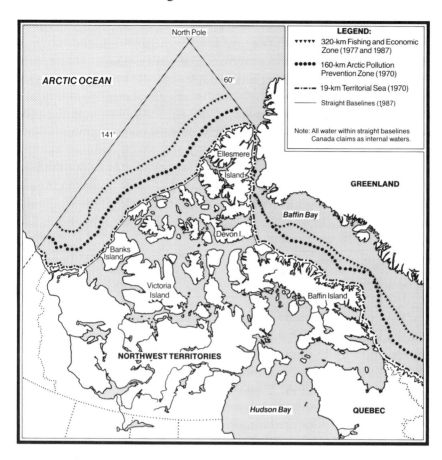

Formal boundaries claimed by Canada in the Arctic (1970-87)

of the 'headland-to-headland' system to determine the line from which both the fisheries zone and territorial waters would be measured. Under this system instead of the zone following exactly the contour of the land, imaginary baselines would be drawn from the headlands or points that protruded farthest out to sea.

Seven years later, the Trudeau government extended Canada's territorial waters to the same nineteen-kilometre limit, following a world-wide trend which had as its authority the international Territorial Sea and Fishing Zones Act.[23] For the Northwest Passage, this had the immediate impact of creating at least one and often many areas of *territorial* waters in each of the seven routes described above. Since the nineteen-kilometre limit is accepted globally, there was then impeccable authority for saying that many parts of the passage were in Canada's *territorial* waters.

And, in fact, the government issued a statement saying precisely that, adding that the effect of the new limit on the Northwest Passage is 'that under any sensible view of the law ... it is subject to complete Canadian sovereignty.'[24] Any nuances as to the difference between territorial and internal waters were carefully omitted.

However, it would not be until 1973 that a statement from the justice department declared in unequivocal terms 'Canada also claims that the waters of the Canadian Arctic Archipelago are *internal* waters of Canada, on a historical basis, although they have not been declared as such in any treaty or by any legislation.'[25] Since then, successive government ministers have repeated Canada's claim that the waters are *internal*.

Having succeeded in extending Canada's fishing zone once, the fishing lobby set to work again and their efforts came to fruition in 1977 with the declaration of the Arctic Fisheries Zone.[26] This declaration extended Canada's exclusive fishing zone out to 320 kilometres (200 miles) and by implication, further extended Canadian control over Arctic ice and waters. How this control was to be exercised was left unsettled.

About the same time, pollution control, particularly worries about the effects of oil spills in the fragile Arctic environment, also became an issue. Although other countries were sympathetic to Canada's concerns about its North, various international attempts to provide a compromise had ended predictably in failure. International law at the time also severely tied Canada's hands. So, in 1970, soon after the *Manhattan*'s passage, Canada took matters into its own hands, passing the Arctic Waters Pollution Prevention Act,[27] which established a series of tough regulations regarding maritime traffic in the Arctic. Shipping-safety zones were delineated and minimum standards on everything from hull and fuel-tank construction, to maximum load, to manning levels were established. The law also provides that if Canada feels any vessel represents a pollution hazard, it can deny it the right of passage. Again, how this law would be enforced was left unclear. None the less, the key was that these regulations were to apply on the high seas up to 160 kilometres from Canada's coast, in effect encompassing all seven routes of the Northwest Passage.

True to form, the United States vehemently opposed the reach of this new law and still does. However, in one of its more impressive diplomatic displays, Canada was able to lobby for and subsequently succeed in pushing passage of a special 'Arctic clause' of the 1982 Law of the Sea Accord. That clause (article 234) gives to Arctic coastal states the right to 'adopt and enforce' laws for the 'prevention, reduction and control of marine pollution from vessels in ice-covered areas.' The article allows such anti-pollution laws to be enforced up to 360 kilometres from shore. For Canada this clause represented a major victory and virtually insured acceptance of the 1970 law. The only fly in the ointment is that the United States has never signed the 1982 Law of the Sea Accord and consequently refuses to accept the reach of Canada's anti-pollution law. Since the Americans are the major foreign presence in our North, this situation presents real policy headaches for Ottawa.

To re-emphasize its seriousness in this matter, the Canadian government moved in 1986, following the transit of the *Polar Sea*, to clear all hurdles for a possible legal challenge to its anti-pollution law. Prime Minister Mulroney's government notified the World Court that Canada would now accept its jurisdiction to hear cases involving the law – a reversal of the position Canada had adopted when it first passed the act in 1970.[28] Canada had originally insisted on the exemption because it feared the possibility of an adverse ruling. Now armed with the special 'arctic clause,' Canada obviously feels more confident about its chances.

The *Polar Sea*'s trek prompted other sovereignty-protection moves, despite the almost facile comment from external affairs minister Joe Clark that its voyage 'has left no trace on Canada's Arctic waters and no mark on Canada's Arctic sovereignty.'[29] The most significant response was the vital declaration of straight baselines to enclose all islands and waters within the archipelago. As discussed above, this move has substantial foundation in international law and further supports Canada's case in the dispute over the waters of the Northwest Passage. More importantly, it represents the first concrete legislation to declare the waters inside the boundaries to be *internal*. The absence of such a declaration was the principal reason why legal scholars for so long advocated the passage of straight-baseline legislation. Other parts of the government's sovereignty package included construction of a Class 8 ice-breaker – twice as powerful as any existing Canadian ice-breaker – and more surveillance patrols by Canada's long-range patrol aircraft.[30] The final component was the immediate adoption of the Canadian Laws

Offshore Applications Act, which extended Canada's civil and criminal law to the limits of the economic zone.[31] While the United States will undoubtedly refuse to accept the act's applicability, the government's purpose was clear enough. When introducing the package in the House of Commons, Joe Clark said 'the policy of this government is to maintain the natural unity of the Canadian Arctic archipelago and to preserve Canada's sovereignty over land, sea and ice undiminished and undivided.'[32]

If legal means alone could ensure sovereignty, then it would be safe to say the case is secure. Unfortunately, such is not the law. Usage, occupation, and exclusion of others can be just as important when it comes to deciding if a water-way is an international strait. For several decades, Canadians have believed that time was on their side in the battle for sovereignty. The feeling was that such passage of time combined with the absence of any real challenge to Canadian authority served only to solidify Canada's position. Today Canada has a good case for saying the waters of the Northwest Passage are *internal*. Yet, as mentioned before, the figures on increasing commercial traffic and unchecked submarine transits through the passage present a real warning. And, as the oil, gas, and mineral wealth of the Arctic is opened up, those figures are bound to show an even greater increase. Then the test will come. Canada still has time to prepare. But to rest on its statute books is to follow a recipe for surrender.

5

Arctic gushers

With heavy mists rising from the Beaufort Sea partially obscuring the summer sun, a Gulf Canada tanker, *Gulf Beaufort*, loaded up with 320,000 barrels of Arctic crude. It was late July 1986 as the tanker set off for Japan from the Kulluk rig, which towered over it like a modern-day pyramid. This voyage, however, was no ordinary one. For only the second time in Canadian history, Arctic crude was being shipped from northern markets to outside markets.[1] A year earlier, Panarctic Oils had loaded up the MV *Arctic*, an ice-strengthened tanker, from its far northern Bent Horn project on Cameron Island in the Arctic archipelago. The MV *Arctic*, with the Coast Guard ice-breaker *Des Groseilliers* in escort, travelled through the ice-choked waters to Little Cornwallis Island, where the crude was transferred to a more conventional tanker for the trip to Montreal. Panarctic's shipment was a largely symbolic, if costly, display of the practicability of such operations. Gulf, too, wanted to show its operation was feasible although no one could say it was yet profitable. However, after spending more than $700 million on rigs and other support materials, Gulf could finally say the Arctic drillers' dream was nearer reality.

The crude aboard the *Gulf Beaufort* was from Gulf's celebrated Amauligak field, just northeast of Tuktoyaktuk in the misty Beaufort. After several years of promising but disappointing drilling, Gulf finally hit paydirt in the Amauligak field. In its release of drilling results, Gulf estimated reserves of between 110 million and 125 million cubic metres of high-quality oil.[2] The size of this discovery meant that Gulf finally had a find that could qualify as the lead project for Beaufort Sea oil development – providing the world price for oil is high enough.[3] With the

GW Ltd's Moliqpak rig in the Amauligak field in the Beaufort Sea
(Photo courtesy of *The Toronto Star*)

ongoing lower prices in 1986 and 1987 that is a big 'if.' Yet, as if to
demonstrate its enthusiasm, Gulf announced in early 1987 it would
spend $110 million to undertake 'seasonal' production at Amauligak for
at least 120 days the following year.[4] Ice-breaking barges are to carry an
initial production of 20,000 to 40,000 barrels a day along the Alaska
coast where cargoes could be transferred to tankers. A rather optimistic
Paul Reichmann of Gulf declared: 'We will be in full commercial production by 1992 or 1993 in the Beaufort unless some nut gets in the
way.'[5]

For the Northwest Passage and Canada, these developments have
major implications. The European adventurers' two-centuries-old dream
of a fast route to the Orient is becoming more of a reality. In the legal
debate over sovereignty to the passage, the increased traffic poses a
potential threat to Canada's claims. While commercial traffic right
through the passage has been very limited to date, partial transits have
increased substantially with the servicing of petrocarbon exploration and
the shipments of ore from the Arctic's handful of operating mines. Can-

ada must be concerned that increased commercial traffic, especially unauthorized foreign transits, could affect the passage's legal status. It must be remembered that a waterway can be considered an international strait if there is a pattern of regular commercial transits. Such transits, consequently, if not controlled and approved by Canada, represent a real threat to its sovereignty over the passage.

The economic development of the North also affects how Canada frames its security policy. If Canada decides to set a goal of self-sufficiency in energy based on development of Arctic wells, then the Arctic's natural resources and their protection would be key to Canada's overall security. By granting drilling permits and carefully regulating the pace of Arctic navigation, Canada is also manifesting its control over the region – a key aspect of sovereignty. It is precisely that control that was challenged again in 1987 by the United States when it announced it would grant drilling permits in 1988 for parts of the sea bed of the Beaufort Sea claimed by Canada. This dispute has simmered since 1965, when Canada sold oil leases in the contested area. Then, in 1984, the United States also sold leases there. No drilling has actually taken place and none is likely to do so until the world price for oil rises. Yet there is more than Arctic gushers at stake for the dispute represents another clear threat by the United States to Canadian sovereignty. The two countries will try to settle the controversy but no solution is yet in sight.

A more troubling aspect to Arctic drilling is the apparent built-in conflict between the subsistence economy of the Inuit and the infrastructure needed for drilling oil. Despite all official denials to the contrary, this conflict does exist and will be extremely difficult to resolve. For example, given that the average life of a mine is ten years and an oil well twenty, is it worth the long-term ecological risks to foster such development at the expense of disrupting the hunting, fishing, and trapping of the Inuit? If so, what are the alternatives for the Inuit? When considering this question, it is important also to remember that the delivery system to take resources out of the Arctic may be more of a danger than the extraction process. Oil companies have gone to great lengths to show the pollution hazards from drilling rigs are kept to the bare minimum. Can the same be said for pipelines and oil tankers? That question becomes all the more difficult to answer because the track record shows that technology that is well suited for more temperate climates is often unusable in the Arctic. Even something so seemingly basic as permafrost still provides riddles for scientists. None of these questions is easy to answer; nor will an attempt be made to do so here.

However, what is important for this discussion is how these questions affect the protection of sovereignty. Not surprisingly, there are more built-in conflicts. The promotion and development of resource extraction represent one of the best examples of Canadian control over its North. Plans to open up and control shipping in the Northwest Passage would be another manifestation of Canadian sovereignty. However, both policies could be diametrically opposed to Inuit desires to protect their subsistence economy. Similarly, the successful conclusion of land-claims settlements with the Inuit could provide valuable ammunition for Canada in proving its historical use of Arctic waters. Yet these same settlements at Inuit insistence could contain provisions restricting or banning future drilling in the North. For the late 1980s at least, the federal government has approved drilling in the Arctic and limited tanker traffic, pending a final decision on energy policy and reserves.

As it balances these conflicting interests, Ottawa will also have to be mindful of what is happening in other parts of the circumpolar world. To the west, in Alaska, there is great interest in more Beaufort Sea drilling. This could well bring more traffic into Canadian Arctic waters. Nor can Ottawa be oblivious of the millions of dollars spent by Canadian oil firms in developing the specialized equipment required for Arctic drilling. Under the old National Energy Program, oil firms were encouraged through extremely generous tax schemes to drill in the far North. While the program has since been disbanded, it has only been low oil prices and slack demand that has slowed the pace of Arctic development. When all these factors are considered, it seems safe to conclude that Arctic drilling and eventual commercial production will take place. What is much less certain is the timing and scale of such development. The resolution of these issues may depend to some extent on how the conflicts mentioned above are resolved.

What does this mean for Canada and sovereignty? Because Arctic drilling has tailed off, there might be a temptation to think Canada has plenty of time to plan for the Arctic. However, such thinking is short-sighted and could have damaging consequences in Canada's efforts to control Arctic navigation. One reason is that commercial activity in oil and gas exploration is always the heaviest in the first stages of the development. Be it for mines or wells, expenditure on supplies and man-power required to build the necessary installations, service them, and house workers is always the highest at the outset. Once the rig or mine is in operation, activity lessens to a certain degree. In practical terms, this means that marine transportation to and from the construction sites will also be most active at the initial stages. For drilling in the Beaufort, for example, most of the materials required were shipped into the Arctic from either Atlantic or Pacific ports or down the Mackenzie River to the delta. For Panarctic's gas drilling in the Arctic archipelago, marine trans-port was also the primary means of supply. Thus, in making any projec-tions about transits through or near the passage, it is deceiving to rely solely on the start-up date for commercial production. Heavy commer-cial traffic will predate such activity by several years.

Another reason to give the procrastinators cause for concern is the uncertainty over world oil prices. As recently as the early 1980s, experts were confidently predicting widescale commercial production of Arctic crude by the late 1980s or early 1990s. That was when the world price for oil hovered near $30 u.s. a barrel and Arctic drilling was blossoming under the incentives of the National Energy Program. When the world price for oil tumbled to $10 a barrel in 1986 at the same time North America was awash in natural-gas supplies, all projections were put on hold. Since then oil prices have bounced back and the demand for both oil and gas has picked up. This dramatic see-saw in just half a decade is evidence enough of the volatility of world energy and mineral markets to make any predictions perilous.

However, the statements of Gulf's Paul Reichmann that at least Gulf is aiming for commercial Arctic production in the 1990s give pause for concern. It has generally been thought that production in the Hibernia oilfield off Newfoundland would precede any full-scale Arctic produc-tion. While proven reserves do exist in the Hibernian field, icebergs still present a real problem. Iceberg tracking, trajectory projections, and iceberg towing have all become standard operating procedure for East Coast drillers. However, while floating drilling vessels can move out of the way of an approaching iceberg, the risk of iceberg collision poses a major challenge for the design of permanent production facilities.[6] It is this factor and cost considerations which make the Arctic a viable alter-native, at least according to Gulf's Reichmann. While the technology is far from perfected to make full-scale Arctic production a reality either,

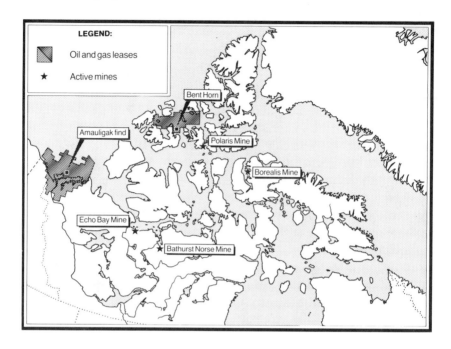

Oil and gas and mineral exploration in the Arctic

the voyages of the *Gulf Beaufort* and MV *Arctic* show that small-scale seasonable production is possible.

With drilling sites and the North's few mines sprinkled throughout the Arctic, as shown on the accompanying map, there is little doubt marine traffic will use parts and pieces of all seven passage routes. Their use will depend on ice conditions and to some extent, the availability of good navigational aids. However, the use of the MV *Arctic* since it was first brought into service in 1978 shows how the pressure is on government authorities to extend the Arctic shipping season. In its initial year of service, the MV *Arctic* only operated from early July to mid-October. With a few years of experience in hand, the same vessel operated from early June 1986 right through to the end of the following January.[7]

While there is still an ongoing debate over the cost effectiveness and environmental safety of tankers compared to pipelines, both options are being studied. In fact, these options are not mutually exclusive. What is most economical to one company in one location may be prohibitively costly to another firm located somewhere else; or both options could be used at the same general site. In making its 1984 report on drilling in the Beaufort Sea, for example, the Beaufort Sea Environmental Assessment Panel concluded oil and gas production there was both imminent and acceptable, provided it was carried out on a small scale. The panel approved the use of a small-diameter pipeline but ruled more research would have to be done before tankers could ply the passage.[8] Tankers were permitted, however, to take Beaufort crude westwards, towards Bering Strait. At Panarctic's Bent Horn site, tankers represent the only real option in the foreseeable future. At one point, Panarctic had proposed using a Finnish tanker to transport crude, but the proposal was unacceptable to Ottawa because of sovereignty concerns. While debate over the relative merit of the two transport modes will undoubtedly continue, marine transport of Arctic petrocarbons seems virtually inevitable.

Unlike the government, though, the oil companies have not restricted either their imaginations or their bank accounts to the confines of the three-month Arctic summer shipping season. With a flair that Jules Verne would have admired, some of the Arctic drillers have plans on their drawing-boards for supertankers that could navigate the passage year round.[9] In the Beaufort, for example, the oil companies proposed the use of ice-breaking tankers, each with a capacity of 1.5 million barrels split into sixteen separate cargo tanks. At the outset, the companies saw a need for two such tankers and then a gradual increase in the size of the fleet as production increased. The companies said the tankers would carry crude through the same route taken by the *Polar Sea*. These tankers would be constructed with a double hull which would include a double bottom to reduce the danger of a spill. The cargo tanks would be within the inner hull, so that no oil would be carried next to the outer hull. These tankers would be massively stronger than conventional tankers and approximately two to three times stronger than required by Canada's anti-pollution laws. As an added protection, each tanker would have separate oil-cargo and ballast tanks so that in the event of damage to a cargo tank, the oil could be transferred to an undamaged ballast tank. Each tanker would be more than a football field in length and be powered by 100,000 horsepower engines. In heavy ice of up to three metres in depth, such a tanker should be able to proceed at a steady pace of three knots. These precautions led the Beaufort Sea Environmental

Assessment Panel to conclude 'the risk of an oil spill would not be appreciably higher for Beaufort Sea region oil production and transportation than for other parts of North America and abroad. In fact, with the technological advances that are being made, the risk may be lower.'[10] However, the panel noted human error remains the greatest risk and 'must be addressed on a daily basis.'

For Panarctic's Bent Horn project, the early plan is to use the MV *Arctic* for limited shipments. Some thought is now being given to use the high-quality oil as generating fuel for the far North's electricity system. The other major proposal has been to deliver Arctic gas in liquified natural gas (LNG) tankers to eastern and European markets. By cooling natural gas, one can reduce it to liquid, at which point it occupies a small fraction of its original volume if maintained at frigid temperatures. The Arctic Pilot Project envisaged a fleet of LNG tankers, each with a capacity of 140,000 cubic metres. These LNG tankers would also be especially reinforced to four times the strength of comparable open-water LNG tankers to be able to cope in one of Canada's most severe ice zones.

Finally, in framing a sovereignty strategy, Canada must also consider U.S. plans – some call them dreams – to use both supertankers and even submarines to transport oil and gas from the giant Prudhoe Bay fields off the north slope of Alaska. Many of these plans may never leave the drawing-board, but some U.S. oil executives have been quite public about their plans to ship petrocarbons to eastern U.S. cities via the Northwest Passage. The 1969 passage of the *Manhattan* was designed to test the feasibility of precisely these plans. While a pipeline has been constructed across Alaska, it does not allow for servicing of eastern U.S. needs. Furthermore, some U.S. oilmen maintain that marine transport is more economical than pipelines. At ongoing low prices for both oil and gas, many of these plans are still forming. Yet they cannot be ignored.

In projecting Arctic navigation, one cannot also ignore the North's often forgotten but rich mineral deposits. While the effects of the ongoing slump in world mineral prices have already been felt in the Arctic, it is still recognized that all lands around the North Pole are rich in a variety of minerals. No country exploits its deposits to such a degree as does the Soviet Union, where rich veins of iron, nickel, platinum, silver, gold, and zinc are mined. While formidable conditions combined with economic costs have not made mining on such a scale feasible in Canada's far North, it is still a significant part of the region's economy. In fact, for several decades, mining has been the most important private-sector activity in the North.

While some mines are in danger of closing, mineral production in the Northwest Territories has been worth most recently about $600 million a year and provided close to 1,500 jobs.[11] Although the Territories are home to less than 1 per cent of Canada's population, the area has been providing 8 per cent of Canada's total metallic production. Before the recent downturn in prices, mineral production in the North accounted for 99 per cent of all Canada's tungsten, 26 per cent of the lead, 23 per cent of the zinc, 13 per cent of the gold, and 5 per cent of the silver.[12] The Territories is also home for the world's northernmost mine, the giant lead-zinc Polaris Mine on Little Cornwallis Island. Shipments to and from Polaris, which began operations this decade, started at an annual rate of eight trips but have since doubled. About the same traffic is reported for the lead-zinc Nansivik Mine on the northern tip of Baffin Island at the eastern entrance to the Passage. The other major mines – the Bathurst Norsemine, just north of Bathurst Inlet, and Echo Bay on Coronation Gulf – with their proven veins of lead, zinc, and silver, will probably be serviced by the most southern of the passage routes. While geological surveys hint at vast stores of other underground wealth, there is no doubt that until prices recover, especially for lead and zinc, any grander development of mines in the far North is a dream of the future.

Fishing, however, is today's reality. With its vast coastline and exclusive Arctic Fishing Zone, Canada has control of the world's largest and potentially most valuable fishing grounds. Aside from Inuit vessels, Canadian fishing boats have taken most of their catches in more hospitable climes. However, the fishing fleets of European countries from both sides of the Iron Curtain have become more adept and accustomed to the rigours of Arctic fishing. Canada gained exclusive rights to control fishing within both the archipelago and vast stretches leading up to the Northwest Passage with its declaration of a 320-kilometre Arctic Fishing Zone in 1977. Such exclusive zones have become fully recognized in international law and are now the basis on which coastal states have absolute authority over all living and mineral resources within them. When a state's zone overlaps with its neighbour's zone – such as Canada and Greenland do in both Davis Strait and Baffin Bay, proven rich fishing zones – the equidistant line is used.

The practical effect of this drawing of lines is that 'free fishing' becomes a thing of the past. Foreign states wishing to fish within such zones need apply for licences and adhere to strict quotas imposed by the coastal state. Of necessity, the receipt of this privilege brings with it responsibilities and burdens. The job of enforcing quotas, regulating fishing practices, and keeping up with necessary marine-biological surveys now falls exclusively to the coastal state. If it doesn't do it, no one else will.

It is on the eastern approaches to the passage that foreign trawlers have been sighted by both Canadian and Greenlanders. The Davis Strait, for example, contains several rich grounds as does Baffin Bay farther north. Canada has granted licences to several countries, as has Greenland, to fish the more northern waters. While foreign fish factories have not made their way into the passage, the possibility remains that they could. Some Greenlanders report the intrusion of unlicensed trawlers close to their shores[13] and certainly Canada has had its share of illegal foreign fishing farther south. The principal job of maintaining control over this immense fishing zone rests with the Coast Guard and its handful of ice-breakers and other vessels. Certainly in any legal challenge over the passage, Canada would want to say it had fully enforced its fishing rules in the Arctic. The current Coast Guard fleet is simply not adequate to do the job.

To lessen the danger of pollution from all this Arctic marine traffic – oil, gas, mineral, and fishing – the federal government has already passed stringent laws, in the form of the Arctic Waters Pollution Prevention Act. Nothing should strike more fear in the hearts of most Canadians than the prospect of oil spills in the Arctic. As discussed, most of the proposed supertanker designs incorporate double protection to mitigate against precisely this possibility. But since many spills in the past have been attributable to human error, no such shipping is risk free. Even the trail of open water left by recently passing ice-breakers or tankers has caused concern. The fear is that whales will be trapped and the migratory habits of caribou and musk ox disrupted. Those fears have been allayed by the experiences so far, but the fears of oil slicks festering for decades on ice floes haven't. An oil spill in the water-way could at a time of breeding, exact a heavy toll on marine wildlife and sea creatures. Recovery would be much slower and the damage to the cycle of nature inestimable. While precautions are being taken by tankers now plying through northern waters, it is still a matter of speculation how effective they would be in the event of human error or collision with an iceberg. The effects of spills and the like in the Arctic have much more devastating consequences than in more temperate climates because the extreme cold can effectively 'trap' pollution and lessen its biodegradable absorption.

To be fair, Canada has taken a leading role in the world in environmental safety and has launched a sustained international campaign to gain acceptance of its anti-pollution laws. While the Canada Shipping Act contains provisions for Arctic shipping, the most prominent statute is the above-mentioned Arctic Waters Pollution Prevention Act. Its primary function is to set out strict standards of design and operation for any ship carrying petrocarbons in the North. It also requires companies owning such vessels to demonstrate to the government their financial ability to pay for any clean-up costs. The Department of Transport has also come up with its Arctic Marine Services Policy to deal with navigation through the passage. Unfortunately, most of this policy exists on paper only.

In recognition of the fact that pollution knows no boundaries, Canada has also successfully negotiated one international anti-pollution agreement with Denmark (Greenland). Signed in 1983, this agreement basically provides for joint Canadian-Danish (Greenland) marine environmental co-operation in both Davis Strait and Baffin Bay. While the 1983 agreement has not been used to any great extent, at least it provides the framework for both sides to develop their expertise. More initiatives of this type can only help.

For many years, it has been said the age of the Arctic was around the corner. And, for many years that corner has been far off. The trips of the *Gulf Beaufort*, the MV *Arctic* are surely harbingers of what is to come. With so many variables at play in the oil, gas, and mineral markets, any attempt to project an actual number of passage transits in the future is a mug's game. The underlying assumptions are always changing. Even with these limitations in mind, a 1985 Arctic Marine Traffic Forecast predicted one-way vessel voyages in the North to be more than 300 by 1990, more than 350 in 1995, and more than 400 by the turn of the century.[14] While these projections are by their very nature speculative, none the less they reveal the potential scope of increased traffic. With slumping oil prices, those figures would undoubtedly be altered downwards. However, even substantially lowered estimates still represent a sharp increase over the pattern of the previous eighty-five years. Since control of maritime traffic may become the key in any legal battle over the passage's status, these estimates cannot be dismissed out of hand.

If Canada wants to control the development which will occur, then it is essential both to have the capacity to enforce its anti-pollution laws and to exercise full control over the Northwest Passage. Anything less is unacceptable and a potential menace to our environment. Unchecked, uncontrolled shipping through the passage is not only a challenge to our sovereignty, it is also a threat to our heritage.

6

Time to plant the flag

It is April 1991 and, at the rather underwhelming International Court of Justice in the Hague, the acerbic lawyer representing the United States is about to complete his argument to the panel of eleven judges. It is the case of the U.S.A. *vs*. Canada. At stake is the legal status of the Northwest Passage. There is an air of anticipation as everyone in the crowded courtroom realizes the lawyer is about to conclude his argument. 'And you realize, my lords, there is this fundamental requirement in international law that for any country to have a water-way declared *internal*, it must not only occupy it and manifest some presence there, but also be able to defend it and exercise some control over it. So, as you ponder the Canadian arguments, I would ask you all to consider three basic questions: Can it *truly* be said that Canada has the capacity to enforce its pollution, fishing, and civil laws in the Northwest Passage? Can it *truly* be said that Canada has the capacity to know what is happening in the passage year round? And, can it *truly* be said Canada possesses any capacity to deny entry to the passage to any vessel it considers hostile? If the evidence allows you to answer these questions with a "yes," then Canada has a valid case. But if, as I believe, the evidence can only lead you to conclude that the answer must be "no" to all three questions, then I humbly suggest the Canadian case is fatally flawed. I thank you.'

This scene, of course, is apocryphal but it is by no means unimaginable. Some argue the United States would never go to court on this issue; others disagree. However, no Canadian government can afford to ignore the risk. Is Canada ready to face it?

For any self-respecting nation, sovereignty is a precious commodity. So long as its existence and authority go unchallenged a nation can exercise freely those powers that sovereignty bestows. But once sovereignty is lost, it is usually lost forever and with it, those invaluable powers that enable a state to protect and govern itself as its people see fit. For Canada, nowhere do these truisms apply with greater urgency than in the Arctic. Canada's sovereignty over the lands and islands of the Arctic archipelago stands unquestioned. However, its sovereignty over the Northwest Passage, while now arguably intact, is being challenged by our most immediate neighbour and could be lost in any court challenge.

The cruel irony is that while, often in response to well-publicized foreign incursions and to changing economic and environmental circumstances in the North, Parliament has moved legislatively to ensure sovereignty, it has not shown the same perseverance or inclination to back up these laws. The passage of the Arctic Waters Pollution Prevention Act in 1970 is a prime example. With a single stroke of the legislative pen, Canada unilaterally and boldly increased its maritime obligations more than a hundredfold with this far-reaching anti-pollution law. A concerted international diplomatic strategy was also mounted, which resulted in successful passage of the 'Arctic clause,' which gives the act much-needed international acceptance. In 1986, Ottawa moved to clear the last hurdle for a possible u.s. court challenge to the act by accepting jurisdiction of the World Court.

But what tangible steps were taken in that same sixteen-year period to give some credibility to Canada's ability to enforce the act? The answer is: precious few. If anything, Canada's navy withered even more in that period: no new vessels were brought into operation and none were slated for the North. Ottawa did announce plans for a new Class 8 ice-breaker in 1986 but they were mired in the tendering process for over a year as Ottawa scrambled to find the funds.[1] In any court challenge, Canada would stand in the dock in the unenviable position of having to admit its navy does not possess a single ice-strengthened vessel capable of operating in moderately ice-infested, let alone ice-covered, waters.[2]

The task of enforcing the act has fallen to the Coast Guard, which has eight heavy ice-breakers and thirteen medium-sized and smaller ones. Although an average of nine or ten see active duty during the three-month Arctic shipping period, none of them can operate effectively at other times. Furthermore, the Coast Guard is an entirely civilian service whose vessels are neither armed nor fit to be armed if such was needed. Nor is enforcement of the act the Coast Guard's only task. Those ice-breakers on active duty are also responsible for ensuring safe and efficient maritime transportation, operation of navigation aids, marine search and rescue, escorts during shipping season, operation of the vessel-reporting system, not to mention the co-ordination of the Eastern Arctic sea-lift – the annual resupply to the communities, firms, and individuals working and living in the high Arctic.[3] All this for a handful of vessels working to monitor the world's longest coastline!

To put this scene further into perspective, one must also remember that, in the same sixteen-year period, Canada also declared the new exclusive 320-kilometre Arctic Fishing Zone and adopted the Canadian Laws Offshore Application Act, which extends Canada's civil and criminal law within the same 320-kilometre limit. Enforcement of both these acts in the Arctic is left to the same handful of ice-breakers and supply vessels.

Surely in any legal challenge of Canada's sovereignty over the Northwest Passage, one important consideration would be how well Canada has enforced these laws and how strongly it has been challenged over them. The reality is that Canada simply does not possess an adequate capacity to monitor the passage of submarines, clean up Arctic spills, or maintain year-round surveillance of the area. What has evolved is a variation of the 'commitment-capability gap,' a term often used to describe the difference between what Canada has promised to do militarily and what it is capable of doing. The term is equally applicable to sovereignty over the passage. There is now a serious gap between what Canada has legislated and what it can enforce.

By any objective standard, a state must have some year-round surveillance capacity of its territories. Such a task is traditionally the domain of a country's military. In fact, surveillance is a necessary ingredient of any country's basic defence effort. Yet, on this count as well, Canada has done little to upgrade its capacity. There is no naval vessel or submarine capable of plying the waters of the North, except during the three-month shipping season. Apart from the Canadian Rangers, there are only about one thousand land-based defence personnel in the Arctic at any one time. On the air side, there are the once-every-three-weeks Aurora patrols, although these patrols, too, have their limitations. With the upgraded North Warning System, Canada will have access to intelligence on air traffic in the North through our joint arrangement with the United States in NORAD. However, the system's primary function is warning of a Soviet low-flying attack, not traffic patterns in the Northwest Passage. Nor has Canada yet developed its own satellite network to provide intelligence. It is planned that some of Canada's new CF-18s will be able to use newly upgraded operating bases in Iqaluit (Frobisher Bay), Rankin Inlet, Kuujjuaq (Fort Chimo), Yellowknife, and Inuvik. However, this high-tech fighter has been stripped of its surveillance component, although that capacity still exists. When considered altogether, then, it is little wonder so many Canadian legal scholars are urging that Canada take more concrete measures to guarantee its sovereignty. To do so, Canada must be prepared to pay the price both in monetary terms and in terms of commitment. There is no free lunch in the preservation of sovereignty. One need only look to other circumpolar countries – Norway, Sweden, Greenland, and the Soviet Union – to learn some valuable lessons. All these countries have defined their sovereignty and surveillance objectives to include the northernmost stretches of their territories. For example, both Norway and Sweden have established relatively sophisticated military infrastructures along the top of the Scandinavian peninsula. Norwegian troops regularly patrol there, partly in response to the proximity of the Soviet Union but also 'to show the flag.'[4] Greenland has maintained its 'Sirius sledge patrol' to keep watch over the entire east coast of Greenland because of a legal challenge half a century old. In the Soviet Union, the development and surveillance of the Arctic has attained a level of sophistication unheard of in other parts of the globe. The degree, for example, to which the Soviets have provided necessary ice-breaking and navigational aids for year-round operation in the Northeast Passage is unparalleled.

In any new defence and external-affairs policy for Canada, therefore, these deficiencies must be addressed. It will be costly, although not every step need be taken immediately. If Canada is serious, it must be judged by its deeds not by its words. Outsiders could well assume from our track record that Canada's real commitment has been minimal. What is needed is a renewed will and a fresh manifesto to guarantee sovereignty over the passage. The time has come to plant the flag firmly. The necessary steps are outlined below.

SUPPORTING THE INUIT

As Canada's longest and most visible presence in the Arctic, the Inuit must be given priority where possible in any new sovereignty manifesto. As Mark Gordon, the Quebec Inuit spokesman, says, 'Canadian Inuit

have always used these waters as their ice cover in winter, thereby
providing Canada with the case in international law required to secure
Canadian rights.'⁵ It is precisely those rights which the Inuit are seeking
to preserve in their various land-claim settlements with Ottawa.

By successfully pursuing such agreement, Ottawa will also be able to
identify clearly Inuit interests in any future maritime traffic through the
passage. Those interests are not always going to coincide, and some
tough choices will have to be made to protect traditional Inuit fishing and
hunting patterns. However, successful negotiation of the land claims,
despite some federal misgivings, would certainly represent a valuable
first step in the sovereignty battle. It would also send an unmistakable
message to the outside world that Canada has bound itself in law to
protect the Inuit and consequently their protected use of the passage.
Such a commitment would be very powerful since, in making it, Canada
would be upholding a centuries-old tradition. The final negotiation of
such claims would also produce a greater social and economic stability
in the North.

Ottawa could also recruit and train the Inuit and other interested
northerners to do needed oceanographic and ice research in the passage.
Although most of the seven passage routes have been surveyed, more
detailed work is needed in several channels, most notably the Parry
channel, James Ross Strait, and Dolphin and Union straits. The last
three, in particular, would be vital if a southern navigation route – using
any of routes three, four or five described above – was developed. As
much as possible of the nuts and bolts work of sovereignty should be
performed by those who live nearby.

As part of Canada's new policy to think of itself as a circumpolar
nation, it should establish closer links with our northern neighbours.
Since the Inuit have led the way in this regard through the Inuit Circumpolar Conference, these links should be encouraged and financially sup-
ported. As Mark Gordon says: 'I think the Canadian government must
first realize its only true allies are the Inuit. These people have a direct
interest in whatever policy is made in the Arctic. It is not a hinterland to
us; it is our homeland.'⁶

EXPANDING THE ARCTIC RANGERS

There is probably not a better bargain for sovereignty patrol than the unheralded and often forgotten Arctic Rangers. This band of 640, with their vintage Lee-Enfield rifles and red baseball caps, has been patrolling the North since the Second World War. Yet they have never received the recognition, let alone the respect they deserve from southern Canadians. Too often one hears whispers that the $34 a day militia pay is simply a better substitute than social assistance. Yet Canadians could well take a page from the Greenlanders' book. They know and speak proudly of their largely indigenous 'Sirius sledge patrol,' which is responsible for sovereignty patrols over the vast, largely uninhabited east coast of Greenland. Here is how Lars Vesterbrik, head of Greenland's Home Rule Office, describes the patrol: 'Everyone realizes the only effective way of patrolling is to walk up and down the land. Air patrols can't see footsteps and things can be hidden. We feel this job is essential and those who do it are held in high esteem. After all, this is defence of our land.'[7]

Canada's Inuit leaders are anxious to see the role of the Rangers expanded. At its current cost of $200,000 a year, the Rangers' budget represents a fraction of the total defence budget and involves the Inuit in the defence effort. As the Inuit have so eloquently testified, they have a bigger stake than anyone in the maintenance of Canadian sovereignty as it involves their 'living room' and their 'dining tables.' The Ranger forces and its role, should be expanded. Every effort should be made to publicize their presence and let the rest of the country know who its sovereignty soldiers are.

INCREASING AIR SURVEILLANCE

Despite its limitations, the Aurora long-range patrol aircraft is another very useful tool for ongoing sovereignty patrol. Although Aurora operations are hindered by both bad weather and darkness in winter, the military is enthusiastic about its surveillance and photographic capabilities. However, sixteen patrols a year just isn't sufficient by any measuring stick. While the Auroras patrol the entire North, a greater emphasis should be placed on surveillance of the main passage route. Under current arrangements, the Auroras land at both Iqaluit and Yellowknife, although none is permanently stationed in the North. With its current complement of eighteen aircraft, the military is hard pressed to live up to its commitments on the Atlantic and the Pacific, let alone the northern patrols. Serious thought should be given to stationing at least one Aurora in the North on permanent duty patrol.

Canada invested millions of dollars in the Aurora program and yet ended up ordering only eighteen of them. The current unit cost is approximately $25 million. When one compares the number of similar patrol aircraft which other countries with much smaller coastlines have on duty (the Netherlands has 13; Japan, 130),[8] the need for more for Canada becomes obvious. Since the Auroras are an essential and effective part of anti-submarine warfare – a role Canada has specialized in – then the argument for more Auroras is even stronger. Following the *Polar Sea*'s voyage, the government did in fact announce a program of increased surveillance. It has not yet got off the ground, but its time has come.

So, too, has the time to reconsider a sovereignty role for the CF-18s. The reconnaissance equipment was deleted from the specifications for the plane for reasons of economy. When he was head of the Air Command, Canada's chief of defence staff General Paul Manson foresaw a strong need for the Hornets to take this role:

Our new fighter aircraft does have the capacity to be equipped with a reconnaissance pod and this could be done relatively easily should the need arise. I think it will, not so much for battlefield reconnaissance but rather for what might be called strategic or sovereignty reconnaissance, specially in the Canadian northland ... with the CF-18's long range, rapid reaction and excellent navigation systems, it would be a natural vehicle for such tasks, complementing the Aurora's existing surveillance capacity in the North.[9]

As the new North Warning System is brought onto line, more CF-18s will be stationed in the North. The reconnaissance pods would be an ideal and relatively inexpensive addition to the surveillance and sovereignty arsenal.

INTEGRATING THE ROLES OF EXISTING FORCES IN THE NORTH

By any measure, the total number of government personnel monitoring and guarding the North, and more particularly the Northwest Passage, is modest. Yet each of the three main contingents – the RCMP, the Coast Guard, and the forces – is carefully confined to certain roles. Take the ice-breakers, for example, which are now operated exclusively by the Coast Guard. They are unarmed and have no capability to allow for the landing of military helicopters. As members of a totally civilian service, the Coast Guard are not usually given any para-military training. Yet under the present arrangement, it is these ice-breakers that represent Canada's first line of defence in the enforcement of the Arctic Waters Pollution Prevention Act. That act allows Canada to deny entry into its waters of any vessel it considers a pollution hazard. But how can Canada do this with a small unarmed Coast Guard cutter?

Surely it makes sense for these ice-breakers to be lightly armed and in future configured in such a way as to allow for the landing of helicopters to aid in patrol of the passage. The suggestion that members of the navy be seconded to the Coast Guard for special practice and training in the Arctic is also a good one.[10] Since there is little likelihood that there will be an increased naval presence in the Arctic in the short run, the brunt of the surveillance work will be left to the Coast Guard and to a much lesser extent to the Mounties. They should both be given the training and the tools to do the job. And, to back them up, members of the military should be assigned on a regular rotational basis to help with this role.

SIGNING A USER AGREEMENT OR OFF TO THE WORLD COURT

To help 'clarify' the status of the Northwest Passage, Canada has decided to seek some agreement or treaty with the United States over its use. Various options have been discussed. One initially favored by Ottawa would see the United States accepting Canada's claim of sovereignty in return for unfettered American naval access to all Canadian Arctic waters.[11] Obviously the ideal solution from a Canadian perspective would be for the United States to simply accept Canada's claim. Failing that, Canadian jurisdiction could be recognized in return for limited or regulated u.s. use of our waters. By pushing this question to the top of the Canada-u.s. bilateral agenda in 1987, the Canadian government signalled clearly that it was anxious to conclude some type of deal.

Would it be in Canada's best interests? At first glance, there is a surface attraction to this strategy. Since the United States is the only major power so far to take public exception to Canada's claim, American acceptance of it would remove a major hurdle. An agreement would also gain, presumably, u.s. acceptance of our Arctic anti-pollution laws and recognition of Canadian authority to fully regulate maritime traffic through the Passage. If u.s. submarines were to be allowed access to Canadian waters, Canada might also be able to secure more knowledge of their transits.

Yet behind those advantages lie substantial hidden drawbacks. Such an agreement would only be binding on the two countries that signed it. Consequently, other maritime powers, such as Japan, or for that matter the Soviet Union, would not be bound by it. Nor would it likely have any practical effect on the transits of friendly or unfriendly submarines through the area. What makes nuclear submarines so attractive to the superpowers is their ability to lurk in hidden places and remain undetected. The routes of these submarines are some of the u.s. military's most closely guarded secrets and not likely to be readily revealed. Even if they are, there is no guarantee the subs will stick to the designated routes.

Another problem with a long-term lease is that it could restrict Canada's military options in the future. If, for example, an agreement allowed u.s. submarines total access to Canadian waters for the next century, this would severely limit Canadian initiatives in arms control or moves to keep the Arctic as demilitarized as possible. While Canadians could rest assured that the United States was protecting our northern shores, the country would effectively be handing over its northern naval defence to the Americans. From both a sovereignty and military point of view, this is not a decision to be taken lightly.

In the final analysis, there is also something unseemly about a country negotiating its own sovereignty. A long-term treaty or lease-back arrangement might reduce Canada to some sort of northern Panama. That alone is incentive enough to examine other options. u.s. reticence to sign any agreement may also force Canada to study alternatives. After having Canada's position personally explained to him by Prime Minister Mulroney in mid-1987, u.s. president Ronald Reagan has conceded there is 'a great deal of merit' in Canada's claim for sovereignty. He cited the fact that many of the northern islands 'are connected by permanent ice conditions with people living on that ice.'[12] However, Reagan was quick to add that America's primary fear was the creation of a dangerous precedent for 'about 16 choke points in the world that must be kept open.'[13] While his concession that the Northwest Passage is 'somewhat different' may give some solace to Canadians, overriding u.s. military interests are more likely to prevail. America's strategic role around the world does not allow it to be party to agreements which close off important waterways to the right of innocent passage. The United States is afraid of the precedent it would set and the compromises any such agreement may impose on a future u.s. security role in the Arctic. This latter factor may be of critical importance if a fully developed Star Wars program is ever implemented. The statement of a senior Pentagon official illustrates the intensity of u.s. feelings: 'The Northwest Passage is not Canadian territory. It's international water and for you to presume to prevent use of international water, this puts you on a collision course with the other maritime powers of the world ... There is no nation that accepts Quaddafi's Line of Death [in the Gulf of Sidra] and no nation that accepts that the Northwest Passage is a territorial sea.'[14]

The Pentagon has identified sixteen strategically important 'choke points' – such as the Dardenelles (Turkey), the Kattegat (Denmark), and the Strait of Gibraltar – which it says must be kept open. The fear that one country may use the 'Canadian precedent' as grounds for taking control of one of these choke points and forbidding the right of innocent passage frankly terrifies the Pentagon.

Another option is to go to the International Court of Justice and let the court decide the issue once and for all. The most obvious risk, of course, is losing. Although Canada's case is strong, it has its weaknesses. Even if Canada decided to take the gamble, the United States would first have to agree to the court's jurisdiction. Many u.s. officials may be afraid to do this because of, surprisingly, the prospect of winning. If the United States succeeded in having the passage declared an international waterway, it would give the Soviet Union the unimpeachable right to use the waterway. Strategically, this would give the United States pause for concern. While Soviet missile-carrying submarines regularly patrol off both eastern and western coasts of the United States, the prospect of them sitting in Canada's North is not particularly inviting. It would come down probably to a question of balancing this concern against American wishes to keep the choke points open. It is hard to predict what the Pentagon would ultimately say.

Another problem is that the United States has withdrawn acceptance of the court's jurisdiction over the Nicaraguan affair. It is questionable whether, as with a previous boundary dispute with Canada over the Gulf of Maine, the United States would do an about-face and agree to the court's authority. If it did and Canada eventually won the case, it would obviously resolve the issue. But the risks are considerable.

Another variation of this option has both the United States and Canada seeking binding arbitration from a limited panel of international judges. While such an option allows both sides to have a say in selecting their adjudicators, a final decision would be binding only on the two countries. And, while persuasive, it would lack some of the authority that a judgment from the International Court of Justice would have.

The final option is to sit tight and do nothing for the time being. While the legal status would remain clouded, this strategy has the built-in advantage of buying time. Canada could use some time to beef up its capacity to control and enforce its rights over the passage. So far, Canada has felt in the absence of any challenge that its claim to sovereignty only got stronger. Yet as the transit figures reveal, time may be running short as exploration of Arctic petrocarbons becomes more viable. Arguably, there is still a window of opportunity for Canada to build up its case.

On balance, it seems advisable for Canada to adopt a flexible approach. If a satisfactory agreement can be reached on which there is *no* compromise on our sovereignty and *no* wholesale right for u.s. subs to use Canada's Arctic waters, then an agreement should be sought. But any inclination to bargain away a piece of our sovereignty in the interests of securing an agreement should be steadfastly avoided. The prospect of having some seemingly innocuous compromise later used to justify American use of our waters for some Star Wars-type plan is too distasteful. If a satisfactory agreement can't be reached, then Canada should bide its time. To opt for the World Court now is fraught with too many risks. Since time could be used to lessen some of those risks, there is little percentage in taking such action. The same reasoning also precludes any move to binding arbitration.

One final point should be made. If the Americans attempt one more transit through the passage without prior approval, Canada should register its objection in every international forum available. At that point, the government should follow up with an immediate appeal to the World Court. To allow the United States to carry out a repeat of the *Polar Sea* without objection could prove fatal to Canada's sovereignty case.

APPLYING AND ENFORCING SHIPPING REGULATIONS
IN THE PASSAGE

To understand the potential for exercising control over a northern waterway, one need only look to the Soviets. Although they have declared the Northeast Passage to be *internal* waters, they have also said that foreign commercial ships have the right of innocent passage. But the Soviets insist that any such vessel use its ice-breaking and pilotage services –

and for a fee. A published brochure lists the schedule of fees.[15] Canada does precisely the same for all ships using the St Lawrence and other parts of the Great Lakes system. Why not do the same for the Northwest Passage?

The Department of Transport has already prepared a list of all services that would be required, under the name 'Arctic Marine Services Policy' – everything from buoys to ice-breaking and escorting, to pilotage boats, to inspection terminals and, finally, weather- and ice-forecasting services. Needless to say, these services would carry price-tags, some of which might be prohibitive at this point. However, Canada should speed up the policy's implementation by providing pilotage services and building incrementally on that base. The benefits would be control of all foreign shipping through the passage and adherence to our anti-pollution laws. A similar commitment is maintained without question on the St Lawrence, where admittedly the traffic is large. As traffic increases through the passage, though, Canada should be ready with the necessary equipment to provide a range of basic services. Since the planning and design of some of the equipment will take time, work should begin immediately.

This policy also has the advantage of spreading the cost over a number of years. International law recognizes the right of a coastal nation to charge foreign vessels for such pilotage services. For ships plying the Great Lakes, such costs are part of doing business. It should be the same for any ships using the passage. Such a regime would also send an unmistakable message to the rest of the world: Canada is taking concrete steps to control its passage.

BUILDING THE POLAR 8 ICE-BREAKER

Has its time come? The answer must surely be 'yes.' As part of Ottawa's sovereignty package following the *Polar Sea* incident, the commitment was made to go ahead with the construction of a $450 million Polar 8 ice-breaker equipped with 100,000-horsepower engines and designed to smash through twelve-metre-thick ice. Plans for the Polar 8 had been in the Coast Guard's files for more than a decade. Under its original specifications, it was intended to escort tanker and other commercial traffic through northern waters. Revised plans have included other tasks, including scientific research and enforcement of environmental laws.

Artist's conception of new Polar 8 ice-breaker
(Photo courtesy Department of Transport)

From a sovereignty point of view, the ice-breaker provides Canada with its first year-round capacity in the passage. Only three of Canada's current stable of ice-breakers are capable of operating in the North beyond the summer shipping season. Only the *Louis St Laurent* has the ability to operate in ice-covered waters, although it is not strong enough to navigate year round through either of the main passage routes. Although the Polar 8 was described by one general as a 'sitting duck' from a military point of view,[16] it does offer some strategic possibilities. Plans are now in place to arm it so as to give Canada a year-round military presence in the Arctic. It could also perform surface and underwater surveillance, monitor Soviet communications, transport troops when needed, and even lay mines in the event of a war.

The objections to this ice-breaker have been threefold: its cost, its limited military value, and its restricted sovereignty usefulness. Some critics have already labelled the Polar 8 the 'billion dollar flag'; however, the reply to such a complaint must surely be that sovereignty does not come at bargain prices in the North. The Soviets, by comparison, have a small flotilla of ice-breakers. No one is suggesting that Canada must have as many but if we are to get serious about this part of the country, then it is time to stop insisting that Canada cannot afford its own Arctic.

From solely a military point of view, it is difficult to justify the expenditure. Further, any attempt to do so is a throwback to Canada's traditional pattern of analysing every expenditure in the Arctic from separate pigeon holes. Privately, Canada's military leaders could come up with a metre-long list of better ways to spend the money. Such an ice-breaker, with limited arms and no air protection, would be highly vulnerable to attack, they add. However, the response must be that the Polar 8's prime purpose is not military. In fact, when it was first announced by the Mulroney government no provision was included for its arming. That addition came as an afterthought.[17] What is clear is that the Polar 8 does offer *some* limited military capabilities, which the forces now lack. In that sense, it will help with the defence of Canada.

Perhaps the most cogent criticism of the Polar 8 is that it would not by itself be sufficient for year-round surveillance and control of foreign shipping. Given the immense size of the coastline, this is undoubtedly true. At this point one is tempted to paraphrase Chairman Mao's famous saying that a long voyage is always started with a single step. To continue to argue that one ice-breaker will never be sufficient is never to begin, never to take the first step. Commercial interests have many plans on the drawing-boards for year-round tankers and container vessels in the North. Is Canada prepared to let those plans be implemented without any presence of its own? Is it prepared to let foreign countries determine whether their vessels meet Canadian anti-pollution standards? Does it want to stand in the dock if and when its sovereignty over the passage is challenged and have to admit it didn't feel it could afford to have *one* year-round ice-breaker in the passage? Those are the risks and the questions Canada may have to face.

ESTABLISHING A PASSAGE HEADQUARTERS

With a sustained and increased presence in the passage, Canada would need a central operations and supply centre – a sort of 'Northwest Passage headquarters.' Since the Coast Guard will be performing most of the patrol duties for the foreseeable future, it could best use this depot for the servicing of ice-breakers and other vessels. The headquarters could also provide a base for the pilotage services, weather surveillance of the passage, search and rescue, and other general assistance operations. It could also act as a base for one of the Auroras sent north on sovereignty patrol.

From a geographical point of view, it makes sense for the headquarters to be on the passage or as close as possible. The military has already done some research and suggests that the best location for a base would be on Devon Island.[18] While there is no question a passage headquarters would be an expensive proposition, it could be developed incrementally with services added over time. However, Qausuittuq (formerly Resolute) – situated right on the passage with its existing weather and communications equipment and long runway – offers many advantages. Many of the basic facilities needed for a headquarters are already there. The only drawbacks are that its airport is often shut down because of bad weather and its wharf – the only one in the high Arctic – was knocked out a few years ago by ice. There may be other options but Qausuittuq should be considered. A passage headquarters would go a long way to cement Canada's presence on the waterway.

SATELLITES, SUBMARINES, AND SOUND SURVEILLANCE
UNDER THE SEA (SOSUS)

Although praised most often for their military value, each of these systems has important spin-offs for sovereignty protection. While each will be analyzed in greater detail in later chapters, their sovereignty value is worthwhile outlining now. Satellites, with their superior surveillance capacity, undoubtedly represent the wave of the future. Mention has already been made of the limitations of the Aurora patrol aircraft in bad weather and winter. Proposed and existing military radar will give intelligence on what is happening in the airspace around the edges of Canada. But for all weather and all-season surveillance of the entire country, remote-sensing satellites are the answer. Canadian space-company executives say the technology is already in place, which would allow, for example, for detection of surface vessels anywhere in the Arctic archipelago up to an accuracy of 500 metres.[19] In the North, such a system could also provide vital information on ice conditions in the passage, oil spills, and natural-resource deposits. Canada has already indicated interest in development of such satellites in a joint venture with the United States and Britain. This project should be pursued. With it, Canada would finally have the capacity to know what was happening on all the waterways of the Arctic on a year-round basis.

To complement the 'eyes' overhead, Canada should also install some 'ears' underneath the water. While satellites are ideal to detect surface traffic, their usefulness is severely restricted for clandestine submarine operations. Since uncontrolled foreign-submarine traffic is one of the real theats to Canadian sovereignty, knowledge of such traffic is a prerequisite of any control. To provide such intelligence, Canada should install up-to-date sonar surveillance systems at all major entrances to the passage. Usually called SOSUS (Sound Surveillance Under the Sea) arrays, each one would be composed of a network of hydrophones (similar to microphones) fixed to the seabed and linked to listening posts on land. Various SOSUS systems have been in use for decades although there have been ongoing problems with their operation under ice. Canada already has an experimental system in place under Lancaster Sound and the United States has installed them farther north. Placed at both the eastern and western approaches to the passage, these arrays would act as a sort of 'electronic trip-wire' to warn of all underwater traffic. Like satellites, the arrays also have the advantage of being immune to weather conditions and thus able to provide year-round data. Again, the government has already expressed interest in Arctic SOSUS. The time has come to translate interest into action.

The final peg in the sovereignty board is submarines. In its 1987 White Paper on Defence, Ottawa signalled formally its intention to buy a fleet of up to twelve nuclear-powered submarines.[20] 'The military role in sovereignty,' the paper argues, 'is that of the ultimate coercive force available when the capabilities of the civil authorities are inadequate ... or when Canada's right to exercise jurisdiction is challenged by others.'[21] Certainly satellites and SOSUS will let Canada know what is happening on and under its waters. But neither gives Canada any capacity to do anything about it. This is where submarines would fit in. While the strategic importance of buying such expensive nuclear-powered submarines is highly dubious, as will be discussed later, there is none the less an argument to be made for subs as tools of sovereignty control. If Canada is to have the capacity to deny entry to an unwanted intruder into its waters – arguably a key component of sovereignty – then submarines are needed. Some critics argue submarines have a very limited role in sovereignty for they are 'invisible.'[22] Certainly the 'hunter / killer' type of submarine sought by Ottawa is only effective in doing its job if it keeps its position secret at all times. In that sense, it is not a very visible tool to 'show the flag' in the Arctic. A huge ice-breaker can do that much better. Yet in replying to the 'invisibility argument,' defence minister Perrin Beatty makes a good point: 'It's rather like saying if you have a burglar alarm in your house, it won't dissuade burglars unless all the wires and sensors are evident.'[23] Surely the advantage for Canada is that such submarines give Canada the *capacity* to control underwater traffic. Possession of that capacity would go a long way to strengthen Canada's claim of total sovereignty. Whether or when it ever chose to use that capacity, or whether the subs have to be nuclear-powered are entirely different questions. It comes down to this: now Canada does not have a viable year-round sea-denial capacity in the Arctic. With subs capable of operating under ice, it would.

Submarines have been part of Canada's navy for decades. It is remarkable that with the world's longest Arctic coastline, no Canadian sub can even operate in the North for any extended time. For Canada to buy submarines that have no under-ice capability would represent another denial of our geography. It would also leave patrol of Canada's territorial waters and ultimate enforcement of Canada's laws in the Arctic to the Coast Guard. That would surely be settling for second-best while also compromising our commitment to sovereignty control. In short, submarines would give Canada a vital boost to its legal case while virtually cementing its control over the passage, once and for all.

It is at this point where the Canadian spirit has most often faltered – paying the bill. There is no doubt that the cost of the manifesto presented would run into the billions of dollars. But spread out over a decade or more, the pain becomes more bearable. Three comparisons should also be kept in mind. Canada's total defence budget is roughly $10 billion a year and funding would almost certainly be available from the department of transport for some of the proposals, such as the Coast Guard. Canada now spends annually $1 billion on its European commitment to NATO and is committed to spend $1.1 billion on a new low-level air-defence system to protect our troops and fighters in Europe. One might well ask where our priorities lie.

In conclusion, it is worthwhile to return to those three fundamental questions Canada might face in that International Court. Can Canada truly be said to possess the capacity to know what is happening in the Northwest Passage year round? Can Canada truly be said to possess the capacity to enforce its pollution and fishing laws? Does Canada have any year-round capacity to deny passage to a vessel it considers undesirable? If the manifesto outlined above were implemented, then Canada could reply with a resounding 'yes' to each of the three questions. Then and only then, could Canada argue with conviction that it had taken all steps to occupy and enforce its laws in the passage. No one should doubt that if and when that court challenge comes – and there is a chance it will – those questions will be asked. But will Canada be ready?

SECURITY

7

Canada's Arctic: The new military frontier

For centuries, the only thing strategic about Canada's Arctic was its impenetrability. It was to all intents and purposes a natural barrier. Early recollections of pirate voyages to Hudson Bay in search of unknown bounty were about the most any adventurist could conjure up. As one Canadian military man in the 1940s mused: 'there's nowhere to go and nothing to do once you get there.'[1] But just as military technology has evolved, so too has strategic interest in the North. The idea that it would become an increasingly vital military frontier would have seemed far-fetched only four decades ago. Yet, with the advent of intercontinental ballistic missiles, nuclear-powered submarines, cruise missiles, and space-based defence systems, that is precisely what Canada's North has become – the newest of the military frontiers.

To understand this frontier, one must first comprehend the Arctic Ocean. Forbidding, barren, with the face of an alien moon, it covers the top of the globe for some fourteen million kilometres. It is the only one of Earth's oceans that can be crossed by foot, yet no man has dared try. Its permanent crust of ice, perpetually shifting, crumbling, throwing up ranges of jagged ridges, has been the death-bed for many a ship. Whipped on the surface by fierce winds and nudged slowly by the under-lying currents, it will suddenly open up to reveal waters trapped under the thick crust. Through these apertures, known as polynia or leads, there is uncovered an underwater domain which, close to the North Pole, plunges to almost five thousand metres in depth. Slicing the domain in half is a spectacular soaring ridge – the Lomonosov Ridge – stretching from eastern Greenland to the heart of the Soviet Union. As the accompanying diagram reveals, this prehistoric vestige of an old continental

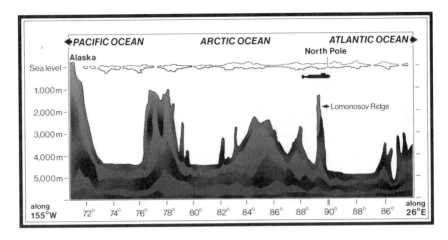

Depth profile of the Arctic Ocean

shelf is flanked on either side by two other mountain ranges. yet despite
the Alp-like heights of the bordering ranges, the water depth is a yawn-
ing kilometre, ample room for a submarine to pass.

The first vessel to confirm the navigability of this mammoth underwater throughway was the U.S.S. *Nautilus* which in 1958 made the
underwater passage from Point Barrow, Alaska, to the Svalbard Islands.
Since then, scores of other submarines have traversed the expanse, making such passage almost routine. While the ocean is covered by sea ice
virtually year round, there are always cracks and openings through
which a submarine can surface, if only temporarily. The deep sea-bed
also provides an immense haven, making detection virtually impossible.
While the continental shelf is quite narrow off the Canadian and Greenland coasts, it extends much farther off the Soviet coast. The very large
amounts of fresh water pouring into the ocean from Soviet rivers have
also had a dramatic effect, tempering the climate on that side, and
allowing for almost year-round shipping through the Northwest Passage.
On the North American side, where only the Mackenzie River pours in
fresh water and the continental shelf is narrow, the conditions are more
frigid, resulting in a colder climate and more severe ice build-up, These
conditions have allowed ice stations, such as the United States-operated
Fletcher's Ice Island, which has flourished for more than two decades, to
carry on research without fear of sinking. The constant ice also allows

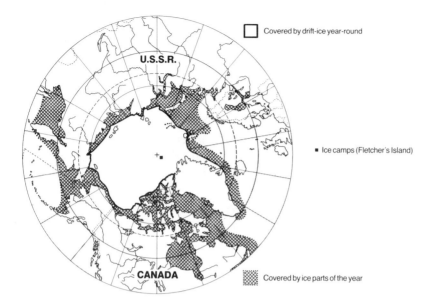

Covered by drift-ice year-round

U.S.S.R.

■ Ice camps (Fletcher's Island)

CANADA

Covered by ice parts of the year

Ice conditions in the Arctic Ocean

airplanes to land on ice fields, and tracked land vehicles to meander for hundreds of kilometres. Thus, the Arctic Ocean has the characteristics of both land and sea, in ways totally unlike other parts of the globe.

For any nation to contemplate crossing this vase expanse with a land invasion force is to reckon with the near impossible. No man has yet crossed from one side to another and for an army to do so would be a Napoleonic nightmare. Studies have shown that when Canadian troops have trained in the high Arctic, approximately 80 per cent of their energy is consumed in mere survival.[2] That leaves little with which to do battle. Throw in all the equipment, weapons, provisions, and fuel needed for an invasion, and the task becomes that much more daunting. Furthermore, traditional tanks and armoured vehicles can't function well or travel far in such extreme conditions. Inuit on sleds or snowmobiles can travel twice the distance in the same time. The sun presents another complication. For nearly one-third of the year the region is in total darkness, while for another third it is in perpetual light. In both cases, the chances of making an undetected crossing would be slim to non-existent.

Assuming the crossing were made, what would be its strategic purpose? The islands of the Canadian archipelago are a desert of endless permafrost, an equally inhospitable terrain. More importantly, there is little of strategic importance to anyone other than a few radar stations farther south. Assuming an enemy base camp was set up, the problem of resupplying and servicing this camp from a distance of more than two thousand kilometres would tax any military's imagination. The only variable in this strategic equation is Canada's proved oil and gas reserves. If and when these reserves are fully tapped, and they become a vital component of North American energy supply, then, of necessity, they would gain strategic value.

Canadian military strategists have privately mused that in the unlikely event of a protracted war, the Soviets might well dispatch commando-type units to land in the Arctic. Their purpose would be to sabotage pipelines or act as a diversion to keep some Canadian and u.s. resources focused on the North, instead of elsewhere. Such a scenario is unlikely, but not so far-fetched that Canada should forget completely about training its forces in Arctic combat. Clearly, nearly one-third of Canadian territory cannot be left completely unmanned. However, it seems safe to assume the threat of attack on or through the ice of the Arctic Ocean against Canada is indeed negligible.

Under the ice, however, is a different matter. What had been for centuries a benign area of limited strategic value has suddenly become, in the words of one u.s. strategic analyst, 'the latest growth area in Pentagon war thinking.'[3] The technological catalyst for this transformation has been the development of the nuclear-powered submarine. The old Second World War-vintage diesel submarines were never able to travel very far underwater because their electric batteries would give out. Nuclear propulsion has now made it possible for subs to stay submerged for months and to travel thousands of kilometres without surfacing. With this new capacity, submarines from both superpowers have already demonstrated for years the feasibility of operating under ice. The strategic advantages are enormous. Submarines hidden under ice are extremely difficult to detect, invisible to over-passing planes or satellites, and still able to confound many underwater radar detection systems.

What's more, the Arctic Ocean's location between the superpowers offers these submarines an enormous strategic advantage. With the development of more sophisticated and longer-ranged ballistic missiles, it is now possible for a Soviet Typhoon-type submarine sitting in Murmansk Harbour to launch its ballistic missiles to *any* target in North America or Europe. Several strategists have plotted graphs showing that the Arctic Ocean is in some cases the *sole*, and in other cases the *best*, staging area from which the widest variety of targets is available.[4] Conversely, for the United States, the Arctic Ocean provides in some cases the sole and in other cases one of the prime staging areas where a single u.s. submarine could hit *any* target in the Soviet Union. The scenario varies with the class of submarine and the range of the ballistic missile. While the Soviet Union has invested more in under-ice technology, the United States is not far behind. Obviously since the ocean is right in the Soviets' backyard, they have a much greater stake in its use. However, any military strategist, Soviet or American, is bound to look at the Arctic as a window of opportunity for target choices in plotting submarine strategy.

A further aid to missile-carrying submarines in the Arctic is the relatively easy access to patches of open water from which missiles can be fired. With the pack ice constantly heaving, such patches are formed regularly, usually within a forty-kilometre radius of any point in the polar ice pack. In other places, the ice pack is surprisingly thin (i.e., two metres), making it possible for a submarine to simply push its way through the ice to fire. Whatever the means, it is clearly established that such test firings have occurred and are well within the technological capabilities of both superpowers.

What does this mean for Canada's Arctic waters? Answering that question requires a critical look at the perspective of both superpowers. First, the Soviet Union, initially somewhat behind the United States in building up its force of ballistic-missile-carrying submarines (ssbns), has entered the fray with a vengeance and now has a fleet of sixty-three,[5] almost double the u.s. complement of thirty-six.[6] More revealing is that more than half, or thirty-nine, of these ssbns are based on the Arctic Ocean.[7] The pride of their fleet is what inside the Soviet navy is called the 'Zolotaya Ryba' ('Golden Fish'), the largest and most expensive submarine in the world. With a hull of costly titanium and the capacity to operate under ice, this Typhoon-class submarine can dive deeper and run faster than its u.s. counterparts. Its one drawback has been that it's a noisy dragster without a muffler. When a Typhoon went on patrol in 1985 off Norway, its movements were reportedly picked up by u.s. sonar devices in Bermuda.[8] Since then, the Soviets have moved to correct the problem. Each Typhoon – four are in operation and two more are being built – can carry up to 180 warheads on 20 missiles, with a range of more than 8,000 kilometres.[9] Again, what is revealing is that all four are based in the Arctic. So, too, are most of the Delta-class subs, for some of whom the Arctic Ocean is the *sole* staging area, one where targets in both Europe and North America are within range of their missiles.

To back up this fleet of ballistic-missile-carrying subs, the Soviets have an awesome complement of 214 attack subs,[10] whose job it is to sink enemy submarines and protect Soviet SSBNS. Not surprisingly, more than half of these (117) are based in the Arctic.[11] To be fair, one must stress that the Kola Peninsula on the Arctic Ocean is the Soviet Union's preferred naval base because it is the only ice-free area from which its vessels can get to other oceans without passing through so called 'choke points' (e.g., the Dardenelles guarding the Black Sea). So, for example, the Soviet subs that regularly patrol the Mediterranean are based in the Arctic. None the less, the data are so convincing that most analysts now accept the Arctic as one of the Soviet Union's *primary* staging areas for its SSBNS. Don Kerr, a naval analyst with the London-based International Institute for Strategic Studies, is one:

There is really no magic to it. For the Soviets to be able to position its SSBNS so close to its home base, just off the edge of the continental shelf, protected by attack submarines in a sanctuary, has to be a very attractive option. By staying up North, they [SSBNS] don't have to pass through any of NATO's existing surveillance systems and by being stationed so close to the home base, the communications problems, which are always tricky in the Arctic, are somewhat diminished.[12]

The proponents of this so-called 'bastion strategy' have ample evidence to back up their claim. Until the mid-1970s, Soviet SSBN's were regularly detected by NATO's underwater sonar systems as they traversed the Greenland-Iceland-United Kingdom (GIUK) Gap. Since then, the detections have dropped sharply, confirming the view there is no longer such a need to stray far away from home.[13] The Americans, with an acknowledged lead in attack subs and anti-submarine-warfare capacity, have also helped push the Soviets into a more defensive posture.[14] It is no secret U.S. attack subs have been probing the Soviet fleet under the

Arctic ice and right into the Barents Sea. Well-known Washington strategist William Arkin argues that this 'misguided' strategy is one of the prime reasons for the Soviets' move to the Arctic:

The Soviets are going to the Arctic in large part because the United States has increasingly integrated strategic anti-submarine warfare in its overall war-fighting deterrence strategy. The end result is that the u.s. has forced the Soviet Union to move to longer-ranged sea-launched ballistic missiles operating more and more in their home waters. And when even their home waters become more threatened by virtue of forward u.s. operations in the Norwegian Sea and other northern seas, then they have to move to another area where they can avoid the long arm of the u.s. Navy. And, increasingly that is the convergence between the oceans and the Arctic.[15]

Another factor not to be forgotten is that the Soviet navy is composed largely of conscripts. Navigating a submarine under ice is not an easy task, nor is it a simple matter to train new recruits in the use of the sophisticated systems that are now an integral part of most modern nuclear-powered submarines. It is an established fact that all Soviet ships spend far less time at sea than their u.s. counterparts.[16] These factors also mitigate against the Soviets wanting to send its SSBNs too far from home. There is no question the ideal location for a Soviet submarine is off either the Atlantic or the Pacific coast of North America. Three or four subs are always there and will continue to be.[17] This forward deployment two hundred kilometres off the shores of North America has the advantage of reducing the warning time of a strike in the so-called 'decapitation' deployment. However, even though both oceans are huge, noisier Soviet subs are more susceptible to detection and potential destruction by the United States. Furthermore, being so distant from home base is a disadvantage. None the less, they will always be there as part of the Soviet deterrent.

Another potential forward position is, of course, anywhere within Canada's Arctic waters. One curious geographical fact confronting both u.s. and Soviet strategists is that the Arctic Ocean in many ways resembles the Mediterranean. Both have few exit points. What points there are, are guarded and narrow. Exit from the Arctic can be made from only four points: out the Bering Sea, which is treacherously shallow; out through the thin gap between Greenland and Canada; out through the maze of the Canadian archipelago and the Northwest Passage; and finally, out the widest route, the Greenland-Iceland-United Kingdom (GIUK) Gap, which is carefully monitored by NATO.

Despite expressed public concern about Soviet subs roaming through Canada's North, there have been few if any confirmed cases of such intrusions. Sightings of submarines have certainly been made in the Arctic, but most often the nationality of the vessels is not known. There is one documented case of a Soviet sub plying the gap between Canada and Greenland as far as Disko Island off Greenland.[18] Greenland fishermen have also picked up sonar buoys with Eastern Bloc markings.[19] Certainly a look at the circumpolar map reveals that this gap offers a direct route for Soviet subs en route to u.s. shores. And, Canada's *Sailing Directions* confirms that the narrowest part of the gap, the 500-kilometre-long Nares Strait, has 'deep water to within a short distance of both shores of the strait.'[20] The strait has been navigated for the past thirty years by ice-breakers serving Canada's northernmost outpost, Alert. Although neither Canada nor the United States will officially confirm the fact, both countries have submarine-detection systems in place along this route. Canada's is somewhat farther south across Davis Strait. While this gap undoubtedly offers a direct route for the Soviets, the narrowness of the channel also makes it relatively easy to mine in times of crisis.

Another slightly longer route to u.s. shores for the Soviets is via the Canadian archipelago and through one of the routes of the Northwest Passage. Under the ice of the waters separating the Queen Elizabeth Islands, the permutations are considerable and many of the channels are navigable. Likewise, it is conceivable that a Soviet sub could simply position itself among the islands, hiding under the ice. Yet all those arguments which make deployment of Soviet SSBNs so attractive close to home would apply with equal force against Soviet deployment in Canadian waters. The fear of a Soviet sub plunked right in the heart of Hudson Bay ready to discharge its missiles should concern Canadians. But there has simply not been any evidence that the Soviets have exercised this option. Confirmation of this came from John Anderson, assistant deputy minister in the department of defence, in late 1985:

The Soviets are using their side of the Arctic Ocean for their submarines at the moment. It may happen that they will find it advantageous as time goes on to deploy missile launching submarines, either ballistic or cruise, through Arctic waters ... But there is no evidence that I am aware of that this is what they are doing now so one is talking about how much one should do to deny them a possible option which they may wish to use later.[21]

What has concerned Canadian officials, including defence minister Perrin Beatty, is the threat of longer-ranged cruise missiles and their placement aboard Soviet submarines.[22] Much smaller than ballistic missiles and also much slower, cruise missiles can be carried on battleships, merchant ships, planes, or submarines. They are insidious weapons because they are almost impossible to count, easy to hide, deadly, and with the development of new guidance systems, very accurate. Once aloft, they fly at very low altitudes and are small radar targets. They are normally only detected at very short ranges by ground radar stations. Fighter aircraft require pinpoint and timely direction to have any chance of knocking them out. Elaborate space-based or airborne early-warning systems could give some warning but at great cost and with little surety of complete success. In the words of retired Admiral Robert Falls 'that means there is no effective defence against the cruise missile.'[23]

The major feature that distinguishes the larger and more destructive ballistic missiles from cruise missiles is their speed. A ballistic missile launched from the Soviet Union takes only between thirty-five and forty minutes to reach its target in the u.s. heartland. A cruise missile, shot from the same spot (assuming it had the range), could take hours to reach the same u.s. target, thereby giving more time to take action to retaliate. Traditional strategic doctrine has it that the ballistic missiles in each superpower's arsenal – be they fired from land, air, or sea – could be used first in any major attack. This capacity is often referred to as the 'first-strike capability.' Cruise missiles, slower but lethal, form part of the 'second strike' capability. This so-called 'second-strike' capability is just as critical in deterring any attack, for it further lessens any expectation by a superpower that it might get away with a successful sneak attack. Even if first strike were successful – which itself is extremely doubtful – the target nation would still face the prospect of an avalanche of cruise missiles wreaking nuclear horror.

Because of the cruise's slower speed and much more limited range, there is an obvious strategic need to launch it as close to its intended target as possible. Until very recently, the Soviets have concentrated on very short-ranged sea-launched cruise missiles. In fact, 85 per cent of their arsenal has a range of below six hundred kilometres.[24] Obviously, then, there is little reason to deploy them in the Arctic since there is very little of military importance within range. The preferred deployment position is, of course, the Atlantic or the Pacific. However, recently the Soviets have upgraded their technology and are soon expected to deploy two new kinds of submarine-launched nuclear-tipped cruise missiles with a range of three thousand kilometres.[25] For such missiles, the Arctic may well be an option to consider as a means to diversify their force. A sufficient number of key targets would be within range. While, as yet, this option is hypothetical, no Canadian or American strategist can afford to ignore it.

What does this strategic situation mean for the United States and its use of Canada's Arctic waters? The proof is plentiful that, unlike those of the Soviets, u.s. subs have regularly roamed through Canada's North. In 1986, three u.s. subs travelled under ice from separate directions, achieving a rendezvous at the North Pole.[26] In the subsequent furore in parliament, both Prime Minister Mulroney and external affairs minister Joe Clark admitted they are 'aware' of u.s. submarine activity in Canada. While not confirming any routes, Clark said cryptically: 'There are provisions in place that allow us to know the information and to assert and protect our sovereignty and those provisions are respected.'[27] In the past four decades, at least twenty-five u.s. submarines are known to have operated in the Arctic, many of them in Canadian waters.[28] Those are only the known ones. It is reasonable and, in fact, logical to assume that the Americans have dispatched other subs on Arctic missions. While Clark and Mulroney insist that provisions are in place for Canada to be informed of such submarine activity, there is no way to know if these provisions are being used. Since Canada has no independent surveillance system, it must rely on information provided by the United States. To expect the United States to routinely inform Canada every time one of its submarines traverses Canadian waters in the Arctic is to fail to understand how the u.s. military operates. Like any military, it thrives on secrecy and likes to keep the number of those 'in the know' to a minimum. Peace groups in Halifax regularly monitor the traffic of u.s. submarines coming in and out of harbour, and they record a constant flow. While not all of these subs are headed to the Arctic, it is reasonable to assume that some are.

One of the reasons for this u.s. submarine traffic, as noted above by

William Arkin, is the U.S. adoption of a new 'forward' naval strategy to go right at the Soviets in their 'bastions.' According to the strategy's author, ex-U.S. navy secretary John Lehman, the navy would move aggressively into northern waters with submarines and then aircraft-carriers at the outbreak of war.[29] The purpose would be to roll back the Soviet northern fleet and attack its home 'bastions,' striking ports and any airfields within reach of the carriers' attack planes. Such a strategy requires that U.S. vessels, particularly submarines, be able to reach the Soviet domain as quickly as possible. Again, any map shows that one of the most direct routes is via Canada.

There are, needless to say, heavy risks in going right at the Soviet fleet. By accident or design, an attack on a Soviet SSBN – most of which are indistinguishable from conventional attack subs – could be interpreted as the opening volley in a nuclear confrontation. Yet, there is little doubt U.S. subs are regularly probing Soviet defences and are familiarizing themselves with the Arctic terrain, where any such naval encounter would take place.[30]

The prospect of Soviet subs with cruise missiles venturing into the northern reaches of North America is yet another reason for U.S. interest in our waters. Allowing such subs to roam freely through Canada's North does not fit in with Lehman's 'forward strategy.' Regular patrols to watch for any intruders will undoubtedly become commonplace. As Prime Minister Mulroney implied in his answers to questions on this matter, such patrols as now exist have the tacit consent of the Canadian government. Since Canada has no naval vessel capable of conducting such operations, it is easy to see why the Americans feel they must undertake them.

A final reason for U.S. submarine activity in Canadian waters stems from a fundamental U.S. strategic belief that defence of *all* of North America represents defence of the U.S. heartland. One senior Pentagon official put it this way: 'I don't look at it as defence of Canada, I look upon it as defence of two alliance members, collectively joined in defending a common treaty area. Yes, by all means, defence of Canada is virtually defence of the American homeland.'[31] When one considers that the United States is the prime target for most sea-launched cruise missiles, such a comment is easy to understand. Handing over this area of defence completely to the United States, however, means losing control over how it is performed. To insist one is regularly informed of U.S.

operations is hardly reassuring to those who live close to where any interception may take place.

Overall, it seems apparent that strategic importance of Canada's Arctic waters has increased dramatically in the past decade and with it, the prospect of greater submarine activity. While there has been no proof of Soviet activities there yet, u.s. patrols have become a fact of life. No longer are the waters for only seals and whales.

A system of defence must anticipate a threat coming not only on and under the ice, but also over it. Here again the evidence is mounting that the strategic importance of Canada's Arctic has taken a dramatic upturn. It is worthwhile to analyze the situation from the perspective of both superpowers.

Since the mid-1950s, when fears that black clouds of Soviet bombers would surge over the Pole and drop their payload of nuclear horror on both Canada and the United States led to establishment of the DEW Line, there have been two decades of inactivity. It seemed Canada's Arctic air space was of limited interest to anyone. While the flight paths of the ballistic missiles of both superpowers went over Canada, albeit high in space, there was no point worrying because there was no defence to intercept them. Furthermore, the fears of the 1950s and the 'bomber threat' proved to be greatly exaggerated; the Soviets spent most of their resources on land-based ballistic missiles instead.

What has occurred to change this situation? The answer is the cruise missile. With the development of new Soviet air-launched cruise missiles reportedly capable of flying three thousand kilometres, the Soviets' seemingly forgotten bomber force is gaining renewed attention. The fear is that the bombers would fly to Canada's North or points nearby to bring u.s. targets within range. For many northern u.s. and Canadian targets, the bombers would not even have to penetrate Canadian airspace before firing their missiles. Recent figures reveal there has been an increase to 160 in the number of long-range bombers capable of delivering nuclear weapons.[32] About 40 of these, Bear-H bombers, are capable of delivering long-range cruise missiles.[33] The rest can only deliver gravity bombs and shorter-ranged air-to-surface missiles. What is worrying Western strategists, though, is the latest-generation Soviet bomber, the Backjack, soon to roll off the production lines. Unlike the Bear-H, which was seen as a slow and somewhat vulnerable target, the Backjack has the speed and range to make a more effective threat.[34]

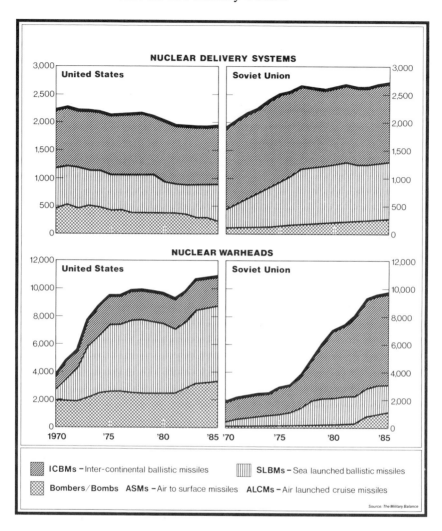

NUCLEAR DELIVERY SYSTEMS

United States   Soviet Union

NUCLEAR WARHEADS

United States   Soviet Union

ICBMs – Inter-continental ballistic missiles   SLBMs – Sea launched ballistic missiles

Bombers/Bombs   ASMs – Air to surface missiles   ALCMs – Air launched cruise missiles

Source: The Military Balance

Comparison of superpowers' nuclear arsenals

To put this threat in perspective, one must remember that the Soviets have always paid less attention to their bomber force than to their ballistic-missile and naval arsenals. As the accompanying chart illustrates, the Soviets have invested so heavily in land-based missile systems that almost 80 per cent of Soviet nuclear weapons are allocated to them. The bomber force, however, represents only 15 per cent of the nuclear-delivery systems. Although the Soviets appear to be diversifying, there is a general consensus that they will not dramatically increase their bomber force. At least one lesson was learned from the 1950s.

What does worry some analysts, however, is the capability of the Backjack in tandem with the newer, more accurate cruise missiles.[35] The fear is that with the current 'holes' in North American bomber defences and the difficulty in detecting cruise missiles, the Soviet Union might think of using its new bombers in a surprise 'precursor' strike. Such an attack would aim to knock out key North American command, communications, and control facilities, effectively paralysing U.S. ballistic warning systems. The Soviets could only contemplate such an attack if they felt confident of being able to launch one undetected, thereby avoiding retaliation. Such a plan, though, involves risks no sane strategist could accept. In this regard, the threat of such an attack must be viewed as marginal.

However, the potential threat of Soviet bombers carrying payloads of cruise missiles into the North American heartland cannot be dismissed too easily. To fail to have adequate detection systems to warn of such an attack would surely be unwise. It is primarily for this reason that both Canada and the United States have agreed to a new North Warning System to plug the 'holes' in the old DEW Line. However, the improvements are basically qualitative. Even if massive resources were spent to upgrade the efficiency of the system to 100 per cent, the total nuclear threat to North America would only be reduced marginally. The ballistic missiles flying in overhead would still do most of the damage. The purpose in plugging the holes is simply to deny the Soviets a 'free ride' into the U.S. heartland with their cruise missiles and bombers in the event of a war. And, as the chart above shows, those missiles and bombers still constitute a relatively small percentage of the total Soviet nuclear arsenal. So, while it is fair to say the Soviet threat to Canadian airspace is escalating, it is important to keep that threat in perspective.

The same, however, cannot be said for U.S. potential interest in Canada's North. The Strategic Defense Initiative, known more commonly as Star Wars, will be discussed in much greater detail later; however, it must be mentioned here as one of the prime reasons for the increased strategic importance of the Arctic. If Star Wars is ever deployed, it will require a variety of warning and detection systems. Some of them will be space-based but others will probably be land-based to provide a back-up and countercheck.

Because of its geographical position so far north, Canada offers one of the best vantage points for basing these warning sensors and missiles. The reason is simple. The closer one is to the launch site of the enemy's missiles, the more time one has to intercept and detect them. From Canada's North, Soviet missiles can be tracked much sooner, and rockets can intercept them much earlier in their flight path. The difference, compared to say North Dakota or Maine, is measurable in thousands of kilometres and valuable seconds. In a system as intricate as Star Wars, such a difference could be critical. Thus, from a strategic point of view, there is no doubt Canada's Arctic would be integral.

In conclusion, the evidence is substantial and persuasive that the strategic importance of the Arctic has increased dramatically. It has, in fact, become the newest military frontier. As the analysis reveals, the Soviets have developed both under-ice and over-ice weapons systems that could easily be used in Canada's Arctic. While these weapons systems are as yet untried, their significance as a threat is real. The United States, too, has developed under-ice and over-ice systems, some of which are already present in Canada's waters. The possibility of confrontation between the superpowers in the North has raised tensions around the Pole. This possibility must give Canadians cause for concern. It is also reason enough to take another hard look at Canada's defence priorities. The days of the impenetrable Arctic are over.

8

NORAD: security at what price?

Deep within a hollowed mountain in the Colorado Rockies lies the nerve centre of the world's most sophisticated surveillance network. Backed up by an intricate patchwork quilt of radar systems, satellites, computers, fighters, and communications links, the network can detect and track missile launches throughout the world while keeping tabs on every satellite and object, even one as small as a baseball, circling in space. The reinforced site for the network's headquarters near Colorado Springs can withstand all but a direct hit from multi-megaton warheads. Under the mountain's crust is a labyrinth of fifteen steel buildings resting on anti-shock springs, interconnected by a maze of steel walkways. Some 1,400 people keep the complex 'alive' on a twenty-four-hour-per-day basis, and in the event of an attack, the installation can sustain itself independently for at least a month. Of its 146 uniformed staff, 46 are Canadian. The operation is known formally as the NORAD Cheyenne Mountain Complex.[1] Its task is vital: to provide advance warning of any hostile missile or bomber attack against North America.

Despite the awesome complexity of this collection of technology, the network has 'holes.' In other words, there are limited spaces through which low-flying hostile bombers and cruise missiles can slip undetected.[2] Some of these holes are in Canada's Arctic. They aren't new; in fact, NORAD has known about them for some time. Yet, as already mentioned, Canada and the United States have agreed to spend $1.5 billion to plug them up with a new gridwork of radar systems called the North Warning System.

In the past, the upgrading of such a 'passive' radar system would have created little controversy. Canada and the United States have always had a mutual interest in knowing of any threat over the Pole. Yet the precise

Control board at NORAD's Cheyenne Mountain complex
(Photo courtesy U.S. Air Force)

location of the new system, its potential use as the 'eyes and ears' for the Strategic Defense Initiative, the future operation of U.S. interceptors in Canada, and NORAD's role in changing U.S. strategic thinking, all raise troubling questions. More importantly, the answers all point in one direction: Canadian and U.S. interests are beginning to diverge in the Arctic. The policy options that emerge from the divergence are discussed in a later chapter. First, however, the reasons for the development of this situation will be analysed.

To understand NORAD and the current debate, one must look back to 1958 when the first North American Air Defence Agreement was signed. Then, the perceived menace was a rush of Soviet bombers invading over the Pole. To provide the earliest possible warning and time for U.S. interceptors to fuel, arm, and take off, the United States decided to build a linked chain of thirty-one ground-based radar stations, positioned as far north as possible. The Distant Early Warning System (DEW Line) was constructed along the perimeter of northern mainland Canada, Alaska, and Greenland, with picket ships carrying powerful radar offering added protection at both sea ends.

Even as workmen started to lay foundations for the twenty-one Canadian stations, the strategic planners had revised their thinking dramatically. (Some have even argued persuasively that the United States wildly exaggerated the bomber threat to entice a reluctant Canada into NORAD.[3]) Attention then focused on the deadly, swifter, more accurate intercontinental ballistic missiles (ICBMs) – a far more formidable threat than the manned bomber. In 1972, when the two superpowers agreed to severely restrict their defences against ICBMs in the ABM Treaty, the rationale for having an extensive air-defence system against bombers evaporated. As the then U.S. secretary of defence, James Schlesinger, reasoned: 'Since we cannot defend our cities against strategic missiles [ICBMs], there is nothing to be gained by trying to defend them against a relatively small force of Soviet bombers.'[4] Against the ICBMs, the DEW Line was of no value. The need, however, for advance warning of an ICBM attack was greater than ever, and so a new system was developed, also under NORAD's jurisdiction. The function of missile warning was then, and arguably still is, NORAD's most important role because of the size of the Soviet ICBM arsenal and the speed of such missiles.

To blanket all Soviet missile sites, the United States relies on two

A typical Distant Early Warning (DEW) Line site at Shingle Point, Yukon, as
seen from an Aurora aircraft on routine northern patrol
(Canadian Forces photo, by WO Vic Johnson)

different technologies – infra-red satellites and long-range radar. The
United States has launched a set of such satellites so that several are
always in the critical observation position over the Soviet Union at any
one time. Picking up the heat from the rockets at the initial boost phase,
these satellites are the first to detect any launch and to provide a launch
count and rough idea of trajectory. Within minutes, the missiles are
picked up by land-based radar which tracks them up to five thousand
kilometres away, confirms an attack is underway, and provides impact
predictions. The radar system, operating for more than twenty years
from three sites in Alaska, Greenland, and England, has been one of
NORAD's most reliable ones. Now in the process of being upgraded and
improved, it is called the Ballistic Missile Early Warning System

(BMEWS). Although Canada is a full partner in NORAD's command structure, it has had virtually no input into either the development or the cost of this two-tiered warning system.

The same situation applies to the third tier, another long-range radar system designed and positioned to track ballistic missiles fired from the three or four Soviet submarines routinely lying off each shore of North America.[5] Named PAVE PAWS, these radar systems can also see five thousand kilometres out to sea. There are currently four, all located in the continental United States: one in California, looking west; one in Massachusetts, looking east; one in Florida, looking south; and one in North Dakota, looking north. Two more are under construction, and this system, too, is being overhauled to upgrade its tracking and discrimination capacities. It is interesting to note that when the ICBM threat was first identified, NORAD was originally assigned the task of detecting a raid so the United States could retaliate in kind. Later, however, when the Soviet ICBMS acquired the capability to knock out their U.S. counterparts in their silos, NORAD was asked to report not only that the missiles were coming but also where they were going.[6] Again, this system was fully developed and paid for by the United States under NORAD's umbrella.

In the late 1970s, strategic planners were back at their drawing-boards, concluding that the future for NORAD lay in space. By this time, both superpowers had launched a bevy of satellites and were depending on them to a much greater degree for military surveillance. The Soviets, for example, have about 150 space platforms, 80 per cent of which serve military purposes.[7] The United States has fewer but is every bit as involved in satellite surveillance. To deal with this new reality, NORAD was assigned the additional task of monitoring space to keep track of all man-made satellites in Earth's orbit and to provide warning when these satellites might be endangered. To reflect this new world, NORAD's name was also changed to the North American Aerospace (not Air) Defence Command. The United States has since positioned radar systems, sensors, and cameras all over the world to keep track of all objects in space. At any one time, officers in Cheyenne Mountain can be tracking more than five thousand objects, everything from satellites to equipment discarded by astronauts. The system is so refined it can pick up objects the size of grapefruits more than three thousand kilometres from the Earth's surface. The Space Wing of the U.S. Air Force, for example, operates a network of ground-based sensors that provide between twenty-five thousand and thirty thousand space observations every day. The navy has its own independent system, and the United States also has a cluster of powerful cameras, one of which is in St Margaret's, NB, although it is soon to be phased out. (As an aside, NORAD provides NASA with its intelligence to help the Space Shuttle avoid any unforeseen head-on collisions while in orbit.) Again, this space aspect of NORAD is financed and developed totally by the Americans within NORAD.

Within this overall perspective, it is easy to see why NORAD's air-defence role against bombers and cruise missiles – the only role in which Canada is actively involved – often takes a back seat. Why then, after almost two decades of inactivity, did Canada and the United States decide to upgrade the system? Does its installation have hidden consequences?

As to the need for an overhaul, there is little doubt the old DEW Line had too many 'holes' to be deemed satisfactory by anyone. A joint U.S.-Canadian study in 1979 concluded there were 'significant gaps in coverage for bomber warning.'[8] At about the same time, NORAD was plagued by false missile warnings and in a now infamous June 1980 incident, a faulty forty-seven-cent computer chip triggered an alarm, indicating the Soviets had launched a full-scale attack. There was a general consensus that the entire operation needed fixing, regardless of any changes in the Soviet arsenal. As NORAD's chief, U.S. General Robert Herres, testified: 'We were particularly concerned because given the coverage we have today with the traditional conventional radars, low-flying cruise missiles launched by [Soviet bombers] flying at moderate altitudes cannot be detected if the routes are carefully selected by Soviet planners. They cannot be detected before the missiles detonate on their targets.'[9]

The proposed $1.5 billion North Warning System certainly fills the gaps, both in the Arctic and along the two coasts. As the accompanying map illustrates, the system provides overall coverage along the 70th parallel for the key transpolar routes of attack. To do the job will require thirteen minimally staffed longer-range radars (eleven in Canada) and thirty-nine unattended shorter-range radars (thirty-six in Canada). It is important to note, however, these radar stations are to be constructed in roughly the same position as the old DEW Line across the perimeter of *mainland* northern Canada, down through Baffin Island into Labrador. Most of Canada's Arctic archipelago is to be left uncovered, the implications of which will be discussed later.

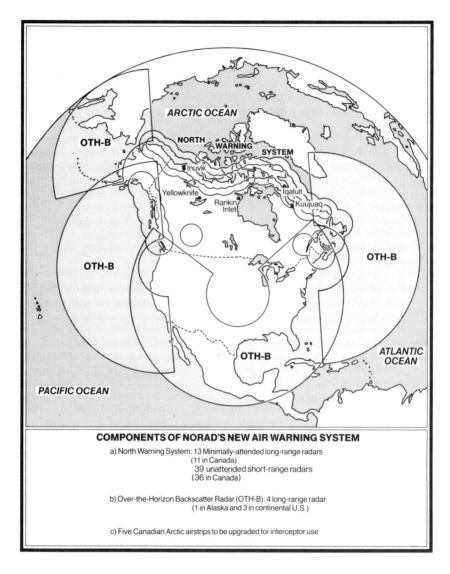

COMPONENTS OF NORAD'S NEW AIR WARNING SYSTEM

a) North Warning System: 13 Minimally-attended long-range radars
(11 in Canada)
39 unattended short-range radars
(36 in Canada)

b) Over-the-Horizon Backscatter Radar (OTH-B): 4 long-range radar
(1 in Alaska and 3 in continental U.S.)

c) Five Canadian Arctic airstrips to be upgraded for interceptor use

NORAD's modernized air-defence warning system

To round out coverage of North America, NORAD is relying on new state-of-the-art Over-the-Horizon Backscatter (OTH-B) radars. This new radar technique, as its name implies, looks over the curvature of the earth to provide low-altitude coverage ranging from 800 kilometres to

2,800 kilometres. The technology depends on the reflection of energy off the troposphere back down to the surface of the Earth. While such technology works well in the more stable atmosphere of temperate climes, it doesn't work as effectively in the Arctic, where the aurora borealis makes the reflection of energy off the ionosphere less reliable. That is why so many shorter-ranged radar stations are planned for Canada's North. The United States is planning to install four of these new backscatter systems, one in Alaska and three in the continental United States.

To round out the package, the upgrading also specifies that five northern airfields be hardened and enlarged to allow for the landing of conventionally armed interceptors. In most cases, Canada CF-18s would be called upon to identify a low-flying intruder and assess its intent. In some cases, United States-based F-15s could also be used. Since Canada is paying 40 per cent or $680 million[10] of the cost, the North Warning System has given some meaning to the idea of military sovereignty and Canada has been guaranteed some control over its operations. Ottawa has been promised that the communications side of the system will be designed in Canada and Canada's Anik satellite will be used to transmit the intelligence from the station to Cheyenne Mountain.[11] Furthermore, Canadian personnel will operate those stations requiring manning; unlike the old DEW Line where the only ones allowed were U.S. military personnel who sometimes made it difficult for Canadians to even drop in.[12]

Unhappily, from a sovereignty point of view, the specific positioning of the North Warning system seems to be predicated on cost more than a desire for surveillance over *all* of Canada. While undoubtedly from a military point of view the 'holes' will now be plugged, most of the northern part of the Arctic archipelago will be left totally unmonitored. It's as if no one cares about what may be flying over the top quarter of the country. As Inuvik's territorial representative, Tom Butters, puts it: 'Why has Canada apparently already offered up its western and high Arctic to a potential aggressor?'[13] The military wisdom of allowing Soviet bombers to cross so much Canadian territory undisturbed was first raised by two retired brigadier-generals, Clay Beattie and Keith Greenaway.[14] They showed that by approaching Canada on an angle from the Beaufort Seat or along the archipelago, such bombers could penetrate undetected through the top quarter of the country and avoid the radar. From positions just north of the North Warning system, most

Canadian and some northern U.S. targets would be within range of the new Soviet cruise missiles.

It is no secret that it is much more difficult for radar to pick up a cruise missile than a bomber. As Greenaway argues 'the further back we drop to engage these missiles, the greater chance we have of contaminating a great raft of Canadian territory.'[15] Strictly from the point of view sovereignty, Canada will not even be able to detect regularly scheduled commercial flights taking the polar route. While NORAD does have plans to periodically dispatch U.S. radar planes (known as U.S. Airborne Warning and Control System or AWACS) from Alaska to the archipelago, these can only provide a stop-gap service. Furthermore, their radar range is quite limited. Although Canadian observers will probably be aboard, the AWACS would be under U.S. control.

Another sign of this abdication of responsibility for the archipelago is reflected in the choice of airfields to be upgraded for possible interceptor use. In the North, five sites – Inuvik, Rankin Inlet, Yellowknife, Iqualuit, and Kuujjuaq, Quebec – have been picked. All are at the southern edge or well south of the warning system. Militarily this decision makes some sense since it takes time for interceptors to scramble to meet an intruder. Fighter pilots would prefer to meet incoming cruise missiles head on rather than chasing their tails. However, the current configuration of the warning system means existing military airfields farther north at Qausuittuq (Resolute) and Alert are ignored. Canadian sovereignty was simply sacrificed.

Surprisingly, very little attention was focused on this aspect of the system during a parliamentary committee's review of it. It is another classic example of Canada's penchant for segregating military concerns from overall sovereignty concerns. One might have expected some tough questions to be asked about a plan that permits substantial undetected flying within Canadian airspace and leaves important parts of the Arctic, the Northwest Passage, and the archipelago without continuous radar coverage. For one to reply that United States-controlled AWACS will fill in is to concede we have granted the United States the right to defend the archipelago. Canada may have problems claiming political sovereignty over lands and waters, particularly the Northwest Passage, for which it has already surrendered its military sovereignty.

It is accepted that new Soviet Backjack bombers carrying long-range cruise missiles represent the main threat to the Arctic in the near future.

Did the military misjudge the Soviet threat or even consider the archipelago? When asked about Beattie and Greenaway's argument, Canadian
defence officials cited both the extra costs of going even farther north
and the fact military satellites may well do the surveillance job by the
turn of the century.[16] However, Major-General Larry Ashley of the
department of defence conceded in testimony: 'General Beattie's point
has a good deal of merit. But I would remind the committee that in
arriving at this architecture we have attempted to match sensible assessment of threat and need today, in terms of capital investment in bucks
and so on . . . It may be that the next major step is a reorientation along
the lines of what General Beattie has said.'[17] One may ask: why wait for
the future? Why not renegotiate the second part of the agreement to have
some radar installed on the archipelago? If the United States refuses,
then Canada should take the initiative. It would be costly but the stations
could be phased in over time.

The relocation issue is a revealing example of how U.S. and Canadian
interests are beginning to diverge in the Arctic. The United States and
Canada have a mutual interest in plugging the surveillance gaps so the
Soviets don't have the option of a 'free ride' into the heart of North
America. However, as discussed earlier, the Soviet bomber force is still a
relatively small part of the Soviet arsenal. So long as there is no defence
against the more destructive, faster ICBMs, then former defence secretary
Schlesinger's dictum that 'nothing is to be gained' in trying to defend
against bombers still has some validity. Even NORAD head, General
Herres, admits, 'I do not know of anyone who regards the strategic land
attack cruise missile as a credible strategic threat by itself.'[18] Thus, the
evidence seems to indicate that the United States was prepared to spend
relatively little in terms of its overall defence budget, especially since
Canada was prepared to pick up part of the tab, to deny the option of
that 'free ride.' But from a U.S. perspective, the acknowledged weaknesses of the North Warning System – its maximum 320-kilometre
range, its detection weaknesses for very low-flying planes, and its difficulty in tracking small cruise missiles fired from outside the radar zone –
aren't of great concern. Canada, however, should be more concerned
about monitoring *all* its territory and not leaving one-quarter of the job to
U.S. radar planes. One can understand the Americans wanting to minimize costs by incorporating as much of the DEW Line infrastructure as
possible in the new system. It was up to Canada to press its own case. Yet

there is nothing in the public record to suggest that any such argument was ever put forward.

Of even greater concern is the fear that through NORAD and the North Warning System, Canada may be involved in systems, which, in the last resort, result in a nuclear war fought on Canadian soil. If that was to happen, Canadian and U.S. interests would be diametrically opposed. Recently such fears have surfaced in three areas: an apparent change in basic U.S. nuclear strategy, the gradual integration of NORAD into the new U.S. Space Command, and the possible development of Star Wars. In each area, there is legitimate cause for concern.

First, the issue of U.S. strategic doctrine is a troubling one. Until the mid-1970s, the fundamental backbone of deterrence was based on what has been called Mutual Assured Destruction (MAD). MAD's logic is based on the simple fact that since there is no defence against the giant ICBMs, the only option for either superpower, if attacked, is to retaliate massively. Because each side realizes it would be devastated by such a retaliatory attack (i.e., facing mutually assured destruction), there is a real disincentive to attack. For such a doctrine to work, it doesn't really matter if your weapons are very accurate. All that is required is the potential for massive retaliation.

The United States accepted this general doctrine without reservation until the early 1970s when U.S. strategic planners pointed out that a U.S. president had only two options in the event of even a 'small' nuclear attack – massive retaliation or no response at all. What emerged first was the 'Schlesinger doctrine,' named after the former defence secretary, which called for greater flexibility in response to an attack. This seemingly reasonable variation was refined even further by U.S. president Jimmy Carter in his Presidential Directive 59,[19] in which he authorized production of weapons designed solely for use against military targets. These new weapons are called 'counterforce' systems and they demand a much greater degree of accuracy. Suddenly people were talking of 'limited' nuclear war and 'countervailing' strikes.

The shift in doctrine was, however, considerable. No longer was deterrence based solely on a massive retaliation against populations. Now the United States, if provoked, was prepared to engage in a 'limited' exchange of nuclear weapons and prevail if possible. As some have argued, such a shift appears to be an improvement because, on the face of it, it seems morally preferable to attack missiles than people. However, as Trudy Govier and Anton Colign of the University of Calgary point out, some of the advantages are illusory: 'People and cities will also be destroyed if nuclear weapons are destroyed, since most weapons systems are located near cities. In any event, the fallout, nuclear winter effects, and likelihood of escalation, make the distinction between (the old and new theories) purely theoretical as far as killing, destruction and environmental damage are concerned.'[20] Mutterings from some officials within the Reagan administration about 'winning' a limited war only reinforced the fears of many that the United States might be interested in a pre-emptive first strike with its new accurate weapons.

Then, in 1983, President Reagan came out with his Star War proposal, which stated that for the first time the United States was going to build an active defence against all ballistic missiles. If successfully deployed, Star Wars would mean the United States would be able to survive *any* attack. In addition to worrying the Soviets, such a defence system represents a complete reversal of the MAD doctrine; namely, that there is no way to defend against ICBMs. Suddenly some in the United States were talking of 'assured survival' and a subsequent generation of more accurate weapons was born.

A huge debate has erupted as to the real intentions of the United States with these strategic changes. Traditionalists have defended them, arguing they are only 'marginal.'[21] They say the United States had to upgrade aging weapons systems and that it is still committed to a defensive strategy (i.e., it would only attack if provoked). Furthermore, it is argued, it only made sense for a U.S. president to have a range of retaliatory options to pick from in the event of an attack.[22] Opponents, however, have viewed the changes as a real shift away from MAD to a 'nuclear-war-fighting strategy' in which the United States might attempt to dominate.[23]

Certain facts are beyond dispute. First, the Soviets, particularly when faced with Star Wars, do perceive a real shift in U.S. doctrine. Second, the shift has had 'hardware implications'; that is, the development of new weapons 'that are going to present the Soviets with worries unlike they have had to deal with before,'[24] in the words of Canadian arms-control expert John Lamb. While it is overstating the case to argue the United States is actively planning or even considering a pre-emptive first strike, there is ample evidence, particularly with SDI, to conclude that U.S. nuclear strategy has shifted. Deterrence now rests not only on the threat of massive retaliation against cities and people but also on a series of smaller more 'flexible' nuclear responses the United States is prepared to employ if provoked.

For Canada, this shift has wide-ranging implications. Through NORAD and other continental defence agreements and because of our location between the superpowers, Canada is inevitably affected. Take, for example, the question of u.s. attack submarines. As part of the new 'forward strategy' discussed earlier, u.s. submarines will now actively seek out Soviet SSBNs in the Arctic Ocean. One of the fastest and most direct routes to reach them is through Canadian waters. Confronted with this option, the Soviets might well move forward with their own attack subs to meet the enemy – in Canada. Another example is the F-15, the highly sophisticated interceptor, which under certain circumstances can be deployed to Canada by NORAD. The F-15 also happens to be the plane which the United States has employed to experiment with anti-satellite (ASAT) technology. In fact, William Arkin unearthed material showing NORAD is 'responsible for ASAT / F-15 tactics, alert postures and standards of performance and employment.'[25] NORAD commander, General Herres, insists that no such F-15 carrying ASAT platforms will ever be sent to Canada.[26] Others, however, argue that with the small number of CF-18s assigned to Canadian air defence and the absence of military radar in Canada's interior, both u.s. AWACS and F-15s – some perhaps equipped with ASAT platforms – might some day be stationed in Canada.[27]

A third concern is the recent creation of a unified u.s. Space Command. Its overall function is to provide information for all of space, tying together civil, commercial, and military sectors as well as providing the command and control for all space-defence tasks. As discussed, one of NORAD's three primary roles is to provide *surveillance* of all satellites in space. Until now, a non-NORAD branch has been responsible for satellite protection and future anti-satellite warfare. Although the Space Command's exact responsibilities have yet to be worked out, it would certainly make practical sense, given the necessary link between all three functions, for the information to be centred in one command. General Herres, who coincidentally is head of both NORAD *and* the Space Command, stresses that NORAD is only responsible for surveillance.[28] Would these distinctions have any practical meaning in a joint command? Could Canada be drawn into situations over which it had little if any control? These are very legitimate questions for which there are few answers.

Tough questions must also be asked about the possible deployment of a missile defence system as envisaged by President Reagan. It is not only reasonable but inevitable that surveillance data gathered by NORAD, including data from the North Warning System, would form an essential part of a fully integrated missile defence system. General Herres again emphasizes that Canada would not be drawn in unless it expressly consented.[29] However, the Space Command is responsible for any new defence system and in the split-second decision-making undoubtedly required, it is difficult to imagine jurisdictional niceties being honoured. To former defence minister Donald Macdonald, 'there is no question we have to be worried about being integrated into that Space Command. Therefore, we should be taking pains – as we always do – to distance ourselves from all U.S. anti-ballistic missile systems. It's control of our own airspace we should be involved in.'[30]

These concerns, considered collectively, illustrate how Canadian and U.S. interests are diverging in the Arctic. Some issues have yet to be translated into reality. Yet if Canada wants to keep the Arctic as free of superpower confrontation as possible and avoid any involvement in a missile defence system, then it must begin planning immediately. As former ambassador Geoffrey Pearson says: 'When we come to determine what percentage of our defence resources to allocate to continental defence, we must therefore be sure to ask the prior question: what is the best mix of actions for Canada to pursue if our goal is to contribute to a more stable relationship between the superpowers.'[31]

In developing a new northern policy for Canada these factors are critical. Systems designed to protect Canadian sovereignty can and should be made to dovetail with Canada's future security needs. To begin with, Canada has to realize it must develop an independent perspective. Otherwise, it will be left tagging along with whatever the Americans have in mind for continental defence. Evidence is mounting that in the Arctic, Canadian and U.S. interests are beginning to conflict. So Canada must rethink the whole question of continental defence. If we want to plan an alternative, the time is now. If we continue aimlessly on the present path, we will have to accept whatever the Americans have in store.

9

Continental defence: a new approach

It is known simply as Arrangement No. 290. Dated 27 July, 1967, it is a secret arrangement between Canada and the United States. In chilling simplicity it sets out the exact conditions under which the United States is authorized to deploy thirty-two nuclear depth bombs to Canada to be used against enemy submarines. Half would go to Comox, BC, and half would go to Greenwood, NS, where Canada's long-range patrol and anti-submarine Aurora aircraft are stationed.[1] The bombs are almost 5 metres long, weight 235 kilos each, and have an explosive yield of almost 10 kilotons.

Despite the unmistakable tenor of the agreement, it flatly contradicts Canada's stated policy not to allow the deployment of nuclear weapons on Canadian territory. Yet when its contents were publicized in 1985, the Canadian government responded bluntly, 'the U.S. can't make any decisions on that without consulting us.'[2] What followed began as a diplomatic gavotte, and turned into a virtual free-for-all. First the defence minister denied the plan's existence.[3] Then the chief of defence staff alleged that he had only just become aware of it.[4] Then the government admitted it – and even added a detail: Argentia base in Newfoundland had also been included until it was shut down.[5] Finally, came a statement from the external affairs minister that the agreement 'is in the process of ending.'[6] For good measure, the government also admitted that there is another agreement which permits U.S. bombers carrying nuclear weapons to over-fly Canada.[7]

The spectacle of the government of Canada expressing surprise that the United States still believed Agreement No. 290 was valid was comic. It also belied the fact that Ottawa had obviously forgotten about it. What that says about Canada's management of its defence relationship with the United States is in itself a cause for concern.

Yet the arrangement and the controversy surrounding it also give a rare if brief glimpse into the complexity of that relationship. After the controversy broke, external affairs minister Joe Clark revealed there are more than 70 treaties and at least 2,500 documents covering Canada– United States defence matters dating back to 1940.[8] Many are out of date but it took the uproar over Arrangement No. 290, to prompt Ottawa to at least sort out which ones still apply. u.s. strategist William Arkin was the one who revealed Arrangement No. 290's contents after a parliamentary committee was denied access to it. As Arkin explains: 'Trying to decipher the treaties, agreements, arrangements, notes and plans is like peeling away the skin of an onion – layer after layer. But there is no centre, each layer raises and exposes new agreements with new questions … I constantly had to ask myself whether Parliament, the defence experts, the press, the peace movement or the public were aware (and approved of) the extent of military integration and planning.'[9]

For Canada, the continental defence relationship is like a marriage with no right of divorce. Our geostrategic position makes any break-up difficult to imagine. If Canada is to prevent its Arctic from becoming an arena for superpower tension, or worse a staging area for Star Wars, then we must undertake a major realignment of our defence priorities. At the very least, Canada needs a better political control over management of the relationship. A greater presence, particularly for surveillance, is also required. After an examination of the nature of Canada–United States defence links, policy options will be discussed.

If one is to understand the history and complexity of the continental defence links, one must start with the 1940 Ogdensburg Declaration. In it, both countries agreed 'to consider in the broad sense the defence of the north half of the western hemisphere.'[10] Prime Minister Mackenzie King later declared that Canada, too, has 'obligations' to see that 'enemy forces should not be able to pursue their way either by land, sea or air to the usa across Canadian Territory.'[11] For the United States, this obligation is fundamental. For Canada, it has meant assuming certain responsibilities and in a strict military sense not becoming a security risk to the United States. If Canada ever became such a risk, it would be the equivalent of asking the United States to take over full responsibility for the defence of the continent. No one should assume the United States would stand idly by if it perceived its security was threatened on its northern flank. Such thinking is naive. As noted political scientist John Holmes puts it: 'Without [NORAD and the defence relationship] I think there can be little doubt that in an emergency, the Americans would take over defence of the continent and we would have little alternative to taking orders, willingly or morosely.'[12] Consequently Canada must develop some *modus operandi* in its defence relationship with its southern neighbour. This reality has been a corner-stone of Canadian defence policy since 1940.

It should also not be forgotten that Canada actively sought out a collective defence arrangement for North America with the United States. This policy has been and continues to be based on certain fundamental assumptions. The first is that there is a commonality of interest in the joint defence of the continent, from which Canada has directly benefited 'under' the U.S. defence umbrella. The second is the presumption that Canada alone could not fully defend its domain against a threat. As long as Canada has agreed with the United States on the nature of the Soviet threat to the continent, it has been content with NORAD. Furthermore, this active collaboration gives Canada access to U.S. technology, some say in the joint defence, and intelligence on what is happening in our waters and over our land.

What if some of those assumptions are no longer valid? If one accepts that Canadian and U.S. interests are beginning to diverge, particularly in the Arctic, then what leeway does Canada have? The more traditional view is that our manoeuvrability is 'slim.'[13] Yet surely this is short-changing our status as an independent country and doing a disservice to our security interests. In the final analysis, Canada does have the right to decide how its defence resources are allocated between Europe and North America. It also has the right to develop an independent capacity to monitor its waters and airspace. Ultimately it even has the right to opt out of NORAD with one year's notice.

The first step, though, must be for Canada to identify its own national-security perspective. For too long, Ottawa has been motivated by fears of what its allies will think. This fixation with the European theatre has hampered the development of a truly Canadian perspective. As University of Toronto professor Franklyn Griffiths argues: 'There seems to be a presumption by some that there is an inherent contradiction between a Canadian security perspective and a collective one. However, that is not necessarily the case. The important thing is for Canada to begin with an assessment of its own needs and then to work out from there into our North American relationships and then to our NATO relationships. The time for such an analysis is long overdue.'[14]

Within the confines of such a review, the scope for change is arguably wide. Canada has never really tried to test the middle let alone the outer limits of those confines. In the past, we have differed with the United States, but in most cases politely so. For example, our military spending is much less than the United States would like it to be and we have taken different stands over such matters as Vietnam and more recently Nicaragua. However, so long as our actions do not compromise basic North American security, there is room to manoeuvre.

Before looking at possible options, it is worthwhile examining the extent to which the United States relies on Canadian territory and defence collaboration. It is apparent for both historical and technological reasons that the United States has taken Canadian collaboration for granted. A visit to Washington reveals there is astonishingly little material on NORAD and most Congressmen have scant if any knowledge of its operations. This attitude was no doubt fostered by the fact that until very recently the U.S. military viewed defence of North America, as one brochure put it, 'as a single entity, with little concern for national borders.'[15] In the past few years, steps have been taken to realign NORAD's defence sharing more along national boundaries and increase the level of Canadian control. Surveillance of Canadian airspace, for example, is now controlled from North Bay.

As outlined earlier, U.S. interest in Canada has risen somewhat with the upgrading of surveillance of the North through the North Warning System – but only a little. With the advent of new satellite technology, which will allow the United States to peer down on the Arctic and detect low-flying targets with even more accuracy, the need for a Canadian land-based radar system will diminish. Since all the ballistic-missile-surveillance systems are based in space or in the United States, Greenland, or England, those on Canadian soil are not so critical. This situation has led one U.S. strategic analyst recently to write: 'Today's technology provides an opportunity for long-distance detection without relying on Canadian participation. It is a cornerstone of United States relations with Canada that there should be collaboration in the defence of North America. Time and technology are making that a matter of choice, not of necessity.'[16] Whether that argument holds for U.S. use of Canadian waters for its submarines or for the future use of Canadian soil for Star Wars is highly questionable. In fact, in both cases U.S. interest in Canada could become intense.

So what are Canada's options? To fully protect the Arctic, guarantee our sovereignty, and prevent any inadvertent inclusion in Star Wars or U.S. nuclear-war–fighting strategy, some have argued the only choice is to pull out of NORAD now. While the full implications of going neutralist will be discussed in a subsequent chapter, at this point it is worth asking if the arguments for NORAD membership still apply.

Since Canada has no independent capacity to monitor its territorial waters and airspace, it relies almost totally on intelligence gathered within NORAD. As the overwhelming majority of this information is collected by U.S. monitoring systems, Canadian access to it could be shut off completely outside of NORAD. Thus a precipitous withdrawal from NORAD would leave Canada without access to information on what was happening within its borders. Similarly, access to U.S. military technology, some of which is now shared, and also to hundreds of millions of dollars in U.S. defence contracts would end. These facts cannot be ignored. They underscore the point that if Canada were to contemplate leaving NORAD, much advance planning both to develop some independent surveillance capacity and to cushion the economic blow would be essential.

Some have questioned the value of NORAD's shared command when, in the crunch, the United States makes all the decisions itself. They argue the mandatory appointment of a Canadian as NORAD's second-in-command gives only illusory feelings of involvement.[17] While the overall functioning of NORAD is less than satisfactory from a Canadian viewpoint, it none the less guarantees Canada a 'seat at the table' and the right to be consulted. Critics are quick to point out the Canadian government was not consulted when NORAD went on alert during both the 1963 Cuban missile crisis and the 1972 Middle East crisis. In both instances the U.S. president authorized the alert but failed to consult with the Canadian prime minister. However, a strong argument can still be made that NORAD provides a window of opportunity for Canada to know what the United States is up to. Outside of NORAD, we have no access to U.S. thoughts on defence. Inside of it, at least we get a glimpse and also the right to speak our mind. As former defence minister Barney Danson says: 'Vis-à-vis NORAD, we have to be there to assert our sovereignty as best we can. If we're not there, they [the United States] are going to do it anyway. So we might as well be there, soak up as much as we can, have as much say as we can and keep them out of our backyard unless we say so.'[18]

NORAD was never intended to be a consultative body for North American defence, and past experience shows it is ill-suited for that purpose. As John Holmes describes it: 'It is a body designed not to promote continentalism ... but to stake out a Canadian role as we cannot escape involvement in American defence.'[19] Canada can't fool itself into thinking it will have a veto over U.S. policy. However, inside of NORAD, we get a look and some say. So long as NORAD does not become the 'eyes and ears' of some Star Wars system, then the arguments for staying are still persuasive. That does not mean, however, Canada should be content with the status quo. Far from it. Real changes, including those outlined below, are essential.

NORAD IN NATO

One of the first priorities for change is the need for more Canadian political control over the joint defence effort. Two of Canada's former NATO ambassadors, George Ignatieff and John Halstead, have proposed that NORAD be made a special command within NATO.[20] That way all of NORAD's war scenarios and fighting options would come under the scrutiny of elected politicians – foreign affairs ministers and defence ministers – as they regularly do within NATO. Halstead and Ignatieff both argue that this review process is much more than a paper shuffle and in fact, allows politicians a real opportunity to approve or scuttle various fighting strategies. There is no similar review process under NORAD. As Halstead argues:

In the defence field, we have very limited bargaining power with the Americans. But we are in a very awkward position because we can't defend our own country with our own means alone. So we need to make allies and form coalitions wherever we can and the only forum open to us is NATO ... The American failure to notify Canada about the Cuban missile crisis is unfortunately characteristic of how Americans work. The danger with the U.S. is not isolationism, it is unilateralism. That is why I keep harping on the alliance.[21]

While both Halstead and Ignatieff are avowed NATO boosters, they also candidly admit the NATO planning group concerned with North American affairs just never meets. While there is considerable merit in NATO's political review process, the greatest obstacle to NORAD's inclusion in it is that, in Halstead's words, 'the Americans will just never go for it.'[22] His assessment was backed up by a senior Pentagon official who, when presented with the option, snapped 'it would never fly here. Why would we want the Europeans mixed up in defence of North America? We don't need them telling us how to run things on this side of the Ocean.'

Blunt words, but from a U.S. perspective, one can understand the desire not to bring too many generals into the North American defence theatre. The United States would rather run it, with limited Canadian involvement. Even from a Canadian point of view, it is arguable whether a Europe-dominated NATO is the best forum for North American defence matters. That the Turks or Spaniards have interests in or rights over Arctic warfare is questionable. So long as the United States is unalterably opposed to the inclusion of NORAD in NATO, it doesn't seem realistic to pursue it.

NEW NATO ARCTIC COMMAND

Another option, championed by Canadian strategic analyst Nils Orvik, is the creation of a new Arctic Command within NATO.[23] Such a command would be concerned with defence of NATO's entire northern flank along the edge of the Arctic Ocean. A grouping of nations – Canada, Iceland, Norway, Denmark (Greenland), and the United States – could then divvy up defence responsibilities to meet the growing strategic threat in the Arctic. Such a proposal has initial appeal in terms of a new northern policy for Canada, for it would establish more links along the circumpolar countries of the world. It would also allow Canada to specialize in Arctic warfare, a specialization that would obviously harmonize with Canada's own defence needs. The idea has also sparked interest in some U.S. circles and may well not be viewed in such a hostile light as the Halstead / Ignatieff proposal.

However, closer scrutiny reveals basic problems with such a command. Although Canada has always been sympathetic to its Nordic neighbours, this particular command would effectively cement Canada's involvement in northern Europe. Its focus would undoubtedly be

Europe's northern flank, because of the geographic immediacy of the Soviet arsenal. Such a grouping would thus restrict Canada's deployment options, given ongoing fiscal restraints, to place more emphasis on defence of northern Canada. There is little likelihood that Norway, Iceland, or Denmark would send troops or equipment to Canada. Where such a grouping might be highly useful is in the sharing of information, intelligence from joint satellite ventures, and the like.

The more fundamental problem with such a new grouping though, is that it elevates the Arctic to a new theatre of warfare. As argued at the outset, it is in Canada's interests to see the demilitarization of the Arctic, not the opposite. Canada should alert the international community that the two superpowers are increasingly utilizing the Arctic as an uncontrolled territory for military operations. Canada should be pushing for partial demilitarization schemes or qualified nuclear-weapons-free zones, not new military commands. Without lowering the defence guard, at this stage, it is preferable to pursue arms-control options rather than new alliances which might further exacerbate superpower confrontation in the Arctic. There is no question the establishment of such a command would cause the Soviets some concern and they might be tempted to reply in kind, leading to an even greater escalation in the Arctic arms race. Canada would be better advised trying to set up rules so Soviet and U.S. submarines don't bump into each other in the Arctic rather than joining forces to better detect such subs. It is for these reasons that a new Arctic command within NATO is not advisable.

NEW CANADA-UNITED STATES DEFENCE BOARD

One problem that has to be addressed, though, is the lack of political control over continental defence. It is a concern shared by at least two former defence ministers - Barney Danson and Jean-Jacques Blais - who witnessed first hand how the relationship is handled. Danson, for example, recalls the occasion when a Russian satellite was hurtling wildly out of control. NORAD was keeping track of it but Canada was only officially informed the satellite had landed in the Northwest Territories an hour after it hit. As Danson says: 'The reason I wasn't advised [as defence minister] was because it was one of those random things that could have landed anywhere. The fact is when it came into our territory there was no time to react. So I'm deeply concerned about political control. I'm also concerned about the military control that they sat there [NORAD headquarters] and did not inform us beforehand of the possibility.'[24]

Blais recalls how when he first became defence minister, he discovered the United States was about to let the contracts for all the long-range and short-range radars for the North Warning System to U.S. suppliers without consulting Canada.[25] With Canada footing 40 per cent of the bill for the new system, Blais felt there should be some Canadian input as to how the contracts were to be allocated. When he demanded a halt 'telegrams started to fly from the U.S. saying "you can't do that". I said "yes I can" and reluctantly I was given a briefing by an American to inform me how the contracts were to be awarded. I exploded, but they just kept stalling. Eventually, and it took place after I had left, the Americans got what they wanted.'[16]

Mechanisms are needed that would allow Canadians, particularly our elected representatives, to oversee the entire Canada-United States defence relationship. The concerns that there are not enough political controls over NORAD and various war scenarios are valid ones. The revelation of secret arrangements like No. 290 makes it apparent Canadian officials have to keep a much closer watch over management of the relationship. Was there, for example, any secret accord made with the new North Warning System? Should not this system be reviewed and analysed by our representatives to ensure that the controls are adequate? Should it be secret, if it exists? As argued before, NORAD is a defence arrangement, not an alliance, and is not a suitable forum for such a review. Furthermore, as the existence of 2,500 defence documents attest, North American defence is more than just NORAD.

To help Canada gain more control in this one-sided relationship, a new Canada-United States Defence Board should be set up. Canada's top representatives should be either the defence minister or the associate defence minister. Equivalent U.S. officials should head the other side. The board should meet periodically, hold press conferences, and review ongoing defence planning. As much of the fighting scenarios and war planning as possible should be made public and debated openly. Canada already has two boards which perform essentially the same tasks - the Permanent Joint Board of Defence and the Canada-U.S. Military Cooperation Committee - but these bodies have no political clout. They have withered on the bureaucratic vine, and even top-level defence officials call the Permanent Joint Board a 'curiosity.'[27] The staffs of these boards could be integrated to form an experienced secretariat for the new board.

Some may doubt the value of yet another layer of bureaucracy. However, it should be pointed out that in the context of the ongoing free-trade talks with the United States, many argue some type of new board should be established to identify potential trading flashpoints and iron out problems before they get too big. The Canada–United States trading relationship is so broad and complex, they say, it deserves such an overseeing body. Should not the same apply to the Canada–United States defence relationship and its 2,500 separate arrangements? Does it not justify the attention of top politicians to provide political control and, coincidentally, let the United States know how seriously Canada regards these matters? Surely that is the least Canadians deserve to ensure they are not unwitting partners in some military adventure.

To complement this new board, the parliamentary committee dealing with defence should develop more links with its congressional counterparts in the United States, and hold regular joint meetings. The Canadian committee should also try to oversee the joint defence relationship and have the NORAD commander thoroughly brief it once a year. That suggestion is hardly radical, although former defence minister Blais recalls it was 'like pulling teeth' to get the Canadian military even to agree to invite the NORAD commander to Ottawa.[28]

However, greater political control by itself is not enough. The next step must be for Canada to specify its priorities in the Arctic.

'KEEP OUT' ZONE

A dramatic beginning for a new northern Canadian security policy would be to declare a 'keep out' zone in the Arctic archipelago and northern waters in which no foreign submarines - Soviet or u.s. - would be allowed. Such a bold move would strongly reaffirm the policy of keeping the Arctic as demilitarized as possible. It would also help avoid nuclear accidents and signal to the world that Canada claimed full, unabridged, sovereignty over all waters within the archipelago. Canada has little to gain and much to lose in allowing its territory to be used as a thoroughfare for foreign subs. While it is obviously useful for Canada to know if such submarines are prowling in its waters, we must rely on the United States to tell us. Canada has no submarines with under-ice capabilities. As pointed out by David Cox, who recently espoused such a 'keep out' zone, such a plan does have advantages for the United States: 'From the point of view of the U.S., reassurance that Soviet [attack submarines] were neither patrolling within the Canadian Arctic waters armed with [long-range cruise missiles] nor transiting to the Atlantic, would be a valuable contribution to the U.S. defence effort. It would be particularly so in time of crisis ... In exchange for this, the U.S. would give up the use of Canadian Arctic waters for purposes of transit to the Polar Basin.'[29]

Universal respect for such a zone would only come on two conditions: that the establishment of the zone was perceived to be fair and that a system was in place to enforce it. As argued earlier, there is virtually no evidence Soviet submarines have been using Canada's Arctic waters. Thus, the existence of 'keep out' zone at the present time wouldn't seriously affect them. In fact, the Soviets would see advantages in the United States' being excluded. However, the Americans would still be able to deploy their attack subs to the Arctic by other routes. With a secure zone, the future threat of Soviet cruise missiles launched from subs would also be greatly diminished. Finally, as Cox suggests, the zone would only apply in peacetime. In times of crisis, Canada could allow the U.S. Navy full access to its waters, if required.

Traditionally, the problem of enforcement has frustrated such proposals. To give meaning to what it declared, Canada would have to develop a sophisticated independent monitoring system to guard the approaches to its waters. In the meantime, one ingenious, inexpensive, and relatively easy method would be to mine the entrances to the archipelago or threaten to do so if the zone is violated. Former chief of defence staff Admiral R.H. Falls explains how it works: 'What you could use is a captor mine. It's a M-46 torpedo that sits on the bottom of relatively shallow water and when something goes by within a certain radius, it will detect this and get off the bottom and hit it ... So to say we don't have any control or can't control our waters is nonsense. We've got the means. We've even got the torpedoes.'[30]

In Cox's words, 'mining as a deterrent would transfer the decision-making entirely to the violator.'[31] The beauty of such a system is that it would be up to a violating submarine to decide for itself if it wanted to take the risk. Obviously the mining need not take place but it could be held in abeyance as 'proof' that the zone's sanctity could be preserved. For Canada, the attractiveness of such a zone is too great to ignore.

To give the zone more credibility, Canada must also have independent 'eyes and ears' to know what is happening in its own backyard. Such eyes and ears are also essential in the changing Arctic strategic environment. As defence minister Perrin Beatty says: 'Our sovereignty in the Arctic cannot be complete if we remain dependent on our allies for knowledge of possible hostile activities in our waters, under our ice and for preventing such activities.'[32]

SOUND SURVEILLANCE UNDER THE SEA (SOSUS)

The next logical step is for Canada to install an underwater radar or SOSUS (Sound Surveillance Under the Sea) system. Usually, SOSUS comprises a line of hundreds of underwater microphones (hydrophones) fixed to the seabed at optimum depth to pick up submarine-generated noise. The microphones are connected by cable to shore stations, where the information can be analysed or relayed on. SOSUS arrays have been widely used since the 1950s, and in open waters they can pick up submarines thousands of kilometres away. Until recently, though, standard equipment hasn't worked well in the Arctic because of the unique ice conditions.

The problem has been one of trying to differentiate between the sound of a submarine and the cacophony of crushing ice, while simultaneously ascertaining distances under ice. Sound waves in a normal ocean environment travel in direct lines from the source to the listener or from one submarine to another. Under the ice crust, however, sound waves are bent down sharply and then upward as they travel beneath the ice-cap, much the same as window glass refracts sunlight. The sound waves then strike the bottom of the ice and are either reflected back into the deep, or, more often, are scattered in many directions. Scientists attribute this phenomenon to a combination of the varying level of salinity, the extremely cold temperatures, and the high pressures created by the weight of massive ice fields. Further complicating detection is the symphony of noise, almost a rhythmic rumbling, that is caused by the cracking and heaving ice-pack.[33]

Sweden has used SOSUS arrays for several years and NATO has maintained arrays across the Greenland–Iceland–United Kingdom Gap for years to monitor Soviet submarines. Canada already has one experimental array in place across Lancaster Sound. The technology has now advanced to the point where the processing or filtering of 'noise' picked up by the arrays is more sophisticated in icy waters. With practice, it is now possible to differentiate between the various sounds. Canada could easily place these arrays at all major entrances to the archipelago at relatively modest expense.[34] The system could also be supplemented by ice-penetrating sonar buoys, which are dropped from airplanes. Such a system would enable Canada to 'hear' what is happening in its northern waters and to ensure its 'keep out' zone is observed.

AURORA PATROL AIRCRAFT

The next step is for Canada to purchase more of its long-range Aurora patrol aircraft and station at least one of them permanently in the North. Despite its limitations in bad weather and winter darkness, the Aurora is an effective part of Canada's anti-submarine arsenal. In a previous chapter, it was recommended that several more Auroras, at a unit cost of $25 million, be bought to enhance Canada's presence in the North. Working in tandem with a new SOSUS system, the Auroras could also provide a one-two punch in detecting any unknown submarine activity. Canada invested a great deal in the Aurora program and more benefits can be derived from it. Furthermore, the fact that it is possible to use the same piece of equipment to protect sovereignty, help in overall anti-submarine warfare, and provide a piece in a new independent monitoring system makes it a 'three-for-one' bargain.

CF-18S (HORNETS)

As a next step Canada should deploy as many CF-18s as are needed in the North or the near North to back up the North Warning System. As part of that system, five airfields in the North are to be upgraded for the landing of interceptors, whose role would be to meet and assess any low-flying intruders. It is interesting to note that at the height of the bomber threat in the 1950s, NORAD had almost 2,000 interceptors at its beck and call, 162 of them Canadian.[35] In 1985, however, NORAD could call on just sixteen squadrons – about one-tenth the 1950s figure – of which only one was Canadian. A second Canadian squadron is to be in place by the end of 1987. Under the new North Warning System, though, NORAD may call upon U.S. F-15s for use in Canada in certain circumstances.

There are also compelling reasons to bring home the Canadian Air

Squadron from West Germany. The primary argument is that it should be Canadian airplanes that are used to defend Canadian soil. Leaving part of that task to u.s. interceptors when perfectly adequate Canadian CF-18s are stationed in Europe just doesn't make sense. Giving Canadian fighters the sole responsibility for such defence also eliminates the possibility that those u.s. F-15s – which have been used for u.s. anti-satellite warfare – might be stationed permanently in Canada. With its relatively short range and high operating costs, the Hornet is not an ideal sovereignty / reconnaissance tool. There is, none the less, a surveillance pod which can be installed on it. Modifications would also have to be made on the Hornets brought from Europe for the North so they would be used as interceptors.

It should be emphasized there is no point filling the Arctic with Hornets. Even if they were able to shoot down every incoming Soviet cruise missile – itself a daunting task – this would only account for 15 per cent of the entire Soviet strategic threat.[36] Furthermore, it is not in Canada's interests to militarize the North. Thus the number of CF-18s in the North should be restricted to that required to meet NORAD's limited objectives.

SATELLITES OR AWACS

The final peg in the surveillance board should be filled by an independent satellite system or one shared and jointly funded by other circumpolar countries. There seems to be nearly unanimous agreement that surveillance of the future will be done from space. For a country that has already invested heavily in space technology – Canada ranks eighth in the world in space expenditures[37] – there are strong economic reasons to follow this route.

In fact, the government is already partly committed to what is called the RADARSTAT program. That program involves a satellite carrying a radar system capable of snapping a picture of Canada regardless of light or weather conditions. Its use in the Arctic would be particularly valuable, as it could monitor the navigation of ships through ice, the course of oil spills, as well as provide data on natural resources. It would be able to pick up objects as small as six metres long.[38] So, for example, it could detect a submarine surfacing in some remote bay. The current plan is for the system to be developed jointly by the United States, Canada, and the

United Kingdom. The data would be available to all three countries and each, in fact, could sell them to others. Its acceptance seems inevitable and is to be applauded.

Unfortunately, the military capacities of such a system are limited. Such satellites look at the ground, while the military, anxious to track low-flying planes or missiles, is more interested in a radar which 'removes' the ground and tracks only the moving parts. That requires a different sort of radar, although SPAR Aerospace Ltd executives insist 'the technologies that are required for military applications are so similar or so close that it really makes very little difference.'[39] In fact, SPAR says it already has the ability to satisfy Canadian military requirements. The price, however, would be steep. When investigating this area, a senate subcommittee estimated that eight to twelve satellites would be needed to make the system viable: four to six air surveillance satellites, one or two maritime satellites, and three or four communications satellites.[40] Such a system would cost $150 million per annum for the first five years and $350 million a year for the following decade.

While the expense is considerable, compared to the $200 million price-tag for a United States-built AWACS, it seems reasonable. For minimal coverage of Canada's far North, up to five AWACS would be needed, each with a radius of 320 kilometres. For the system to be foolproof, the AWACS would have to be constantly aloft. At an hourly operating rate of $25,000, the bills would certainly mount.

As part of NORAD's new North Warning System, U.S AWACS based in Alaska, with some Canadians aboard, are slated for occasional deployment to the far North. As a stop-gap measure, they serve the purpose. But as part of an overall long-range surveillance alternative, the prohibitive costs and surveillance limits make the undertaking a very dubious one.

For the present, Canada may want to seek out partners in the development of a military satellite system. With the dismantlement of the Pinetree radar system in the middle of the country, Canada will be left with precious little ability to monitor much of its interior airspace. That alone is reason for its need. However, there seems little reason for the Canadian system to be 'hardened up' against possible attack or explosion. The ABM Treaty has put limits on such radars and it seems desirable for Canada to stick with satellites designed for peacetime. With such a system in place, the surveillance network would be quite secure. We would know what is happening in our backyard.

British nuclear-powered Trafalgar-class submarine, which Canada is
interested in purchasing
(Photo courtesy Vickers Shipbuilding & Engineering Limited)

SUBMARINES

To give credibility to a 'keep-out' zone and perform limited patrols, Canada must have submarines which can operate in the Arctic. Now it has none. With the world's longest coastline and one-third of its territorial waters in the North, Canada has tried to make do with just three submarines. But since they can't operate in the North, u.s. subs have assumed all patrol of Canada's Arctic environs. If Canada is intent to keep its archipelago free of foreign warships, then it must have some means to enforce its will.

The submarines with the capacity for longest under-ice patrol are nuclear-powered, the most advanced of which can now cost up to $1 billion a unit. In the 1987 White Paper on Defence, a preference was stated for the less expensive British or French model, which still would cost taxpayers $6 billion for a fleet of twelve.[41] But that $6 billion pricetag doesn't include the cost of building the necessary infrastructure to station these units, store the nuclear fuel, train the sailors and provide all the necessary backup. Most independent observers estimate these expenses will at least double the final cost.[42] That makes at least $12 billion – and for what?

The government says 'through their mere presence, nuclear-powered submarines can deny an opponent the use of sea areas.'[43] However, that argument is by no means universally accepted. In Sweden, for example, Soviet subs have been regularly tracked in Swedish territorial waters. But even though they have a fleet of thirteen subs, the Swedes have been loathe to attack intruders, fearing the international consequences. Any Canadian government would be faced with exactly the same dilemma and would in all likelihood make exactly the same decision. In fact, the Canadian decision would be even harder because virtually all submarine traffic in the Canadian Arctic is American. Supposing a Canadian 'hunter / killer' attack sub of the type recommended by the White Paper confronted an American sub, what would it do? As John Lamb of the Canadian Centre for Arms Control put it so succinctly: 'there is no submarine alternative to a shot across the bow.'[44] About the only option it would have, short of attacking it, would be to saddle up close. Submarine expert Don Kerr of the International Institute of Strategic Studies asks: 'then what would you expect the Americans to do about it – go away and do nothing? I rather doubt that.'[45] This scenario illustrates the limited use of submarines in peacetime. While in theory their presence acts as a deterrent, in practice their value is diminished by the realization that their use in retaliation would only come as a last resort.

In the past, no Canadian government has been prepared to take the consequences of intervening to stop u.s. ships from using the passage. Even with nuclear-powered submarines, there is no logical reason why Canadian policy would change. Quite simply, the consequences would be too severe. While the presence of a Soviet submarine might imply a greater threat, there is no indication a Canadian government would act any differently. The Swedes certainly have always opted on the side of caution.

Nor is there any guarantee Canadian subs operating in the Arctic will even be able to track their u.s. counterparts. It is an accepted fact that American ssbns are so quiet in operation that detection is all but impossible. 'With the Ohio-class of American ssbn, there has not been one recorded instance of a successful tracking,' reports Don Kerr.[46] American attack subs would be almost as difficult to find. While Soviet subs have been much noisier and thus easier to find, recent developments suggest they too would be difficult to locate.

A final complication with nuclear-powered submarines is that their very existence would probably invite Soviet subs to test their reactions. As with any new military system, an enemy always wants to test its responsiveness and capabilities. From the Soviet point of view, the Canadian purchase of nuclear-powered subs undoubtedly represents a greater threat to Arctic security. It would be only natural for them to take certain precautionary steps, including probing Canadian waters. Thus, while there have been no reported Soviet incursions to date, there may well be in the future as a consequence of Canadian policy. If Canada's aim is to keep its Arctic as demilitarized as possible, then the purchase of such subs may produce exactly the opposite result. Such is the paradox of increasing the level of militarization.

If there was no choice but to 'buy nuclear' to achieve some under-ice capacity, then the government's decision would be easier to understand. Yet there are other options. Diesel-powered subs are being upgraded and in conjunction with the small Canadian 'slowpoke' nuclear reactor, they could operate under ice for considerable lengths of time. Others have suggested there might be a good 'used' market in old submarines as the three Western powers that manufacture them – Britain, France, and the United States – upgrade their fleets.[47] The government argues that state-of-the-art nuclear-powered subs are quicker, better anti-submarine fighters, and more versatile under ice.[48] While admittedly these things are true, it is worthwhile asking what role these submarines are to perform. If, as argued earlier, the subs are to provide limited patrol and give some teeth to a 'keep-out' zone, then top-of-the-line submarines are not essential. When their limitations in peacetime are also considered, the high cost becomes even harder to defend – especially when there are visible, cheaper alternatives.

There are also pitfalls in arguing Canada deserves only the best. In the field of military technology, what is state-of-the-art one decade is outmoded the next. Already some commentators question whether either the British or the French sub will be a match for its American or Soviet counterpart. 'To try and play catch-up with the big guys [the United States and the Soviet Union] in the field of nuclear submarines is a costly and risky gamble,' says Don Kerr, 'especially for a country which up to now has had no tradition in such technology.'[49] At a time when there are other options, the arguments are persuasive for Canada to take a better look at all of them. With Canada's huge Arctic coastline, its longstanding expertise in anti-submarine warfare and within the context of a new northern policy for Canada, Arctic-going subs are needed. In searching for the right type, it would be counterproductive to deny a propulsion system that ignores Canada's basic geography. But it would be wasteful and undesirable to take the alternative championed by the government.

In conclusion, the steps outlined represent the kind of defence realignment necessary for Canada to meet the security challenges of the future. They do not come cheaply. Nor can they be achieved unless there is a major shift in Canada's defence priorities. If Canada wants to keep the Arctic as peaceful as possible, minimize superpower confrontation, and ensure its sovereignty, all within the confines of some working relationship with the United States, such an approach is essential. Anything less means events may well overwhelm us.

10

Star Wars and Canada

With the strains of when 'Irish Eyes are Smilin'' still to come, U.S. defence secretary Caspar Weinberger went on Canadian morning TV in 1985 to talk about one of his favourite subjects – the Strategic Defense Initiative (SDI). It was the opening day of the Shamrock summit, the first meeting ever held between Ronald Reagan and Brian Mulroney in Canada. Everything had been meticulously orchestrated to achieve the appearance of an Irish love-in. But Weinberger was about to undo all those carefully laid St Patrick's Day plans and confirm in one fell swoop the worst fears of many Canadians. In response to a question about the possibility of placing Star Wars missile 'launchers' in Canada, he replied, 'defences ... would be first placed in the most effective way ... Some might be here [in Canada]. Some might be in the United States, some might be at sea. It just depends on where is the most effective technical place for them.'[1] The Americans, realizing what had been said, immediately issued 'clarifications' insisting the United States would never do anything that would interfere with the sovereignty of Canada.[2] Yet the message was not lost. Canada probably would be involved in Star Wars, at least in the mind of the initiatives' most senior and ardent proponent.

Facing up to that possibility has brought Canada to the greatest watershed yet in its security relationship with the United States. Thus far, Canadian defence policy has operated in relative concert with U.S. interests. The 'American factor' has been the dominant one in the evolution of Canadian security policy. Conversely, Canada has been forced to adapt itself to whatever strategic policy the United States pursues. This interrelationship has led David Cox to conclude: 'What is important to Canadians is not what we think the Russians will do; it is what we think the

Americans think the Russians will do, because our strategic doctrine is essentially one of trying to accommodate ourselves to American strategic doctrine.'[3]

Its position as the 'meat in the nuclear sandwich' makes Canada of ongoing strategic importance to the United States. While the proposed upgrading of the North Warning System represents a slight revival of U.S. interest in Canada's North, as the previous analysis reveals, this is but a relatively small part in the overall superpower confrontation. The Strategic Defense Initiative, however, is an entirely different matter. U.S. interest in Canadian soil would become intense, raising fundamental dilemmas for Canada to resolve.

To deal with the overall question of Canada and Star Wars, one has to ask first: does the program necessarily involve Canada? If so, how? Then, what options does Canada have to pursue a policy independent of that of the United States? Any such discussion at this point is fraught with risk, for SDI is still evolving as research continues. It is too early to determine how it will finally shake down. However, this situation provides Canada with valuable breathing space in which to plot its strategy. If Canada is determined not to play any role in a space defence system involving its own territory, then planning must begin now.

There is virtually no doubt that in order to set up a full-fledged space defence system the United States will want to use Canadian soil. In the words of John Pike, who monitors the SDI program for the Federation of American Scientists, 'there is no magic to this conclusion, only the facts of Canadian geography.'[4] In its barest-bones form, the Strategic Defense Initiative is a multi-layered defence umbrella that would guarantee the surveillance, tracking, and eventual destruction of Soviet missiles in all phases of their flight. For purposes of such planning, strategists have broken down the flight path of these missiles into four phases: 1 / the boost phase, lasting several minutes, as the missiles are first launched into space; 2 / the busing phase, lasting several more minutes as the missiles fly free of their boosters; 3 / the mid-course phase, which can take up to twenty-five minutes, as the missiles soar in space towards their targets; and 4 / the terminal phase, lasting up to ten minutes, as the missiles re-enter the atmosphere headed for their targets.[5]

It would be up to sensors based both in space and on land to pick up these missiles. Then different types of interceptor rockets would knock them out at different stages of their flight to the United States. The detection process would be particularly important for the sensors would have to work faultlessly, sifting through hundreds of thousands of decoys and bits of chaff and debris to pick out the 'real' Soviet missiles. Originally it was envisaged that once the missiles were identified, a combination of newly developed lasers, rockets, and particle beams would be used to intercept and destroy them. As testing has evolved, much of the fancy weaponry has already fallen off the drawing-board and officials are now looking at small 'kinetic energy' homing rockets launched from ground or satellites that would destroy targets with the force of their impact.[6]

From a strategic point of view, Canada's North provides an ideal locale for both land-based sensors and interceptor rockets.[7] Lying directly underneath the flight path of incoming Soviet ballistic missiles, the Arctic provides one of the best 'viewing points' from which to pick such missiles as they are first launched. Some sensors will be space-based but others will inevitably be land-based to provide a back-up to other data received.

For example, among the many futuristic acronyms used to describe potential components of SDI is SATKA Project 008 – the Airborne Optical system. Modified Boeing 767 jetliners, carrying high-resolution infra-red telescopes, would track Soviet warheads in the mid-course and terminal phases, detecting the heat of the re-entry vehicles against the coldness of space. Anywhere from twenty to forty of these 767s would operate out of twelve patrol bases. There is even talk of remote-controlled pilot-less 767s that would fly for several days at a time. To give maximum warning, it is thought these jets should be stationed as far north as possible and Canada's Arctic provides the ideal location.[8] Even if they were stationed just south of the Canada–United States border, they would undoubtedly need to fly over Canadian territory to carry out their missions effectively.

Another system best suited for the North is the Exo-atmospheric Re-entry Vehicle Interception system (ERIS). It is an interceptor designed to destroy Soviet missiles during the mid-course phase. Propelled by a two-stage rocket – each stage would burn just fifteen seconds – ERIS would be guided by an infra-red sensing system as well as a homing laser. As the term 'exo-atmospheric' suggests, ERIS would hit its targets outside the atmosphere in the late mid-course phase. If the missiles were based in northern Canada, ERIS would be able to hit targets much earlier in the

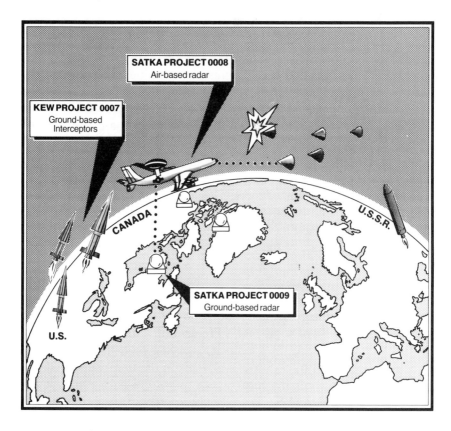

Possible use of Canadian soil in a Star Wars system

mid-course phase, thereby extending the range and effectiveness of these interceptors.[9]

A third system, code-named 'Braduskill' (Exo-atmospheric Non-nuclear Kill Technology) is designed to hit warheads in the mid-course phase. However, unlike ERIS, Braduskill would not hit targets dead on. Instead, it would fly alongside the warheads, taking time to discriminate between decoys and real targets. Once identified, the warheads would be destroyed by numerous small, self-propelled 'kill vehicles' guided by infra-red sensors or other homing devices. Again, the ideal location for such a system would be as far north as possible.[10]

These three systems are only samples of the intended technology; however, they serve to illustrate how vital the deployment area will be.

According to William Arkin, 'Star Wars will not work without the early warning system and that depends on Canada. There is no military scenario in the northern hemisphere in which Canada (or at least Canadian real estate) does not play a crucial role.'[11] u.s. officials have admitted as much and Caspar Weinberger in his morning tv interview virtually confirmed it. In private sdi briefings held in the United States, the 'Canadian dimension' is not even alluded to as an issue. Former defence minister Barney Danson, who attended one such briefing in Boston, reports: 'Anybody who can suggest we're not involved in sdi, if there is an sdi, is just out of their mind. In the Boston briefing, they didn't hide the fact that they had to have sensors in the North. They didn't call it Canada, they just called it North America. There were just spots on the map that were in Canada. If they decide to go that route, that's the area they'll go after or they will find a way around it. We won't have very much say in it at all.'[12]

Another immediate consequence of the deployment of an sdi system would be the inevitable transformation of norad and its detection systems into the 'eyes and ears' for it. sdi is concerned primarily with shooting down missiles in space, and it would be foolhardy to have a total space-defence system against ballistic missiles but nothing against low-flying bombers and cruise missiles. As norad chief General Herres put it: 'It doesn't make any sense to build a house with a roof over our heads – such as ballistic missile defence – while we forget to put walls around the sides.'[13]

For Canada, the most obvious concern is that norad would become an integral part of such a system. Even one of Canada's most senior analysts in the department of defence, Dr George Lindsey, acknowledges this: 'Should ballistic missile defence be deployed, it would be operationally desirable to place it under the operational control of norad ... For mid-course interception it is possible that it would be desirable, perhaps even essential, to locate certain sensors, readout stations or launchers in Canada.'[14]

norad's inclusion would also mean that information picked up by the new North Warning System would be used by the United States to defend against any low-flying threat. Under current plans, the North Warning System is passive; that is, it has no capacity to destroy incoming cruise missiles and the like. In fact, no such foolproof system has yet been devised. But if the United States is successful in developing a defence against ballistic missiles in space, the next logical step is to do the same for those flying close to the earth's surface. At this point, the North Warning System would become critical.

Paul Nitze, senior arms-control negotiator for the Reagan administration, pointedly refused to rule out such a possibility during a visit to Ottawa in 1985.[15] Other Reagan administration defence officials, including the outspoken Richard Perle, have openly talked about the need for plans to 'defend against aircraft and cruise missiles.'[16]

Under the old NORAD agreement, there was a provision stipulating that everything under NORAD should be construed in accordance with the Anti-Ballistic Missile (ABM) Treaty. That treaty severely limits the rights of the superpowers to develop or test strategic defences. The clause was dropped in the 1981 renewal of NORAD and kept out again in the 1986 renewal, the excuse being that the United States is already an ABM signatory and to re-include it would be unnecessary, if not insulting. One must wonder why, if the United States is so comfortable with its position, it saw fit to ask that the ABM clause be dropped in the first place. One can only assume, lacking a better explanation, that the United States saw some advantage, perhaps the precluding of a future problem, in the clause's early elimination.

At this point, the question must be asked whether Canadian participation in SDI – voluntary or otherwise – is in this country's best strategic interests. On the face of it, it is directly contrary to what should be Canada's principal aim – the lessening of superpower confrontation on Canadian soil. It also flies in the face of any desire to keep the Canadian Arctic as demilitarized as possible. Until now, Canadian and U.S. interests in northern Canada have coincided with a passive radar system whose sole stated purpose is to give early warning of – not defend against – a Soviet attack. For the United States to incorporate Canadian soil and Canadian-based radars in an active defence system would represent a radical departure from the past. It would also involve Canada directly in U.S. war-fighting strategy. How such a scenario is in Canada's best interests is hard to imagine.

First, the whole concept of SDI is destabilizing. The logic of current deterrence theory is that each superpower believes the other will launch its missiles if attacked. That presumes each superpower has 'second strike' weapons, and that it possesses adequate warning and detection systems to give it enough time to retaliate. Just as important, it is essential these two facts are perceived to be true by both sides, since deterrence ultimately is a psychological phenomenon. When looked at critically, Star Wars undermines all three underpinnings of deterrence theory.

Since active ballistic-missile defence involves attack on ballistic missiles, it would necessarily reduce the surety that the opponent's second-strike weapons would get through. Each side, faced with this new reality, would inevitably embark on a program to increase and diversify the number of its offensive weapons to ensure it had enough to be considered a threat. Assume, for example, an SDI shield is 90 per cent effective, allowing only 10 per cent of one side's weapons to get through. The temptation would be for that side to increase its number of weapons tenfold to guarantee the same number, pre-SDI, would arrive at designated targets. Thus a never-ending escalation in the arms race begins.

Second, although SDI is primarily directed at missile destruction, it would also include elimination of the opponent's warning and control systems, especially those based in space. Again, the impact would be to lessen the assurance that each side possesses sufficient warning and detection systems to be able to retaliate in time. Taken together, these factors would undermine that all-important psychological aspect of deterrence – the belief that the other side could and would retaliate. Such an unpredictable state of affairs can only be viewed with alarm.

Next, even if Canada did become a voluntary partner in SDI in the hope of having some say over its deployment, there is every expectation the system would remain under unilateral U.S. control. The very nature of the computer-dependent technology, requiring nearly instantaneous responses after missiles have been launched, precludes much if any intergovernmental consultation. What if, for example, the Canadian prime minister happened to be indisposed at the critical moment? It is virtually impossible to conceive of the United States consulting its allies in advance, given the exigencies of the system. In this sense, Canada has much to lose and little to gain.

Nor is it reasonable for anyone, particularly the Soviets, to distinguish between the functioning of the North Warning System on one hand as a passive detection system and on the other, as an integral part of SDI. The Soviets would logically see the system as a cog in the overall SDI system and would treat Canada accordingly. For anyone to try and pretend otherwise is to ignore reality. In that sense, Canada is included whether it likes it or not. Thus, the point is sometimes made that Canada doesn't really have any choice because the United States will go ahead and do what it wants anyway. The U.S. military has always had a relatively free hand in Canada and knows it can use Canadian soil in times of crisis. It would logically expect such co-operation to continue. Yet in a full SDI deployment, the United States would have to permanently station squadrons of interceptors and new sensors right across Canada's northern rim. For such a major deployment, Canada would have the right to approve it. As a sovereign country, Canada does have a veto over how its territory is used. For anyone to suggest otherwise is to deny the most fundamental of sovereign rights.

One final objection to SDI is that full Canadian membership would represent a denial of many things Canada has stood for; namely, arms control, deterrence, and a role as an independent middle power. For example, while still a member of the western alliance, Canada has pursued a policy of nuclear suffocation since 1978. Canadian interest and viewpoints on the North/South dialogue, South Africa, and Central America have often put it at odds with the United States. While our alliance preference has never been in doubt, Canada has always treasured its independent image and fostered the promotion of it. Surely that image would be damaged by Canada's wholesale inclusion in SDI and the consequent impression created that Canada's participation meant its approval. Such inclusion would certainly also diminish Canada's ability to pursue an independent arms-control policy. The country, in short, would be seen as a military adjunct to the United States.

So what leverage, if any, does Canada have to pursue an independent policy? The answer may be more than many Canadians expect. Here is American William Arkin on the subject:

Does Canada have any leverage? Absolutely. In fact, Canada may be one of the rare only countries with the ability to stop the U.S. in Star Wars because they need you. Just like the U.S. needed Canada when NORAD was established, so it will need Canada in 1998 when SDI is deployed. Canada can either cede its territory to the U.S. in the name of NORAD or SDI, or Canada could have some say over what the policy might be. I can't see it is in Canada's view to militarize the North. But that view would have to be manifested in a real political way and not in some gimmicky way.[17]

When the Mulroney government decided not to participate in SDI research on a government-to-government basis, there were fears in some quarters that retaliation might be in order. Such was not the case. In fact, several other European allies also saw fit to politely decline. It is possible, as Arkin suggests, that since Canadian soil will in all likelihood be needed, Canada does have some clout. But the time to use it is now, not when the system is about to be deployed.

The first step must be for Canada to state in unequivocal terms its adherence to the Anti-Ballistic Missile (ABM) Treaty. The re-inclusion of the 'ABM clause' in the NORAD agreement in 1986 would have been even better. Instead Mulroney acquiesced, opting to join with Reagan in issuing a milquetoast statement that 'the prime minister and the president ... noted that the extension of the NORAD agreement is fully consistent with the ABM Treaty and is in full accordance with other U.S. and Canadian treaty obligations.[18] The statement is sadly lacking for there are very few doubts the *current* NORAD agreement is in violation of the ABM Treaty. The worry is that some of its systems will be used in a *future* missile defence system. On that issue, the statement was stonily silent. As arms-control expert John Lamb noted, 'the statement does contain a sort of veiled expression of Canadian concern about American compliance with the ABM Treaty, but it's extremely veiled.'[19]

It has always been Canadian policy to fully endorse the ABM Treaty. Yet a debate is brewing in the United States over its interpretation, with the Reagan administration arguing for a very broad reading which would allow much more SDI testing and research. The U.S. position has critical consequences for Canada, because the United States may soon want to test the Braduskill or SATKA systems mentioned above, which are ideally suited for northern deployment. As was the case for cruise-missile testing, the United States will likely argue that the testing should take place in the same environment in which the system will be used. At that point, Canada will be faced with a very tough choice. If it waits until then to make its feelings known, the political and alliance consequences of saying 'no' may be too great. If, however, it has been long-standing, often-repeated policy that Canada will not permit any systems testing in violation of the treaty, then its refusal down the road will become all the more understandable and acceptable.

Nor should Canada be drawn into broadly interpreting the treaty.

Many powerful forces within the United States, including the Senate's leading military expert, Georgia Senator Sam Nunn, already stand opposed to Reagan on the issue.[20] Many others within the alliance have similar doubts. Canada could stand against in very good company, reinforcing its long-standing support for arms control and disarmament. Such a stand would also serve as a valuable precedent if and when Canada is ever asked to be part of an SDI system.

Simple words, though, are not enough. However, for Canada to jump out of NORAD now without knowing what SDI might be is precipitous. The same applies to all continental defence studies, including SDA (Strategic Defence Architecture) 2000. At this point, Canada needs to find out as much as it can about U.S. strategic planning and to influence it wherever possible. The second phase of SDA 2000 clearly involves a study of the needs for surveillance *and* a possible missile defence system for North America by the year 2000.[21] Some have worried that Canada's participation in this study implies its acceptance of SDI. Again the argument for Canada being on the inside, knowing what is going on, should still apply. Outside of these studies, all we can do is guess about U.S. intentions until the final plans are revealed. Canada still has the opportunity to pick the appropriate time to say 'no,' when and if any SDI system is deployed.

In the meantime, Canada has to develop its own Star Wars insurance policy. To this end, all the measures proposed in the previous chapter – a 'keep-out' zone in the Arctic, underwater radar surveillance, more use of satellites and some submarines – fit in neatly. If SDI involves the use of NORAD and Canada wants no part of the system, then Canada would have no alternative but to withdraw from the agreement. But if Canada stays with the status quo and fails to develop its own independent surveillance system, then outside of NORAD it will have virtually no capability to know what is happening under its waters or in its airspace. Furthermore, the United States would undoubtedly step in, particularly in the Arctic, to protect against a potential Soviet submarine or bomber threat. Unless Canada had made its 'keep-out' zone secure, the United States would feel it had no alternative but to take over entire defence of the North. This scenario also presents another compelling argument for the stationing of radar stations along the edge of the archipelago to ensure Canada could monitor all of the North and not just part of it. In sum, Canada has to make the North secure, and ensure that this security is credible to both superpowers.

If Canada wants to take out this insurance policy, then the planning has to begin now. The development and financing of some of these systems require lead times of up to a decade. By the mid- to late 1990s; SDI proponents such as Secretary Weinberger are hoping the first parts of SDI will be deployed.[22] If Canada waits until then to act, the strategic die will already have been cast.

Such a strategy does not have to be seen as hostile to the United States. Canada can easily argue it has decided to assume a greater share of the continental-defence burden, silencing those who say we have taken a 'free ride' in defence for too long. It can also say that in keeping with a longstanding desire to keep its Arctic as demilitarized as possible, it has decided unilaterally to secure its northern waters in a 'keep-out' zone. If Canada remains totally dependent on the resources of an integrated defence arrangement such as NORAD, its fate will be sealed. As strategic analyst Douglas Ross argues: 'Integrated defence arrangements amount to an automatic "yes" to American decision-making in crises. It is the national security equivalent of writing a blank cheque. Canada's influence on critical East-West issues to a large extent will hinge on being able to say "no" – or at least engage in constructive delay, when and where Canadian authorities deem it appropriate to do so.'[23] At this point, no one can say with surety where or if SDI will be deployed. But can Canada afford to bank on that doubt? The answer must surely be no.

NATO

11

West Germany: the key to the club

Canada, it has been said, has the geography of a superpower, the gross national product of a middle power, and the population of a smaller power.[1] Those inherent contradictions manifest themselves in many curious ways on the Canadian psyche and nowhere more apparently than in the realm of military commitments. Not that Canada or Canadians have any delusions about being a military superpower. Yet, with the quiver of commitments it has assumed, Canada now stands at the point where, within NATO, only the United States has a comparable range of varied and geographically diverse roles. Just consider the list. With only 84,000 active forces, Canada is committed not only to maintain and supply a land and air contingent on the Central Front in West Germany, send a brigade of 5,000 to Norway in times of crisis (now under review), and supply a contingent of 500 to Denmark in similar times of crisis, but also to patrol 2.76 million kilometres of the northwest Atlantic in times of war and ensure (with the United States) the security of 6.3 million kilometres of Canada's archipelago. Those are only Canada's NATO commitments. The list doesn't include the military's first task, the defence of Canada itself, or Canada's promise to exercise surveillance over 1.66 million kilometres of the north Pacific.

In the words of former defence minister Allan Mackinnon, to cite just one of many who are sceptical of Canada's capabilities, 'I do not believe for a minute we can carry out the commitments we have made.'[2] Nor are the military happy, although for different reasons. In a remarkably blunt speech just before he retired, the former chief of defence staff General George Thériault argued that the costs 'in making viable this highly fragmented effort are associated with an elaborate support infrastructure that does not make military sense per se ... Having paid this large bill and deployed much of our resources in fulfillment of these various commitments, a Canadian government would not be left with much strategic flexibility.'[3]

With politicians and military alike admitting the present set-up doesn't make sense, one might well ask why nothing has been done. It's as if a paralysis has set in among official circles based on a fear of annoying our allies, an inability to come to grips with our limitations, or a combination of both. Certainly Canada's commitment to Europe through NATO has been one of the primary pillars, if not preoccupations, of Canadian foreign policy since the alliance's formation in 1949. The so-called 'Atlanticist' tilt of our external-relations policy has been cemented by a continuing military presence in Europe. Of necessity, that presence, which now costs Canadian taxpayers $1 billion a year,[4] has resulted in fewer resources being dedicated to Canada. It is also based on several assumptions, some of which might have been valid forty years ago, that no longer apply.

The 'Atlanticist' argument has always been that less military effort is needed to protect Canadian soil because the primary security threat to Canada still comes from Europe. The argument continues that since Canada is too large a country for Canadians to defend themselves, it needs membership in a military alliance to achieve collective security. By participating in this alliance, the argument goes, Canada has helped maintain peace and a more strategically balanced world.[5] Furthermore, participation in NATO gives Canada a 'seat at the table'; that is, access to many high-level *international* forums and the opportunity to 'have its voice heard." For Canada to go it alone would be both too expensive and the equivalent of burying our heads in the sand. In terms of designing a defence policy for Canada, therefore, 'Atlanticists' have used these assumptions as a basis for maintaining our NATO commitments. Some even describe it as paying our 'dues' to the club.

It is essential to keep these assumptions in mind when analysing Canada's current commitments to NATO. It is also important to realize that by paying 'dues' in the manner we have, we have accepted a fundamental trade-off. Less attention has been given to the Arctic, and both Canada's sovereignty and its military interests there, despite the fact that officialdom has repeatedly said sovereignty protection must be the military's number-one task.[6] Following a critical review of all Canada's

NATO 'dues' – the West German and naval commitments outlined in this chapter and the Norwegian and Danish ones discussed in a subsequent chapter – the 'Atlanticist' assumptions will be evaluated in terms of their relevance today. The question will then be posed: should Canada stay in NATO and, if so, in what role? The analysis will illustrate how outdated and flawed many of these commitments are and how their fulfilment has compromised Canada's security and sovereignty on this side of the Atlantic. The inescapable conclusion is that nothing short of a complete overhaul of these commitments will suffice.

Nowhere is the need for re-evaluation more evident than on the Central Front, where Canadian troops provide what one senior diplomat has called 'the Canadian key to the club.'[7] Just a few kilometres east of West Germany's principal autobahn, near the town of Lahr in the fabled Black Forest region, lies the heart of Canada's European presence. A huge sign at the gate along with the familiar maple leaf emblem proclaim Canada's commitment to Europe. Canadian military vehicles abound, and in nearby Lahr, the Canadian soldier is an every-day and welcome part of life. Not too far to the north, at Baden-Soellingen, lies the home of two Canadian air squadrons, protected by aging cannons retrieved from Canada's last aircraft carrier, the *Bonaventure*. The peacetime military strength of these two bases is now roughly 6,500. Also sprinkled throughout Europe as part of NATO commitments are another 400 Canadian forces. Some 130 military personnel serve with NATO's special radar and reconnaissance 'Early Warning Force' at Geilenkirchen, West Germany, while another 70 are on the multinational staff of NATO's headquarters just south of Brussels.

Altogether these forces are just a miniscule part of what is undisputably the greatest concentration of military might anywhere in the world. With a population of 62 million, West Germany has 485,000[8] military personnel of its own along with about 400,000[9] foreign troops, most of them American. A country roughly the size of Newfoundland, West Germany also has more than 4,000 individual military facilities and an infrastructure of highways, railroads, airports, and communications networks, all designed for maximum wartime usefulness. Highways, for example, are also built to serve as optional landing strips for military planes. Most bridges, tunnels, and the famous autobahns have been constructed with demolition chambers to enable easy destruction in the event of attack.

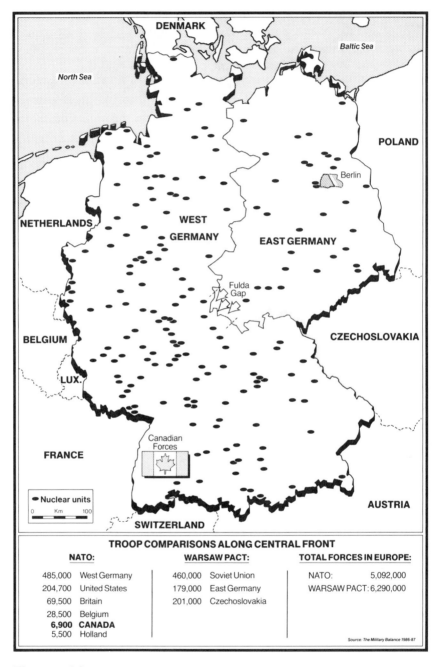

The central front

West Germany is also the nerve centre for the most densely nuclear-ized theatre in the world. Close to 10,000 nuclear warheads have been either deployed in Europe or are targeted on it from both sides of the Iron Curtain. Nuclear weapons are now positioned in eleven European countries and cover the entire spectrum of type and capability. Almost all of them are dual purpose in that they can carry both nuclear and conventional payloads. Naval forces patrolling the waters around Europe also carry nuclear warheads, bringing the continent's total to almost one-third of the world's entire nuclear arsenal.[10]

With more than two million troops[11] facing one another across the final battle line of a war that ended four decades ago, it is virtually inconceivable to think of the Soviets launching a first strike into the heart of West Germany. Former NATO supreme commander General Bruce Rogers said as much in 1986 when he told reporters the chances of such an attack are 'one in a million.'[12] Former Canadian defence minister Paul Hellyer describes this massing on the Central Front as 'the Maginot Line complex. My personal fear is that the Soviets will operate every-where else except along the Central Front in an end run.'[13] Both NATO and the Warsaw Pact have on file the most elaborate of war scenarios, yet nuclear weapons are so closely integrated into each bloc's fighting machine, it is virtually impossible to imagine any conflict remaining at conventional levels for long. And, a nuclear-bombed Europe, given its dense population and industrial development, would scarcely be of use to anyone.

Much has also been made of the Warsaw Pact's lead in both conventional and nuclear forces along the front. Yet the renowned International Institute for Strategic Studies concludes that 'the conventional military balance is still such as to make general military aggression a highly risky undertaking for either side ... The consequences for an attacker would still be quite unpredictable, and the risks, *particularly of nuclear escalation*, remain incalculable' (italics added).[14]

This generally accepted view has led some analysts to pose fighting strategies based on the Soviets nibbling away at various corners of NATO without incurring a nuclear strike. So, various conventional small wars in such areas as Greece, Turkey, or Norway have been put forward as a possibility. However, Europe's integrated nuclear network plus NATO's fundamental premise that an attack against one is an attack against all make such strategizing highly improbably.

In the context of this military monolith sit Canada's 6,900 troops.

Under current NATO plans, they have no front-line role but are to be used as reserves to support the West Germans and the Americans. According to most military experts and retired NATO generals, the valley of the River Fulda is the most likely route in the event the Russians launch a quick blitzkrieg to smash NATO's defences. The so-called Fulda Gap is where East Germany protrudes farthest into West Germany, reducing it to width of 150 kilometres. Pinched by hilly ranges, this fifty-kilometre stretch of gently rolling countryside has been overrun by invaders through the years. The most notable were Napoleon on his way to Russia and U.S. general George Patton in 1945. Canada's troops are situated to the south and west of the gap and within hailing distance of France's half million forces, which undoubtedly would come to West Germany's aid in the unlikely event of a frontal Soviet assault.

From a military point of view, it is impossible to argue that Canada's troops are a significant component. Within the context of 800,000 other NATO troops and the nuclear infrastructure of the Central Front, Canada's contribution ranks at the token level. This is not to demean the Canadian presence, only to emphasize that the contingent's primary role is symbolic, a statement that Canada is committed to Europe. Paul Hellyer puts it a little differently: 'There's no question Canada's contribution is entirely political. This is not to denegrate the force. The real reason they're there is as hostages. It's not politically so much to guarantee Canadian involvement as it is to shore up American involvement. If we pulled out, the Americans would hop on the crusade.'[15]

Whatever the reason, the commitment carries a heavy price-tag. Hundreds of millions of dollars have been spent arming this token force with everything from tanks to armoured carriers, to helicopters, to state-of-the-art CF18s. According to another former defence minister, Donald Macdonald, this massive spending has 'distorted our priorities, our force structure and probably led to a miscalculation of our resources.'[16] The latest project is a $1.1 billion low-level air-defence system to replace those aging *Bonaventure* cannons at the end of the runway.[17] From a military point of view, the expenditure of so much money on so few troops has caused raised eyebrows in several outside quarters. It is, though, revealing of the Canadian military's own perceived raison d'être and its desire to plot and plan with the 'big boys' in the NATO club. When one considers how effectively even part of that money could have been spent to ensure Canadian sovereignty over the Northwest Passage, one is forced to ask a few questions.

Another area worth questioning are the two squadrons of forty-two CF-18s (Hornets) committed to Europe. Despite Canadian military protests that they bought the best, no other NATO ally on the Central Front uses the Hornet. Instead, they operate F-16s, F-15s, or Toronados. While F-18s are used by Americans on their aircraft carriers, they are not currently part of the U.S. air contingent on the Central Front. For Canada that poses some interesting logistical problems, because such highly computerized and modern aircraft require equally sophisticated servicing.[18] While obviously Canadian personnel at Baden-Soellingen are equipped to do the job, no other Allied bases are. There have been attempts to standardize equipment for all NATO fighters, but this process is still in its early stages. Its success has not been proven. Certainly to restrict such an expensive fighter to one airfield makes little military sense. What also makes little sense is that Canada has only twenty-four Hornets in total committed to Canadian soil. That means for the upgraded North Warning system, NORAD may have to call upon American F-15s to do patrol work in Canada. Can only really argue Canada's security interests are better served in keeping these Hornets in Europe restricted to one airfield? And, what about Canadian sovereignty interests in the North?

The other major area that needs re-evaluating is Canada's naval commitments to NATO. Nowhere is the trade-off between Canada's promises to Europe and the stark need to ensure sovereignty control over its own waters more striking. Any discussion of the naval role must begin with the simple yet overwhelming fact that Canada has the world's longest coastline, some 71,000 kilometres – and that doesn't include most of the islands. The waters and islands of the Arctic archipelago add another 6.3 million kilometres to the total. Somewhere in their collective consciousness, Canadians probably realize the extent of their enormous maritime domain but few seem to have come to grips with the enormity of the task in exercising control over it.

In the past fifteen years, Canadian governments have taken a series of legal steps to guarantee legal control over an ever-increasing area of the North. At the same time, the navy has been left to languish and age, with no new additions to its meagre complement to ensure control over these areas. It was this predicament that led the Senate subcommittee studying Canada's maritime command to conclude that 'with the equipment now available, the maritime command cannot meet its commitments to the protection of Canadian sovereignty, to the defence of North America –

156 NATO

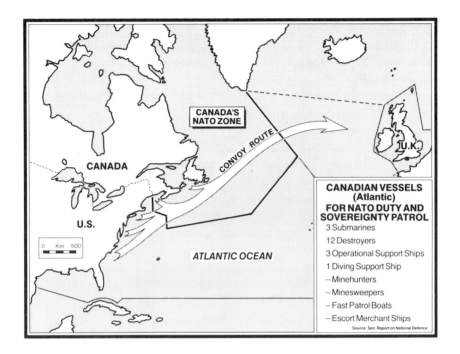

CANADA'S
NATO ZONE

CONVOY ROUTE

CANADA

U.K.

U.S.

0   Km   500

ATLANTIC OCEAN

CANADIAN VESSELS
(Atlantic)
FOR NATO DUTY AND
SOVEREIGNTY PATROL
3 Submarines
12 Destroyers
3 Operational Support Ships
1 Diving Support Ship
– Minehunters
– Minesweepers
– Fast Patrol Boats
– Escort Merchant Ships
Source: Sen. Report on National Defence

Canada's NATO naval zone

much less to NATO.'[19] A much blunter assessment came from the editor of the renowned *Jane's Fighting Ships* in his 1984–85 edition. He wrote that Canadian naval personnel:

have been placed in a most invidious position by the failure of successive governments to understand or accept the basic principles of naval planning. Maritime Command is responsible for naval operations throughout the world; surveillance, control and defence of Canadian waters, defence of North America, in conjunction with the U.S. Navy etc . . . This high-sounding charter gives a totally false impression of the navy's current capability, another case of good men and women starved of tools to do the job.[20]

On the face of it, Canada's pledge to NATO to patrol and monitor a giant quadrangle of 2.76 million kilometres of the north-west Atlantic makes some sense. The area borders Canada's Atlantic coast and, with any continued presence in Europe, Canada would need to resupply its troops. NATO estimates that in the event of war there would be 1,800 transatlantic convoys in the first month alone – most passing through Canada's quadrant.[21] Unlike the Warsaw Pact countries, which are not dependent on open sea lanes of communication, the far-flung fortresses of NATO are only linked by oceanic highways. That means NATO must maintain control of the seas, while the Soviet bloc would obviously try to prevent this. Military planners estimate a favourable balance of at least twice and maybe three times the strength of the enemy to assert the necessary control.

To fulfil this responsibility, Canada has a grand total of twenty-three combat vessels (twenty-six if three rusting destroyers are brought out of mothballs).[22] There are three submarines, and twelve helicopter-carrying destroyers on the east coast and eight on the west. Given the usual timetabling for maintenance and refit, approximately 25 per cent of the fleet would be in dry dock at any one time. And, Rear-Admiral Michael Martin says, of the surface vessels, only four possess a 'marginal capacity' to survive a hostile environment: 'In the Atlantic four of the destroyers could probably do a reasonably effective job; but do not be misled. These ships are at least a generation behind in their capability. The other helicopter-destroyers are so old that all they are really providing is a command and control center and deck room from which a helicopter can operate.'[23]

Canada has contracted to buy six new frigates but the first one won't arrive until 1989. Quite frankly our naval efficiency has dwindled to the point that while in 1963, Canada was able to provide back-up for the U.S. navy during the Cuban missile crisis, it would not have been able to pick up any NATO slack for the British, had it been asked, during the recent Falklands war. Were the Canadian navy called upon now to do convoy duty in its quadrant, it simply wouldn't be up to the job.

What makes this situation critical is that the same vessels earmarked for NATO duty also have the responsibility to ensure sovereignty surveillance over Canadian waters, not to mention control of the flotillas of foreign fishing fleets that regularly venture into prohibited waters. In the Arctic, there are no regular naval patrols, only periodic summer exercises. The only regular presence is the once-every-three-weeks flight of the Aurora long-range patrol aircraft. Again, since the navy's first job has always been to protect Canadian waters, one is inclined to ask whose interests are being served by the present fleet. While it is possible to make domestic naval tasks coincide with NATO roles, currently the Canadian navy is serving in neither role adequately.

To summarize, from a strictly military point of view Canada has 6,900 troops on a front where two million others are gathered and where even the former NATO supreme commander admits the risks of a direct attack are minuscule, two squadrons of CF-18s which can only be serviced in one area, and a navy which its own commander admits can't do its NATO duty. That, in itself, is unacceptable. When it is also remembered that these commitments have been carried out at considerable expense and in lieu of performing other Canadian tasks, particularly in the Arctic, the mind boggles.

As argued above, Canada's principal aim in maintaining its European presence appears to be political – not military. Thus the temptation may be simply to dismiss such criticisms. However, while belonging to the club is one thing, performing outmoded and impossible tasks is quite another. For Canada to continue to be dedicated to roles that relate more to a war than terminated four decades ago just doesn't make sense. For us to persist in those roles is to perpetuate contradictions that should have been resolved long ago.

12

Norway and Denmark:
the 'Hong Kong commitments'

In the middle of August 1986, the order was given to send 5,500 Canadian troops to the mountainous fjords of northern Norway as quickly as possible. Military publicists quickly dubbed it 'the largest movement of Canadian troops to Europe since the Second World War.'[1] The advance party, some travelling by seconded Air Canada jets, arrived on 20 August. The vast majority, along with their 27 helicopters, 1,900 vehicles, and countless tents, voyaged across the Atlantic in four rented ships – one Panamanian, one British, and two West German – to arrive 3 September. Ten days later they were dug in their positions just outside Narvik, Norway, roughly two hundred kilometres north of the Arctic Circle, ready to do battle.

The enemy, of course, were Norwegians, for this was Operation Brave Lion, a $100 million war game.[2] And, although it took only one month from the time of the first order to the troops' deployment near Narvik, actual planning for the exercise began four years earlier.[3] The purpose of the exercise was clear: to dispel any doubts about Canada's ability and will to live up to its NATO commitments on Europe's northern flank. The Canadian show of logistics and military performance was impressive, as the grateful Norwegians repeatedly stressed. However, the entire exercise served only to reinforce longstanding military doubts about this commitment. In fact, the doubts became so apparent to defence minister Perrin Beatty, who witnessed the war game, that he returned to Ottawa convinced Canada must get out its Norwegian commitment. Following the long line of defence ministers before him who had also queried this role, Beatty has now at least formally proposed that it end.[4] When that happens, the backbone of Canada's two-decade–long commitment to Europe's northern flank will be over.

However, the other part of Canada's two-tiered northern commitment is a promise to send a small military force of about five hundred to Denmark in undefined times of crisis. It is to be maintained. Scarcely known to the Canadian public and fraught with military risks, this commitment is just as questionable as its Norwegian counterpart. On one level, Canada has felt some special affinity for both Norway and Denmark, given their similar northern terrain and their proximity as circumpolar neighbours. Arguments have often been put forward that it made sense for Canada to specialize in 'northern-type' fighting, so that the same skills could also be used in our Arctic.[5] Yet, as long as Canada maintains its commitment on the Central Front, the military logic of sending troops to a second front hundreds of kilometres away is impossible to defend. Furthermore, although there are elaborate plans to get Canadian troops *to* both Denmark and Norway, the same type of plans don't exist to get them *out* in an emergency.[6] It is little wonder former defence minister Barney Danson called these our 'Hong Kong commitments,'[7] referring to the Second World War battle where our troops were left hopelessly stranded in Hong Kong with no means of escape.

From the perspective of a new northern policy for Canada, these two commitments are just as hard to defend. Both demand resources and money which could just as well as allocated to efforts in the North. However, the attractiveness of helping two circumpolar countries and the logic of specializing in 'northern-type' fighting makes it impossible to simply dismiss these commitments out of hand. Altered radically in light of a totally redefined European defence policy, they may make some sense. However, before they can be sensibly evaluated, it is necessary to understand their strategic importance and how Canada came to be involved.

As is often the case for Canada, the initial decision to defend Norway was the progeny of a political compromise. Following a review of defence policy in 1968, the Trudeau government decided to halve the number of Canadian troops permanently stationed in West Germany. When the NATO allies, led by the United States, protested, Canada replied by promising to send a brigade of five thousand troops to Norway in unspecified times of crisis. It is ironic that this restructuring, based on the realization that Canada's military capability was already stretched too

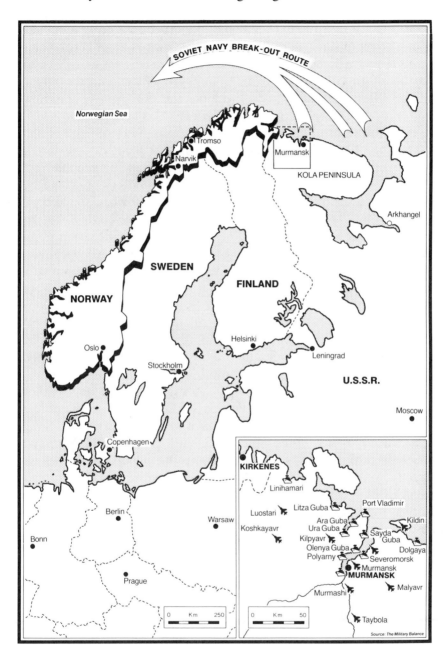

Strategic locale of Norway with inset of military build-up on Kola Peninsula

thin, in fact resulted in the addition of a totally new European military commitment. It is now doubly ironic that defence minister Perrin Beatty wants to return to the original scenario, although he plans to increase the number of troops dedicated to the Central Front.[8] Certainly the military will be relieved at having to deal with one less European theatre. However, no one can be insensitive to Norway's strategic position and its vulnerability if attacked.

Stretched like a zipper along the north-west flank of Scandinavia, Norway offers ultimate command of the Norwegian Sea and the North Atlantic with its myriad safe harbours and deep fjords (see accompanying map). Europe first awoke to this reality in 1940 when, to the cry of 'the flies have captured the fly paper,' it heard that the Nazis had seized Norway. Hitler would later use those many fjords as safe havens for his U-boats to relentlessly attack allied convoys in the North Atlantic. In any protracted war today, those same Atlantic sea lanes would be used in much the same way to bring supplies from North America to Europe. And, Norway would be just as vital, for in the hands of the East Bloc it could mean the potential control of the Atlantic. In virtually every one of its naval exercises over the past ten years, the Soviet Northern Fleet has gathered in the Norwegian Sea to assume positions to fight for control of the North Atlantic.[9]

Consider also Norway's geography. A straight line linking Moscow and Washington over the North Pole passes through the middle of Norway. The bee-line between U.S. ICBM silos in North Dakota and Soviet ICBM silos in Yedrovo runs through Svalbard. Like Canada, Norway is one of the Soviet Union's closest neighbours. But unlike Canada, Norway directly borders on one of the Soviets' most sensitive and highly militarized zones – the Kola Peninsula. In those arctic wastelands between Norway and Murmansk, the Soviets have amassed what has been described as the greatest concentration of naval, ground, and air forces to be found anywhere in the world. Former U.S. navy secretary John Lehman called it 'the most valuable piece of real estate on earth.'[10]

In one of the most detailed analyses of the build-up every undertaken, including satellite photographs, the Norwegian Foreign Policy Institute reported in 1986:

This [area] included two main strategic nuclear submarine bases, two strategic nuclear bomber bases, two strategic early-warning and target acquisition radar complexes, one theatre-nuclear missile launch complex, seven main submarine bases, nine major bases for surface forces, 22 main airbases with hardened aircraft shelters and runways exceeding 1,600 metres, 18 secondary airfields, the pre-positioning and deployment infrastructure for one front-level army and very many further installations.[11]

It must be emphasized that this build-up is not designed primarily as a threat to northern Europe. Again because of quirks of geography, the Soviets have been forced to concentrate most of their naval firepower in the north. Latest estimates are that two-thirds of the Soviet Union's nuclear ballistic-missile submarines (Typhoon, Delta, and Yankee class) are based there.[12] Although the Soviet Union borders on several large bodies of water, access to the open oceans can be cut off at 'choke points' such as the Dardanelles, near Turkey, and the Baltic, near Denmark. Although the Soviet fleet can sail freely from the Kamchatka Peninsula to the Pacific, this area is too far from the Soviet heart. That leaves the vast Arctic Ocean which, in a two-hundred–kilometre–wide band from Murmansk to the Atlantic, is clear of ice year round.[13] When all these factors are considered, it is hard to underestimate the importance of the Kola to the Soviets and the sensitive position that puts Norway in.

Denmark is of central importance precisely because of its location right at the Baltic choke point. Perched atop the northern edge of continental Europe, Denmark sits like a cork blocking the entrance to the Baltic. For NATO, the addition of the cork of Europe to the alliance was vital. All maritime traffic heading from the Baltic to the North Sea and eventually the Atlantic must navigate through Denmark's narrow belts and straits to reach the Kattegat/Skagerrak passage. Tourists savouring mackerel in some of Denmark's sea-side hostelries often view Soviet warships at very short range. Hardly any ship passes through these waters that is not tracked or noticed by both sides. Soviet, Polish, and East German surveillance boats regularly assume positions on each side of the straits.[14] East Bloc signal intelligence aircraft fly over Bornholm Island, Denmark's easternmost island, which was occupied briefly by the Soviets during the Second World War, on a year-round basis.[15] Denmark, likewise, has established a sophisticated system for observing traffic; royal decrees limit the number of warships that may pass through at any one time to three. Submarines are also to proceed in surface position.

Naval routes through Denmark

Thus, it is no coincidence that the latest developments in Soviet naval weaponry are often first detected by Danish ships. Since the Danes also require advance registration for certain warships passing through their waters, NATO has access to key intelligence on the Soviet's Baltic fleet.

In an international crisis, therefore, Denmark would garner more than passing interest from the Soviets – just as it has from invading European powers over the centuries. If the Warsaw Pact countries controlled Denmark, they would have unimpeded access to the North Sea and eventually to the Atlantic. If the Soviets had control, they could establish a strategic link-up between their Baltic and Northern fleets. While the Soviets have concentrated most of their naval firepower in the Northern

Fleet, more than half of their naval repair and maintenance facilities are located in the Baltic, principally around Leningrad. In any protracted war, access to these facilities would be vital. Nor should the air dimension be forgotten. If the Soviets secured an air corridor through Denmark, it would allow them a direct route to attack Britain and southern Norway, thereby bypassing NATO's air-defence systems on the Central Front. Finally, Denmark's strategic geography atop the Central Front would concern Soviet military planners whose tradition has always been to secure the flanks. In short, in any war the Soviets would want Denmark.

Since Denmark, like Norway, prohibits the permanent stationing of foreign troops on its soil, NATO planners had to come up with a different plan for its defence. The answer was to establish a special light brigade of six thousand from as many NATO countries as possible to act as a modern-day rapid-deployment force. Formally called 'Allied Command Europe Mobile Force, (AMF) or more commonly the 'ACE brigade,' it is designed to be deployed *before* hostilities break out. It is supposed to arrive at its designated area within days of authorization and be so small in number and so lightly armed that it could not be seen as provocative or menacing. Canada joined ACE as one of the eight participants in 1964 along with the United States, Britain, Belgium, the Netherlands, Luxembourg, Italy, and West Germany.[16]

The brigade Canada had pledged to Norway was also to arrive *before* hostilities broke out. Code-named the 'CAST Brigade' (for Canadian Air/ Sea Transportable combat group), it was also designed to act as a deterrent force and to arrive in northern Norway as quickly as possible. It should be emphasized that Canada's ACE commitment to Denmark is separate and distinct from its CAST commitment to Norway. In fact, before Canada decided to pull out of the Norwegian role, it was theoretically possible that Canada could be asked to send troops to both countries at the same time. Even NATO planners acknowledged that this situation would have been an impossible one, and privately assured Canada that in such an event the Norwegian commitment would take precedence. But that is only the first of a patchwork of pitfalls any Canadian government must confront before committing troops to either country.

Unlike other NATO decisions, the one to deploy the CAST or ACE force is *political* not military. Since the troops earmarked for either country are stationed in Canada, the decision has more serious implications. Moving

Belgian or Dutch troops a few hundred kilometres is one thing. Transporting Canadian soldiers six thousand kilometres across an ocean, with all the military logistics that entails, is quite another.

The question immediately arises as to what circumstances would ever prompt a Canadian government to make this decision. Both commitments are purposely fuzzy as to the exact types of crisis that would spark their activation. When asked about the Danish commitment, for example, several former defence ministers were at a loss to come up with any likely scenarios.[17] Danish officials dismiss the likelihood of any frontal attack. More likely, they say, Warsaw Pact nations may start to harass Danish warships in the Baltic or stage menacing naval exercises close to the Danish straits. Or they might demand more passage rights for their warships. While any of these scenarios would undoubtedly cause alarm in Copenhagen, it is difficult to imagine any one of them alone being grave enough to justify Canadian intervention.

Similar problems problems plague the Norwegian role. It is difficult to specify exactly what form of hostile Soviet behaviour, short of all-out attack, would cause Norway to ask Canada for help. Since it would take a minimum of three to four weeks for the troops to arrive, the range of imaginable 'crises' narrows. Furthermore, there is a school of strategic thought that argues the very act of deploying the CAST brigade would have given the Soviets cause to counter-attack quickly. Within NATO and throughout Scandinavia, it is felt Norway's prohibition against the stationing of foreign troops on its soil is designed principally to give the Soviet Union absolutely no excuse to put any troops in Finland. This doctrine, often referred to as the 'Nordic balance,' is based on the premise that the presence of Allied troops in Norway might produce Soviet pressure on Finland and possibly result in occupation of Finnish bases near northern Norway. If such thinking is correct, a quick deployment of the CAST brigade might well upset that delicate balance to Finland's detriment. In such strategizing, certainty is a rare commodity but real possibilities can't be ignored.

Deciding when to send troops is only the first hurdle. The next step would be to decide what troops to send. Nowhere would the conflict between defending Canada and deploying troops to Europe become more apparent. Simply put, there aren't enough troops available to adequately fulfil all the promises Canada has made. For example, it took roughly sixteen thousand troops to guard the Montreal Olympics and ten thousand for the FLQ crisis in 1970. In fact, a Senate committee studying Canada's military reported in 1982 that if Canada's brigade in West Germany was reinforced during a prolonged crisis, it would leave only between six thousand and seven thousand trained combat personnel for the defence of the whole of Canada.[18] If CAST had been sent as well, that would leave only two thousand to three thousand troops here.[19] A further complication is that some of the troops assigned to go to Europe also have specific tasks in Canada.[20] In military parlance they are 'double tasked.' That means any government of the day would face a next-to-impossible choice, because once any troops were deployed to Europe, it would become impossible to get them back in a hurry. Needless to say, the Arctic is virtually forgotten in all of these scenarios.

When analysed closely, these two commitments also highlight serious deficiencies in the equipment available to the Canadian military. For example, huge transport planes would be required to dispatch troops to Denmark or Norway. However, if left to its own resources, the Canadian military would be severely strapped to provide them, for in the words of General Manson 'we have some serious shortfalls in air transport.'[21] The necessary Hercules may be found but again that would mean a trade-off between Canadian and European needs. Would any government want to leave Canada with few transport planes in a time of real crisis? The lack of such planes would also make it extremely doubtful that the troops could be rescued quickly. In fact, General Manson conceded there were no formal plans to evacuate Canadian forces from Norway. It is small wonder another former defence minister, Donald Macdonald, referred to this as our 'hostages commitment.'[22]

The final and most fundamental defect in the northern commitments is that when twinned with the Central-Front role the problems of supply and servicing become overwhelming. That a country such as Canada has agreed to maintain troops on two separate European fronts a thousand kilometres apart is clearly untenable. Even before the Norway commitment was dropped, General Manson conceded that the prospect of fighting a two-front war 'is simply not very attractive.'[23] In fact, for any country such a predicament would be daunting. For Canada, given its ongoing state of military unpreparedness, it would be impossible.

Not surprisingly, Danish officials are only too aware of the problems involved in a Canadian deployment. Privately they don't think Canada would come and they understand why. As one senior strategist in Denmark's defence department put it privately: 'Your battalion would be very important for the home front. I could only see it being deployed [here] if you were sure you could get it out before war starts. For Canada, so far away, I can't see that being a risk the government would take.'[24] A Canadian could not have put it any more succinctly.

The Norwegians will undoubtedly be upset with the Canadian decision to pull out because according to defence minister Johan Holst, 'the Canadian brigade is very important because it is the only one of the NATO land forces that is specifically earmarked for Norway.'[25] But Holst is as aware as anyone of the logistical and servicing problems Canada would face. However, he was also very outspoken on the special ties he feels exist between Canada and Norway: 'We share very much in common and I think many Norwegians feel a special affinity for Canada. CAST for us is more than a military commitment. It is a political commitment as well.'[26]

Other Norwegian officials hinted darkly that if Canada did pull out of CAST, Norway might feel so let down that pressure would build for it to consider neutrality. Such an eventuality seems as unlikely as any move on Norway's part to change its constitution to allow the permanent stationing of foreign troops there. The risks of upsetting the Nordic balance are too great.

Overall, the problems and contradictions underlying the Norwegian commitment are so basic that defence minister Perrin Beatty had virtually no reason to maintain it in its present form. What seems to be forgotten in his decision, however, is that both Norway and Denmark offer 'northern-type' terrains and northern climates similar to those found in Canada. Skills acquired for fighting in the rugged and mountainous terrain in northern Norway, for example, could very easily be used in the Canadian theatre, particularly in the North. Furthermore, it seems logical for Canada to strengthen ties between fellow members of the circumpolar world if it is to maintain any commitment to Europe. In their present configurations neither the Danish or the Norwegian commitments is viable. But that does not mean Canada could not play a much more meaningful role in a totally redefined strategy in Europe. To do so, however, Canada must start from a new understanding and within the framework of a workable, integrated northern security policy. For Canada to pay lip service to the present set-up just doesn't make sense.

13

One role in Europe or out

Within NATO, Canada is a country without a region. Whiile the alliance embraces both Europe and North America, it has evolved primarily into a European-only collective-security agreement. There is a separate NATO planning group for North American defence matters, but it rarely, if ever, meets and never produces any papers.[1] The Americans have never wanted the Europeans involved in North American defence, preferring instead to discuss it on a bilateral basis with Canada. This situation has put Canada in a unique position. Unlike other NATO members, such as Norway, Spain, and Turkey, who can readily identify their strategic interests within the confines of their respective European regions, Canada has no such specific region. Instead, its interests are more generalized, defined to mean the security of all of Europe. Consequently, it is more difficult for Canada to particularize the military role it should play in Europe. As the analysis in the two previous chapters illustrates, there is no obvious 'homeland' to defend. So Canada has ended up with a diverse array of commitments - spread over three countries and vast expanses of the Atlantic - several of which are militarily unsound.

The responsibility for this predicament must rest primarily with Canada. Bound politically to NATO but unable or unwilling to translate that commitment into feasible military roles, Canada, until 1987, had assumed three land tasks (West Germany, Norway, and Denmark) as part of the 'dues' of the club. Part of the reticence in trying to redefine a new role stems from a Canadian fear of rocking the NATO boat too much. Mention the need for change in many external and defence circles in Ottawa, and the automatic response will be: 'but what will our allies think'? or 'we might lose our seat at important tables,' or 'what will the

Europeans do in retaliation?' The fact that officialdom, until recently, has failed to come to grips with the military absurdity of Canada trying to supply two fronts in Europe (West Germany and Norway) is further evidence of these fears. In this sense, the situation is little changed from 1968 when, just before launching a review of Canadian defence policy, Pierre Trudeau remarked 'our defence policy now is more to impress our friends than frighten our enemies.'[2]

The question then becomes: should Canada stay in NATO? If so, is there any logical role that would fit in with a new northern policy?

To answer those questions, one must return to the 'Atlanticist' assumptions that have provided the philosophical bedrock for Canada's European presence. Are they still valid? Foremost among these is the belief that Canada's greatest security threat comes from a Europe overrun by the Soviet bloc, leaving North America dangerously isolated and vulnerable. The corollary to this view is that the direct military threat to Canada itself is not as great. As the previous analyses suggest, it is clear that these assumptions are no longer as valid as they once were. In particular, the case has been made that the direct security / sovereignty threat to Canada, especially in the Arctic, has increased markedly in this decade. While there is little worry of a Soviet land invasion or a mass of bombers invading over the Pole, the advent of Star Wars, the increasing submarine traffic in Arctic waters, and the advent of cruise-missile technology has upped the strategic importance of Canada's North. However, the ongoing massing of men and nuclear trip-wires has made the West German front line an increasingly unlikely locale for any Soviet attack to begin, as NATO's supreme commander admits. Undoubtedly, it is still true that any outbreak of East-West tension, as a consequence of another regional conflict, would likely occur in Europe rather than in Canada. In that sense, the assumption is still valid. What has changed from a Canadian perspective is the narrowing of the relative threats to both Europe and the North. That alone demands a reordering of priorities.

The second major assumption is that Canada is too large a country for Canadians to defend alone. Thus, membership in military alliances is essential to ensure security. There can be little argument that Canada's size and geography make it a very awkward land to patrol and defend. In fact, since the Second World War, Canadians have willingly accepted protection under both the U.S. defence wing and NATO's collective-security umbrella. All polls reveal that a healthy majority of Canadians think

Canada should stay in NATO, a level of support virtually unchanged over the past decade.[3]

However, there is another school of thought that sees such alliances leading to war and Canada's maintaining forces in Europe adding to the risk of war.[4] This view turns on its head the traditional argument that the presence of Allied troops has been the principal reason for European peace for the past four decades. While the landscape of history is littered with failed alliances, NATO is somewhat different from some of its bellicose antecedents. Its primary function is defensive – to come to the aid of any one of its members if attacked – and its strategies and formations are so aligned. While NATO has admittedly not forsworn the first use of nuclear weapons, even this strategy is only to be resorted to in the event of Soviet adventurism. It takes an enormous leap of logic then to argue that this defensive grouping of countries with like-minded ideals in itself will lead to war. Viewed from the opposite extreme, if NATO didn't exist, would the risk of war in Europe diminish? Surely not. In fact, the total absence of Allied troops and the nuclear trip-wires that accompany it would logically destabilize the European theatre in the face of the superior numbered and armed Warsaw Pact countries. This is not to say the East Bloc would attack; however, the deterrence to such an attack, small or large, would certainly be dramatically decreased. As an aside, it could also be noted that neutralism in the absence of an alliance did little to help Belgium, Denmark, and Norway in the Second World War and Afghanistan and Tibet more recently.

Alternatively, the traditional view that the Allied presence has been and still is the only thing stopping a Soviet attack is outdated. While the presence of Soviet troops in the immediate post-Second World War environment posed a real threat to several western European countries, the situation is radically different now. The Soviets have established their buffer of European allies to protect them and it is very doubtful the gargantuan and highly risky prospect of gobbling up the rest of Europe is anywhere on their agenda. The Soviets have too many problems of their own at home and with their allies to launch such an attack.

The rejoinder that NATO's greatest success is its success is also suspect. One is reminded of prehistoric societies that offered up sacrifices to ensure the continuing shining of the sun. As the sun still shines today without such rites, so too the peace in Europe might well persist without such a massive NATO presence. It is time Canada recognizes the new realities in Europe. Increasingly the Soviet Union is lessening its iron control over Eastern Europe. A happier reconciliation between Eastern and Western Europe is surely to be welcomed as a step forward from the Maginot Line complex. It would also serve to lessen even more Soviet control in Central Europe. In both Holland and Belgium, there are an increasing number of calls to lessen the number of their troops deployed in West Germany. These Europeans seem anxious not to remain wedded to a concept of NATO based on strategic assumptions rooted in the 1950s. A reduced NATO military presence on the Central Front may well encourage a lessening of tensions while still providing an effective deterrent. For Canada, acceptance of this view opens the doors to many alternatives.

The options, however, of leaving NATO and going it alone as a neutral, non-aligned nation is not a viable one. To argue as external affairs minister Joe Clark did when confronted with such an option – 'leaving the western alliance would make nuclear war more likely' – is to strain credibility. He said such a retreat would inspire the Soviets 'to hawkish demonstrations of strength.' That Canada's 6,900 troops in Europe and political adherence to NATO are so critical would come as a rude shock to many at NATO headquarters. But since Canada's geography makes its military posture of vital importance to the United States, any neutralist declaration might bring on U.S.-inspired consequences never imagined. Finally, neutralism brings with it a hefty price-tag, something most Canadians would not happily accept. Such states as Sweden and Switzerland spend up to three times more than the comparable amounts Canada allocates to defence to maintain their neutrality.[6]

However, neutralism's greatest flaw is that it is isolationist and does not necessarily lead to the goal its proponents espouse – greater world stability. There is no doubt that regardless of what Canada does, the battle between the superpowers will continue. Canada may well want to ask itself if it wants a voice, however limited, in how this struggle unfolds. It is this very point that leads to perhaps the most compelling of the 'Atlanticist' assumptions – that by belonging to NATO, Canada gets a 'seat at the table where our voice is heard.' Certainly by retreating to 'Fortress Canada' in a self-declared military eggshell, Canada would have to give up its seat on many 'Western' bodies, such as Sweden, Austria, and Switzerland routinely do. It could no longer exercise whatever moderating influence it now does on Western security and arms-control thinking. As a member of the western alliance, Canada has gained a seat at such meetings as the yearly economic summit of industrialized nations and European arms-control and human-rights conferences, to name just a few. As a paid-up member of the alliance, Canadian prime minister Pierre Trudeau was also able to pursue his peace initiative and have access to the leaders and capitals that count. Since Canadians have always taken pride in and have come to expect that their country plays a more active role on the international stage, the possible loss of such a part cannot be easily dismissed. Former u.s. president Jimmy Carter's national-security advisor Zbigniew Brezinski is particularly forceful on this point: 'Do you really think Canada would be a member of the summit of the seven if it excluded itself from NATO. I think there are very many tangible benefits for Canada, which give Canadians weight and status in the world – maybe to some extent out of proportion to its size. If Canada were to terminate that presence, I think they would find themselves very much on the sidelines.'[7]

Former British cabinet minister and defence specialist Denis Healey is just as forceful on how Canada's contribution to Europe provides a useful counter-weight to the United States: 'I often think that Canadians do not realize the value of their role to Europeans as a counterweight to the United States. But for Canadians there are also real advantages to using the European link as a counter-balance to American weight on Canada. Obviously by severing the European link, those balances would be lost.'[8]

At the outset, it was maintained that one of the aims of a new northern policy was to establish as many multinational links in the circumpolar world as possible. The purpose was threefold: to provide a balance to the Canada / United States defence relationship, to attempt to lessen tensions in the area, and to seek joint co-operation on matters of mutual interest. With the exception of the neutralist Sweden and the Soviet Union, all other circumpolar nations in the United States, Norway, Denmark [Greenland], Iceland, and Canada) are members of NATO. There is no doubt the alliance has provided one of the best forums to date for Canada to forge links with these countries and to discuss collective northern security. Neutralist Sweden is excluded from this process and cannot share either the discussion or the information. For Canada to follow suit and retreat to 'Fortress Canada' would be to cut off links and inevitably increase its dependence on the Americans. While one of the objects of neutralism is to ensure Canadian sovereignty, the paradox is that by isolating ourselves in the northern half of North America, we may be forcing the United States to take military steps to guarantee security of all the continent. Ultimately we might end up reducing Canadian sovereignty in the far North rather than increasing it. Membership in the alliance, however, allows Canada to pursue a different policy without arousing U.S. fears. It is just another illustration of how membership in international groupings for Canada enhances rather than diminishes sovereignty.

The final assumption is that membership in NATO gives Canada a chance to exercise some political control over the military strategizing of NATO's generals. Although not well known to Canadians, this control represents another persuasive argument for NATO membership. Unlike NORAD, where various war scenarios are not necessarily vetted before politicians, NATO has a fixed procedure for each country's elected representatives to have a say in which war strategies are acceptable and which are not. Such matters are regularly discussed by foreign and defence ministers. One of Canada's former NATO ambassadors, John Halstead, argues that this right of review is 'critical for any self-respecting democracy. It is only proper the elected representatives of the Canadian people should have veto over strategies which could ultimately affect their lives. The power of the politicians is real and it is exercised. Not to be present at those meetings, of necessity, denies you any input.'[9] It is a further example of how a country's sovereignty and security are heightened by membership in an international organization. It seems axiomatic that it is in Canadian interests to be at the table, not only to know, but also to influence what might happen in a whole range of military possibilities. To be excluded is not to know and not to be able to influence.

Having concluded on balance that there are compelling reasons to remain within NATO, one is still left with the dilemma: what European role, if any, should Canada assume? As a starting point, any role must be in Canada's strategic interests as defined by Canadians. Unlike the present panoply of commitments, which have dominated and somewhat distorted Canada's defence effort, a new role should be compatible with Canadian interests on this side of the Atlantic. As part of a new northern policy for Canada, that role should also be compatible with the part the military must play to ensure the sovereignty and protection of the Arctic. That means Canada should stop trying to cover all bases and specialize instead in certain roles that harmonize with its domestic needs. Our priorities should no longer be tilted eastward to maintain the type of membership both the military and external-affairs departments perceive is expected of us within the club of NATO. Finally, the role should also be within Canada's capabilities, and should not be based on some pie-in-the-sky commitment that appears grand on NATO strategy documents but is beyond the military's capacity. These conditions may sound basic; but in order that they be followed Canadian thinking must undergo a fundamental shift.

The whole idea of specialized roles in NATO is not a new one. Military strategists on both sides of the Atlantic have been busy for the past few years coming up with various scenarios. But there has been an overall reluctance to change, a general feeling of 'why rock the boat when what is in place right now has worked so well.' Does it logically follow, though, that what worked in the past will necessarily work in the future? Surely not. Nor is it necessarily true, as discussed above, that the current arrangement was the *sine qua non* of peace in Europe for the past forty years.

Certainly, from a military point of view, specialization makes sense. NATO's founders always envisaged a balanced alliance force, composed of elements from all its members, rather than each member seeking to be competent in every field. Under the present system, each country decides what forces will be 'attached' to NATO, and it is then left to a military command structure (NATO Command) to plan how such forces are to be deployed. Any mention of 'division of labour' seems to arouse fears of encroachment into one country's sovereignty over military planning or suspicions that it is simply an excuse for some members to shirk their responsibilities. With the extremely high cost of maintaining a high-tech military, it has come to the point where it is just not fiscally possible for most NATO states to sustain a comprehensive military. Furthermore, slowly but surely, members are coming to realize that some of their roles should be modified to meet changing strategic requirements.

Surprisingly, former U.S. secretary of state Henry Kissinger has taken the lead in arguing for change. 'Everyone has been afraid to take the initiative in changing the present [NATO] arrangement, lest so doing would unravel the whole enterprise,' he wrote in 1983. 'But since drift will surely lead to unravelling – if move imperceptibly – statesmanship demands a new approach.'[10] Since then, a chorus of others has chimed in with a similar view. Their primary aim has been to emerge from the Maginot Line mentality and face the reality that the Soviet threat is much more likely to emerge first almost anywhere else than in Central Europe. It is not realistic, they argue, for u.s. and Canadian troops to stay indefinitely in Europe. As former u.s. senator Gary Hart puts it: 'We are not the Romans. We do not intend to stay in Germany for 300 years.'[11]

Nor should Canada. While a precipitous withdrawal from Europe without similar cutbacks in Warsaw Pact forces is not advisable, Canada should be thinking about eventual disengagement from Europe. There has been much debate about the Europeans taking over a greater share of their own defence. It is surely an idea whose time has come. Any European role for Canada should also take this factor into consideration.

Finally, Canada should start to remind its NATO allies over and over that the alliance is a 'two continent defence arrangement and not just a North American aid-to-Europe scheme,' as veteran diplomatic observer John Holmes argues.[12] According to two of Canada's former NATO ambassadors, John Halstead and George Ignatieff, Canada rarely gets 'credit' for the efforts it makes in defence of North America.[13] It is often forgotten that when Canada joined NATO in 1949, it did not have *any* troops in Europe, nor was it the government's intention to send any. It was only after Cold-War tensions heightened in the mid-1950s, culminating in the Korean War, that Canadian troops were dispatched to Europe. A reading of the historical documents at the time also reveals that the St Laurent government did not imagine the troops would remain for long.[14] Now the very mention of withdrawal is interpreted in some quarters as a traitorous abdication of our responsibilities. Canada's European allies often forget that Canada's contribution to NORAD in defence of North America is in effect a contribution to NATO and the security of Europe. Canada has always defined its security interests in terms of a secure western Europe. But how often do you hear Europeans defining their security in terms of a secure North America? Does not the same logic hold true for both?

With these considerations in mind, it is proposed Canada assume the following roles in NATO: temporarily supply a rapid-deployment-type force specializing in cold-weather combat to be stationed in Schleswig-Holstein for use on NATO's Northern Flank; redefine its naval role, both in equipment and purpose, to concentrate more on sovereignty patrol and anti-submarine warfare than on convoy patrol; redeploy all the CF-18s in

A Canadian soldier on patrol in Norway, 1986
(Photo courtesy Department of Defence)

the Air Squadron back to Canada; and close down both bases in central
Germany. Here's how it would work.

The new rapid-deployment force would be a mobile unit with special
training in cold-weather fighting. It could include many of the forces now
committed to the CAST Brigade in defence of northern Norway. As a
mobile force, it could be sent wherever NATO Supreme Command felt it
could be best used. However, it would be designed particularly to come
to the aid of Denmark or Norway in times of crisis. Many of the problems with the current Danish and Norwegian commitments are linked to
the enormity of the task in getting troops over the Atlantic. By being
stationed right on the Danish border in Schleswig-Holstein, the force
could be in Copenhagen in a few hours' time. Norway would only be a
day farther as huge ferries make the Copenhagen-Oslo run daily. Since
neither Denmark nor Norway is likely to change its constitution to allow
for the stationing of foreign troops on its soil, this would be the next best

alternative. With a base in Schleswig-Holstein, the force would also bolster NATO forces on the Northern Flank of West Germany, which is now probably the least defended of the entire German front.

Such a force would have other advantages. It would be trained for a specific role – cold-weather combat – which could be useful in Canada while complementing a new northern policy. If needed, the force could be quickly recalled and dispatched to northern Canada, in effect, giving us 'two roles for one,' as one strategist put it.[15] Such a force would also be primarily directed to help two northern allies, Norway and Denmark, countries with whom we have always felt a natural affinity and with whom we share space in the circumpolar club. By doing so, we would also be getting more 'bang' for our military buck. Canada does not receive anywhere near the 'credit' it deserves, commensurate with the expenditure, for its current role in southern Germany. By pinpointing its responsibilities to the Northern Flank, this force would serve to highlight Canada's role. With a reduced European presence, Canada could also use some of the saved resource to bolster its Arctic roles, in which it has been sadly remiss. While many of the logistics would have to be worked out, such a force has the attractiveness of meeting the criteria set out above. It would be a Canadian-defined role; it would maintain our international tradition; it would blend within the precincts of a new northern policy; it would fit within our capabilities; and it would maintain links with NATO allies with whom we have the most affinity.

It should be stated that this force would be located in Europe for only a limited time. Canada should emphasize that the force would remain on the condition that NATO's European partners work to assume a greater share of their defence of Europe and also strive to achieve substantial cuts in conventional forces with the Warsaw Pact. Canada must prepare the path for a return of its forces. Such a plan would be a useful beginning and would undoubtedly have wide support within Canada.

The second step should be the redeployment of Canada's Air Group, the two squadrons of CF-18s to Canada. Nowhere is the conflict between European and Canadian demands so clear. Under the upgraded North Warning System, there is a stated need for more fighter patrols. Under the present configurations, Canada has only twenty-four Hornets in Canada and is therefore unable to carry out all the potential air tasks assigned to it under the new system. U.S. F-15s could be used instead to patrol Canada. Meanwhile, Canada has the bulk of its Hornets in

Europe, where servicing limitations restrict them somewhat to Canadian bases. The priorities are quite simply reversed. Nowhere can one see so transparently how the 'Atlanticist' tilt of Canadian defence policy manifests itself. For Canada to give up patrol of its own terrain – and with it the affront to our sovereignty – in exchange for a symbolic air presence in a European theatre where there are already hundreds of other Allied fighter, defies rational explanation. Whatever logistic or image links went with having both an air group and ground forces close by in southern Germany will evaporate if Lahr is closed down. From a military point of view, the two forces are not interlocked anyway. From both a sovereignty and northern point of view, it makes sense for the Air Group to go where it belongs – home.

The final element is a revised naval role for Canada – more emphasis on sovereignty patrol and anti-submarine warfare and less emphasis on the traditional convoy-protection role. Here is another area where protection of Canadian interests at home has suffered in the face of living up to European-tilted roles. One only has to remember that Canadian naval forces do not possess one single vessel capable of operating in the Arctic on a year-round basis. Nor does it have anywhere near the number of vessels needed to adequately patrol and supervise the waters under Canadian jurisdiction and control. Nor does it have the capacity to deny entry of foreign submarines into its waters. Instead, under the current NATO allotment, Canada is responsible for patrolling and providing convoy protection, as it did so valiantly in the Second World War, for the north-west quadrant of the Atlantic Ocean. As the Senate subcommittee noted, convoy patrol requires an inordinate number of ships at considerable cost,[16] a role that does not represent the best use of limited funds. For example, with the money from just one of Canada's new half-billion-dollar frigates, partly designed for convoy patrol, Canada could have bought two modern non-nuclear submarines or nearly eight more Aurora patrol aircraft.[17]

The second problem with the convoy-escort role is that many NATO tacticians now argue the concept of the traditional Second World War–type convoy is outdated. Other more sophisticated strategies, for example using submarines to 'clean out' zones before a convoy passes, are being involved. The development of anti-shipping missiles also complicates the picture. It is for these reasons the subcommittee recommended Canada would be making 'a serious error if it built a naval force founded on the assumption that close convoy escort would necessarily be the major task in the event of hostilities.'[18] When one remembers that Canada has been seriously neglecting its sovereignty-protection role, the argument becomes almost invincible that more attention should be directed towards building forces suited to patrolling Canadian waters. Ice-breakers and fast patrol boats are two prime examples. To enhance its presence in the North, Canada should also have more submarines and patrol aircraft, both of which could also do double duty in anti-submarine warfare. Aside from being less expensive to acquire than frigates, traditional submarines have more versatility and are cheaper to man and operate. For Canada to assume some anti-submarine-warfare duties in the north-west Atlantic might well provide a defensible NATO commitment. Again, the key would be that the same equipment could be used to ensure the sovereignty of Canadian waters. It would be, in effect, another 'two roles for one.'

In the past, when similar scenarios have been presented, critics have viewed them as subterfuge for Canada's leaving NATO via the northern door. Using a variation on the saying 'out of sight, out of mind,' they argue that unless Canada is visible (i.e., on the Central Front), it will not get its deserved 'credit.' Furthermore, such planning will set a precedent for other small states to retrench and ultimately lead to the unravelling of NATO. This effect on NATO in turn will damage Canada's credibility abroad and adversely affect our relationship with the United States. Such a preoccupation with what others will think has been a hallmark of Canadian procrastination on such matters. Surely, as a sovereign state, Canada has not only the right but also the responsibility to define its own strategic interests and tailor roles to accommodate those interests. No one would deny that being a member of an alliance also brings with it responsibilities to help others. However, that shouldn't stop Canada from defining roles that cater to both needs.

No one should be deluded that Canada's indecisiveness on these matters goes unnoticed in foreign quarters. Canada's efforts to articulate its priorities precisely and firmly – or, to put it more bluntly, to get its act together – would likely be respected by many. Britain's Denis Healey is one: 'For Canada to maintain some token presence in Europe but to assume more well-defined strategically useful roles in North America would be understood in Europe. It would have to be well-defined, however, to counter the impression you were trying to sneak out of the alliance.'[19] French strategic analyst Phillipe Moreau-Desfarge of the Paris-based Institut Français des Relations Internationales, argues that Canada would get more 'respect' from Europe if it started to flex its muscles even more. 'Within NATO, Canada is of marginal importance militarily. If you want to have more influence then it is up to you to define a greater role for yourselves and it would seem to make some sense for it to be in the north. Certainly to carry on in the present form would be to perpetuate Canada's marginality.'[20] A remarkably similar view came from U.S. strategic expert George Carver of the Washington-based Centre for Strategic and International Studies: 'Looking at the situation now, what really should be done is an honest re-look at Canada's NATO and NATO-related defence responsibilities to see if the pie ought to be a little differently apportioned. I think there is a tremendous political utility in having a symbolic Canadian presence on the continent of Europe. But to apportion more resources and roles for a northern role would appear to be valid and have more pressing claims on the Canadian defence dollar. That would be understood here.'[21]

There is little doubt that other parts of official Washington would be upset by a Canadian move to pull most of its forces from Europe. As one senior Pentagon official put it: 'it would just give more ammunition to those with like feelings in Congress.'[22] At various points in Canadian history, similar arguments were used against Canada's recognizing China and selling wheat to the Soviet Union. In both cases, Canada went ahead anyway. The same should apply to NATO. If Canada is ever to give the North the attention it deserves, the first military changes must come within NATO. The options outlined above have the advantage of doing precisely that, plus being within the military's capacity and serving Canada's strategic needs. For Canada to stick with the status quo is to compromise its primary interests and to perpetuate the outdated.

ARMS CONTROL

14

The Arctic and arms control

For a country with so much at risk, Canada has played a curiously passive role in the field of arms control. Rather than striking out to promote agreements that ban or limit weapons systems that directly threaten us, Canada has been content to follow policies primarily developed by the United States. So long as Canadian and u.s. interests coincide, this laissez-faire attitude is easier to understand. Yet if one accepts that u.s. and Canadian interests are beginning to diverge in the Arctic, then this attitude becomes much harder to defend. In fact, for Canada, to continue with it could compromise our basic security.

Three recent examples illustrate the point. When the Strategic Arms Limitation Treaty (SALT) II was being negotiated in the 1970s, there were proposals to ban air-launched cruise missiles. What emerged instead was a brief time restriction on their deployment, which has long since lapsed. Had such a ban been realized, there is no doubt the threat Canada now faces across the Pole from such missiles would have been dramatically reduced.[1] Yet there is nothing in the public record to suggest that the Canadian government even asked the United States to seek such a ban. While it is often misleading to look at just one proposal in isolation, and folly to suggest that Canada alone could have determined the course of the SALT talks, there is no reason why Ottawa couldn't have made its views known - loud and clear.

The same applies to the 1985 Soviet-u.s. negotiations on strategic-arms reduction. The Soviet Union proposed a virtual freeze on its bomber force and cruise-missile arsenal, while the United States proposed an allowance of 1,500 air-launched cruise missiles on 350 heavy bombers for each side. Since the Soviets had only half that number of such bombers and missiles on hand, acceptance of the U.S. proposal would have virtually forced the Soviets to build up their stockpile to the ceiling. Again, such a build-up would have been contrary to Canadian interests for it is precisely these missiles and bombers that pose the greatest immediate threat to Canadian soil. Yet there was no statement from the Canadian government on this issue, nor any declaration spelling out Canada's interests.

The third example is the 1986 Reykjavik Summit, which admittedly President Reagan took in directions not even contemplated, let alone agreed to by America's closest allies. Before the talks began, the issue of cruise missiles and bombers was on the table, and again, there was no public Canadian statement of our position. The then defence minister Eric Neilsen expressed the government's views: 'I think you cannot single out a particular proposal . . . and look at it in isolation, in a vacuum. Any arms control discussion, my reason tells me, has to proceed on the basis that you are looking at all arms, not just at cruise missiles. That seems to me to be the only reasonable way to approach it. You cannot pick here and pick there at one or any other particular element and express a view without taking all the others into consideration.'[2] While admittedly there is some truth in Neilsen's statement, one is left with the clear impression he felt Canada should leave it to the United States to decide on the give-and-take at the bargaining table. That presumes, somehow, that only the United States is capable of balancing all the issues. Surely Canada has the right to formulate its own position and then make it known. The Europeans have done this for years. For Canada to simply accept the U.S. bargaining strategy is potentially to short-change our security interests. In fact, Canada's NATO ambassador says he was instructed a few days before the summit to speak to his U.S. counterpart 'of Canada's concerns about cruise missiles.'[3] But there was certainly no public statement from the government on Canada's stand. As one of Canada's leading arms-control experts, John Lamb, says: 'The question we need to ask is why. The answer, we would contend is that we have failed to appreciate strategic arms control as a truly integral component of our national security policy. Regarding the consequences of arms control as somehow out there, except in some very general sense, we have been deferring to the judgment of our alliance leader on these questions. We have been letting the Americans do our thinking for us.'[4]

As the previous section on security reveals, Canadian and U.S. interests are beginning to diverge in the Arctic. The development and deployment of a ballistic-missile–defence system represents potentially the greatest turning point in Canada–United States defence relations. Most Canadian analysts argue that deployment of such a system on Canadian soil would do precious little to enhance our security – in fact, quite the contrary. Next, there is the increased submarine traffic in the Arctic, both u.s. and Soviet, which has jolted the Arctic Ocean into a new military frontier. Finally, there is the issue of both air-launched and sea-launched cruise missiles, which still sits on the superpower bargaining table unresolved. On each of these issues, Canada's direct security is threatened, and it seems beyond debate that an arms-control agreement on any one of them would be in Canada's best interests. First, however, it is essential for Canada to make its demands specific and known as widely as possible, primarily to the United States.

Experience shows this may be easier said than done. The practice of Canada deferring to the United States in the arms-control field is entrenched and longstanding. NATO members, to varying degrees, have acceded to u.s. bargaining strategy lest any sign of public disagreement gives solace or comfort to the Soviets. However, United States's almost unilateral embrace of Star Wars with very limited Allied consultation and Reagan's 1986 proposal at Reykjavik to do away with all warheads without much thought for the European theatre, should give powerful ammunition to those who say the Allies have the right to an independent voice. Canada has been reticent to interfere, fearing a hostile reaction might invoke u.s. wrath in some other economic sphere. This fear has been bolstered by the fact Canada depends largely on the United States for its defence, gains millions in defence-related contracts, and derives cost-free benefits from the protection afforded it by the u.s. nuclear umbrella. For Canadians to accept, however, that we have no right to define our arms-control interests is to accept that we have handed over our security lock, stock, and barrel. The United States, perhaps more than most others, is very quick to identify its own interests in most international situations. For Canada to do the same would not only be accepted but likely respected in Washington.

No one should forget that the United States is not a monolith. There are many powerful competing factions within the United States, some of whom are quite sympathetic to Canadian concerns, though often for different reasons. They should not be forgotten, Canada alone cannot turn the tide; but in the giant policy struggle played out in the corridors of Washington, Canada can be a factor. To lobby and participate in the debate is to play a role the Americans understand. To fail to do so is to accept by default u.s. leadership and all its consequences.

In order to analyse possible arms-control initiatives for Canada in the Arctic, it is worthwhile reviewing some of the past proposals and their fates. Not surprisingly, most interest in this area has coincided with times when the Arctic is perceived to be of growing strategic importance. So, the first proposal came int the 1950s when the bomber threat over the Pole was most immediate. Most of the others have come in the past decade as strategic interest in the Arctic has revived. The proposals have covered the whole spectrum, ranging from partial demilitarized zones to full nuclear-free zones. Sadly none of them has ever come to fruition since interest in the Arctic as a *separate* arms-control zone has been peripheral at best. The 'open skies' plan of the 1950s, plus other plans for partial demilitarized zones, will be analysed first with a view to understanding the common threads which have led to their floundering. In a subsequent chapter, the idea of a nuclear-free–zone in the North will be reviewed.

The first full-scale Arctic arms-control proposal came from former u.s. president Dwight Eisenhower, who in 1955 advanced his 'open skies' plan. Tabbed the 'Arctic Sky Inspection Proposal,' it called for a mutual inspection system by both superpowers of large zones within the Arctic Circle.[5] The plan's aim was to lessen the fears on both sides of a sudden attack over the Pole, since missile-detection systems then were still fairly primitive. Two years later, after consultations with Canada, Eisenhower advanced a more specific plan, shown in the accompanying map, which included Canadian soil. Former Canadian prime minister John Diefenbaker offered to open up Canada's North to Soviet inspection provided reciprocal privileges were granted in return. Despite the superficial attractiveness of this proposal, the Soviets did not pay much attention to it for reasons that continue to haunt Arctic arms-control proposals.

First, the Arctic is of incomparably greater importance to the Soviet Union than any other state. The Soviets have major cities and many military installations north of the Arctic Circle and use the Arctic Ocean as their major naval staging area. While the 1957 proposal would have encompassed huge parcels of the Soviet mainland, not one metre of the

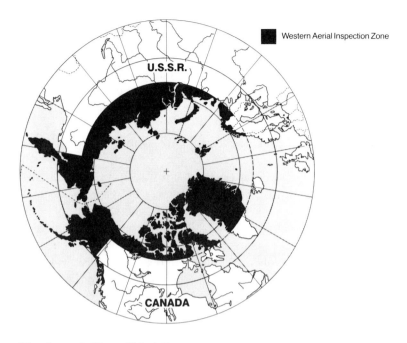

Eisenhower's 'Open Skies' disarmament proposal (1957)

lower United States would have been included. While many Soviet missile and bomber sites would have been subject to inspection, virtually every u.s. base would have been exempt. It is little wonder ex-premier Kruschev complained the proposal was 'calculated to obtain unilateral advantages for the United States.'[6]

Nor is there anything to suggest the Soviets placed much importance on inspection of the Canadian North. Aside from a few radar stations, there was little of strategic importance to inspect. Even if the Soviets were there, they would only gain a few hours of additional warning of a surprise u.s. attack. To ensure total knowledge, the Soviets would also have to have had complete access to all radar stations strung out across the top of North America. Even if such access was granted, it would be paltry in comparison to the invaluable inspection access the United States and Canada would have had to many vital Soviet military installations. This fundamental asymmetry of geography doomed the plan from the beginning and led to its eventual demise.

The failure of the 'open skies' plan illustrates one of the basic yet often ignored aspects of arms control. Any successful plan must contain elements that are advantageous to each signatory. Failure to recognize this maxim guarantees stalemate. Thus, in the Arctic context, any proposal in which the Soviets are asked to concede a lot in return for inconsequential gains will never be accepted. Basic geography alone makes it very difficult for the West to offer anywhere near the equivalent number of concessions in the Arctic arena alone.

There has been, though, one successful early demilitarization treaty. That concerned the 1920 agreement for the use of the mineral-rich, rugged Svalbard archipelago, far north of Norway.[7] The treaty vested sovereignty and administrative control in Norway but gave nationals of all forty-one signatory countries equal rights of access. Today only the Norwegians and Russians maintain substantial permanent presences on the archipelago. The treaty also specifically bans the establishment of any naval base or 'fortification' and while both populations live in a state of frigid solitude, the archipelago has remained demilitarized. This restriction, however, has not stopped both populations from observing and logging in meticulous detail any movement in the strategically sensitive Barents Sea lying directly between Svalbard and the Soviet Union. In the context of current superpower naval confrontation in the Arctic Ocean, Svalbard sits like a sentinel guarding the widest entry to the Arctic Ocean. While it is ice-bound much of the year, its strategic importance would certainly be viewed much differently by the Soviets now than it was more than half a century ago when the treaty was signed. At that point – with the build-up of the Kola Peninsula and nuclear-powered submarines not even imagined – the Soviets could well be excused from thinking they were giving up very little.

The next attempt at Arctic demilitarization came in a 1964 proposal by an American and a Soviet scientist to achieve in the North what had been secured in Antarctica.[8] In 1959, a year after International Geophysical Year, twelve nations signed a landmark treaty that effectively established Antarctica as a demilitarized zone.[9] The treaty specifically banned any military activities and nuclear explosions and provided for verification of installations by observers of all signatories at all times. While the treaty did not attempt to resolve conflicting territorial claims, it has, with few exceptions, withstood the rigours of time and established Antarctica as a special zone for scientific research and co-operation. Signed by the Soviet Union, the United States, Australia, New Zealand,

South Africa, Argentina, Chile, Great Britain, Belgium, France, Japan, and Norway, it is probably the most comprehensive arms-control agreement covering any of the earth's regions. Why not, the scientists wrote, apply the same type of agreement to the Arctic?

The answers were to become all too familiar. The fundamental strategic difference between the two regions is that while Antarctica is of little consequence to the superpowers, the Arctic is exactly the opposite. As already outlined, the Soviet's Arctic regions contain many of that country's principal military installations and the ocean provides the main ice-free thoroughfare for its naval forces. The Kola, in particular, provides the home for myriad Soviet ballistic-missile sites, naval stations, and missile-warning systems. While the United States does not rely militarily anywhere to the same extent on the Arctic, it has been shown that Alaska ranks second among the states, with forty-two facilities in the U.S. nuclear infrastructure.[10] Furthermore, since the Arctic lies dead centre in the path between the heartlands of the superpowers, one can see why a mutual banning of land-based military installations is next to impossible. Compared with the remote Antarctic land mass, the ice-covered waters of the Arctic are of vital strategic importance to both superpowers. This reality makes it difficult for either superpower to accept any demilitarized plan for the Arctic area, after having spent so much there. The 1959 treaty suited both superpowers' interests for it effectively prevented either of them from achieving dominance in Antarctica. In the Arctic, such a congruency of interests simply does not exist.

It was precisely these limitations that sparked Franklyn Griffiths in 1979 to come up with his imaginative proposal for a partial demilitarized scheme in the Arctic.[11] Later redefined by Ron Purver,[12] the plan called for demilitarization of only the *ice* and *surface waters* of the ocean. As shown in the accompanying map, Griffiths proposed such a zone extend up to the edge of each country's 320-kilometre economic zone. Purver suggested it be expanded to take in the ocean right up to the 19-kilometre territorial limit and include the sea bed as well. While obviously limited in scope, the proposal's primary advantage is that it offers something to both superpowers. If adopted, it would effectively ban the use of futuristic weapons and surveillance technologies, which depend on smashing through the ice.

Griffiths also suggested that the way to arms control lay through

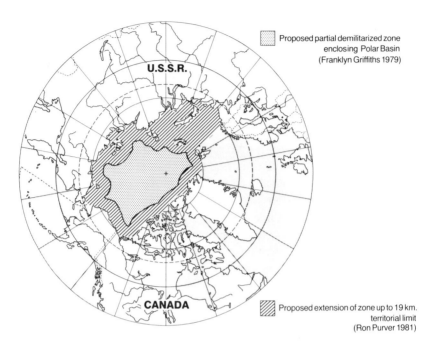

Griffiths / Purver proposals for demilitarized Arctic zone

greater scientific co-operation and the establishment of confidence-building measures between all Arctic countries. Such co-operation could be in the fields of pollution control, other forms of environmental protection, and general polar studies. Despite its apparent advantage, the proposal has been largely ignored, because as Purver himself suggests, 'it is too limited in scope.'[13] While it limits activity where there is in fact almost none – on the ice – it does nothing to restrict that area where the growing militarization is taking place – above and beneath the ice. Thus, acceptance of this proposal would do almost nothing to curb the current threat, only limit a future one. In that sense, the proposal provides only an illusion of actual disarmament. As an example of 'preventative arms control,' by its very nature it also fails to address limits on present strategic threats. It is likely for these reasons and because the Arctic has never gained much appeal as a separate arms-control zone, that the proposal hasn't caught the eye of either superpower.

Griffiths' proposal to limit the use of ice stations and anti-submarine devices is also found in plans to create 'submarine sanctuaries' in the

Arctic. The idea is to create combat-free zones where both superpowers agree their submarines are immune from attack or pursuit by each other.[14] The theory is that if such sanctuaries are guaranteed, then the submarines within them become 'invulnerable,' thereby acting as an insurance policy against a sneak attack. Because submarines carrying ballistic missiles are always on the move, they are generally accepted to be invulnerable to a first-strike attack. Consequently, they would be able to retaliate even if the enemy was successful in knocking out the other side's land-based missiles. Thus they constitute an integral part of each superpower's deterrent. Any proposal to strengthen their immunity of necessity also strengthens deterrence. These sanctuaries, proposals for which have been refined, offer significant advantages for Canada. With their assured existence, there would be less incentive for either Soviet or U.S. submarines to traverse Canadian waters. The Soviets, secure in such zones, would no longer find it as attractive to hide under Canadian ice in times of crisis. The United States, assuming it abandoned its 'forward strategy' of pursuing the Soviet fleet right into its home ports, could be content patrolling the outer limits of North America to guard against intruders. Such sanctuaries would also lessen the pressures on Canadian defence resources to counter a submarine threat in Canadian waters. But because of its adoption of a 'forward strategy' and its acknowledged lead in anti-submarine technology, the United States has consistently opposed such sanctuaries. The Soviets, for precisely the same reasons, have favored them.[15]

Another offshoot of the sanctuary theory is that both superpowers agree to ban the deployment of new anti-submarine–warfare techniques or limit the number of permanent underwater detection systems. The Soviets, at one point, also floated the idea of creating zones where no anti-submarine devices would be allowed.

As with many of these ideas, a big obstacle is one of verification. If one side feels it cannot ensure that the other is living up to its side of the bargain, the deal stands less chance of acceptance. And, the problems with verifying underwater systems or their absences are considerable. Since the Soviets use the Arctic Ocean as one of their prime deployment areas, the West has also consistently felt it would be giving up a disproportionate advantage in guaranteeing sub sanctuaries there. However, as Purver argues, the United States could easily use this concession as a bargaining chip to persuade the Soviets to restrict their production of ballistic-missile-carrying submarines.[16] The Soviets have a big lead in this area (seventy as compared to thirty-six) and a ceiling on all types of submarines, including those carrying cruise missiles, might well prove attractive to the Americans. Whatever the variation, such proposals offer considerable advantages for Canada, given its strategic position between the superpowers. Any scheme that leads to a decreased militarization of the Arctic can only add to Canada's security.

The same reasoning can also be applied to any superpower agreement limiting the use or range of cruise missiles. As outlined, some proposals have been on the bargaining table but have not been acted upon. The most promising, from a Canadian point of view, was the Soviet proposal of October 1985 to ban all long-range cruise missiles (i.e., those with ranges of more than six hundred kilometres).[18] The Soviets have since moved away from this position. Although their technology is still developing, the current three-thousand-kilometre range of the top Soviet sea-launched cruise missile means any Soviet sub would have to be well within Canadian territorial waters to reach most u.s. targets from the North. Thus any agreement to ban them would be in Canada's direct interests. Any similar accord in limiting air-launched cruise missiles would be just as welcome. Since this technology is more advanced, the prospect of banning them altogether is less likely. However, any stringent limit – and certainly much lower than the 1,500 ceiling proposed by the United States – would definitely be in Canada's best interests. There is no doubt verification makes any cruise-missile agreement very tricky to negotiate. The missiles are small, and to complicate matters, they can be used for conventional as well as nuclear purposes. There are thousands of torpedoes and conventional cruise missiles for which it is next to impossible to tell if the conventional warhead has been replaced with a nuclear one. On the positive side, it is one area where both superpowers have expressed some willingness to compromise. Canada's security would be well served to help them find a way.

As with virtually all Arctic-specific arms-control proposals, none in recent times has met with any success. The basic asymmetry of geography and extensive military use of the Arctic region by the Soviets has made it next to impossible to come up with the right balance of compromises to make any Arctic-only proposal viable. This situation has led Ron Purver, author of one such proposal, to conclude that concentration on arms-control proposals of a much wider scope is essential.

For any successful arms control agreement, there have to be trade-offs and there just don't appear to be enough trade-offs available in the Arctic arena alone. So trade-offs from other areas of negotiation and other geographical areas will be required ... Thus, for example, the proposal to create sanctuaries for [submarines] in the Arctic may only be realized if there is a corresponding global limit on the numbers of nuclear-powered attack submarines. That is the kind of mix that is required.[19]

Canada, however, should not use this need for compromise as an excuse to throw up its hands and let the United States do all its talking. With the advent of Star Wars and given our strategic position, we do have some leverage and we do have the choice to develop an independent point of view. It may take time and will require the development of expertise in these affairs. The prime minister should appoint a national security adviser, complete with staff, to work directly in the prime minister's office, a plan similar to that in effect in the u.s. president's office. One such adviser was recently hired by Prime Minister Mulroney but one is simply not enough. The ambassador for disarmament should also be given a full staff within the external affairs department to work out Canadian proposals related directly to our security. Furthermore, the suggestion from Purver and John Lamb that Canada bolster its presence in Washington, possibly with a full-time lobbyist to push Canada's views on arms control, is an excellent one.[20] That approach was taken by those in Canada concerned with the devastating effects of acid rain. Their lobbying efforts on Capitol Hill have dramatically raised awareness of Canada's concerns in this area. Doesn't our security justify the same kind of attention? It is time Canadians realize we do have a choice.

15

The CANDI arc: a nuclear-weapons-free zone for Canada?

A nuclear-weapons-free zone for Canada? It is a goal with tremendous appeal. While its achievement is more revolutionary than many realize, Canadians should not be dissuaded from striving for its fulfilment. The prospect of Canada's being in a region devoid of nuclear weapons is too worthy to ignore. Yet to accomplish it unilaterally starting from the status quo is almost too much to expect. It is necessary to begin with more limited expectations and build up from there. A qualified version of a nuclear-weapons-free zone, particularly with our circumpolar neighbours, may be within reach. At the very least, we owe it to ourselves to see what can be achieved.

Polls say an increasing number of Canadians want some type of nuclear-weapons-free zone,[1] two of the three political parties have passed resolutions favouring it,[2] and in fact, since 1985 it has been a reality.[3] But it has been a nominal reality. While no nuclear weapons are permanently stored on Canadian soil, they are in regular transit, aboard u.s. planes and submarines, through Canadian waters and airspace.[4] Furthermore, the 2,500 pages of defence agreements Canada has signed with the United States may well be interpreted by the Americans as giving them permission to deploy nuclear weapons to Canada in various times of crisis, despite all Canadian assurances to the contrary. Also as a NATO member, Canada has accepted that nuclear weapons could be used here in the event of a Soviet attack. Finally, Canada has no independent means now to either know or prevent the occasional passage of intruders carrying nuclear weapons through its territory.

Despite these limitations, the goal should not be abandoned. As former prime minister Pierre Trudeau said in his celebrated 'nuclear suffocation' speech to the UN's special 1978 session on disarmament:

It is hardly credible that nations that have learnt their destinies are linked, that national aims can no longer be wholly realized within national boundaries, that beggaring our neighbours is the surest way of beggaring ourselves, should have discovered no better alternative to assuring their security than an escalating balance of terror. Security, even absolute security, is not an end in itself. It is only the setting that permits us to pursue our real ends: economic well-being, cultural attainment, the fulfillment of the human personality. But those ends are all incompatable with a world of neighbours armed to the teeth.[5]

In that speech, Trudeau announced that Canada would no longer permanently store nuclear weapons on its soil. That pledge, finally realized six year later, basically fulfils the first tenet of the UN's definition of a nuclear-weapons-free zone – a declaration in which 'the state of total absence of nuclear weapons to which the zone shall be subject, including the procedure for the delimitation of the zone, is defined.'[6] However, he was deliberately silent on the second tenet – 'that an international system of verification and control is established to guarantee compliance with the obligations deriving from the [declaration].' That silence reveals perhaps the greatest single contradiction in the establishment of a nuclear-free zone in Canada: what is the point of its creation, if there is no means to ensure its observance? As one senior Pentagon official put it bluntly: 'You'll be the laughing stock of the world if you go ahead and make some high-principled statement without the slightest means of backing it up or enforcing it. The Soviets won't take it seriously for a second.'[7] What about those agreements with the United States and Canada's membership in NATO? Is Canada prepared now to give up these commitments and the protection they confer in order to rid itself permanently of nuclear weapons?

One of the first to take immediate and perhaps dramatic exception to a unilateral Canadian decision to go nuclear-free would be the United States. Never an ardent advocate of such zones, the United States has agreed to only three in addition to the one created in Antarctica. The others are: in Latin America, designated a nuclear-free zone by the 1967 Treaty of Tlatelolco; in outer space, in which weapons of mass destruction were banned in 1967; and on the sea-bed, where similar weapons of mass destruction were banned by the 1971 Sea-Bed Treaty. In each case, the agreement was preventative; that is it guaranteed against the deployment of nuclear weapons where none had been. And, in each case, the United States felt its military and strategic needs were not being compromised while observing that the Soviets were prepared to bind themselves to the same limitations. That essential meeting of superpower minds has not yet been found in other parts of the globe, be it Central Europe, Scandinavia, the South Pacific, or South-east Asia.

Complete freedom from nuclear weapons, with no exceptions, would be hardest to achieve in Canada alone. For Canada to 'de-couple' itself from NATO and NORAD, while prohibiting the United States from deploying or bringing nuclear weapons to Canada at any time, would surely snap America to attention. First, the United States would view such a move as directly contrary to its strategic interests, since in U.S. eyes defence of all North America is coincidental with defence of the U.S. heartland. Second, such a unilateral declaration, without comparable concessions from the East Bloc, would be seen to be giving the Soviets an enormous strategic advantage right on the U.S. doorstep. When New Zealand signed a nuclear-free-zone treaty in 1986 and banned even the occasional visit of U.S. warships carrying nuclear weapons to its ports, the American reaction was swift and tough. As if to send a shot across the bow of other nations contemplating such action, the United States cut off some military aid and intelligence to New Zealand, and moved to end the special preferences it had granted for New Zealand's exports.[8] The U.S. attitude is best summed up by U.S. strategic analyst Melvyn Krauss who wrote about what he called the 'New Zealand Syndrome': 'Why, after all, should America accept the risks of deploying weapons on its soil to protect other countries, if these countries are not willing to accept the same risks, and for the same purpose, by allowing American nuclear weapons on their soil? It is enough that America alone pays for the nuclear weapons that deter our common enemies. It is too much that we bear all the risks from deployment as well.'[9]

If New Zealand, far from the U.S. prime security zone, brought this kind of response, one can only imagine what an equivalent Canadian declaration might produce.

Canada's ties to the United States, both military and political, are a fact of life that cannot be ignored. Given our geopolitical position between the superpowers, those ties become even more critical. History has recorded over the past few decades the sensitivity of the superpowers when any neighbouring buffer states step out of expected line – Czechoslovakia and Poland to the Soviet Union, and Cuba to a less extent to the United States. For the most part, though, the United States has not had to face any major rumblings as both Canada and Mexico have remained loyal allies. For Canada to tamper too much with that ongoing trust is to flirt with danger. As Canadian political scientist Albert Legault argues:

It is obvious that Canada cannot afford to become in a military sense, a security risk for the United States … As a country we have agreed to assume certain commitments towards the United States, and so we take upon ourselves a military role within the Alliance. The day we would want to shed those responsibilities could become an unacceptable security risk for the Americans. In those circumstances, even our sovereignty could be put at risk. Our independence in matters of foreign policy would be even more threatened.[10]

The New Zealand case is a good one for it provides an insight into U.S. thinking in this area. The South Pacific pact – known as the Treaty of Rarotonga and signed by New Zealand, Australia, and eleven smaller island nations comprising the South Pacific Forum – banned nuclear testing, stocking nuclear arms and dumping of nuclear waste. It appeared, though, to allow the free passage and occasional visit of nuclear-armed ships. Accordingly, Admiral Ronald Hays, commander-in-chief of U.S. forces in the Pacific, at first recommended its acceptance since it did not conflict with U.S. military needs in the region.[11] However, his views were overridden in Washington, where there were fears that the treaty failed to guarantee vital U.S. access to South Pacific ports and airfields. In the past, the United States has refused to identify which of its vessels is armed with nuclear weapons. This long-standing practice has allowed many nations with avowed anti-nuclear policies to provide temporary landing rights for U.S. planes and vessels. When New Zealand decided the treaty banned such visits, confrontation was inevitable. Since then, the United States has hardened its opposition to any nuclear-free zones in areas its ships might go. Arguing that peace depended on the nuclear deterrent, U.S. secretary of state George Schultz has stated categorically: 'Our view is that the nuclear free zones are basically not a good idea at this point.'[12]

For Canada the lessons are clear. It would be folly to ignore U.S. concerns in this area. This is not knuckling under, but *realpolitik*. There is little likelihood of the Americans abandoning their long-established right of access to Canadian ports and airfields, and little chance the United States would see the declaration of a nuclear-weapons–free zone as being in its military interests. Finally, there is even less of a chance that it would sit quietly and accept it – in fact, one might expect quite the contrary. For Canada, these would not be excuses for inaction but facts of life which must be considered. A simple, unabridged, unilateral declaration by Canada of a nuclear-weapons–free zone would simply not wash in the United States. A less sweeping declaration encompassing other circumpolar countries, with accompanying concessions by the East Bloc, might be viewed much differently. It is more within these parameters that Canada must work.

In his 'nuclear suffocation' speech, Trudeau was able to nimbly walk that narrow space. While publicly calling for an end to the stationing of nuclear weapons on Canadian soil, he quietly reassured the United States of the continuance of all defence agreements and all usual access. Ultimately the loss of some old air-to-air missiles on a few aging Canadian aircraft meant very little militarily to the United States. The subsequent agreement by Canada to allow U.S. testing of cruise missiles seemed to reconfirm Canada's loyalty. It is these types of compromises which have led most analysts to look beyond a Canada-only nuclear-weapons–free zone and speak in terms of Arctic-wide zones. While all previous proposals of this type have not fared any better than those for partial demilitarized Arctic zones, they still offer arguably the best prospects for success. For Canada to think in circumpolar terms is also consistent with a new northern approach.

Interestingly, plans for a nuclear-free Arctic have flowed from all quarters of the circumpolar world. In its inaugural 1977 meeting the Inuit Circumpolar Conference, the congress of the world's Inuit, called on the governments of the United States, Canada, and Greenland to strike an agreement to ban 'military bases, nuclear weapons and military manoeuvres' in the region.[13] Various political parties in all of Scandinavia and Iceland have put forward proposals for nuclear-weapons–free zones covering varying parts of the Arctic. Canada's distinguished former diplomat George Ignatieff, in a 1980 magazine article, called for the 'gradual denuclearization' of the North by the banning of nuclear forces there.[14] However, it was Ontario peace activist Hanna Newcombe who came up with the most comprehensive and detailed proposal for a nuclear-free zone in the entire area north of latitude 60 degrees.[15] While she conceded there might have to be 'flexibility' in the exact drawing of the exclusion line, Newcombe's plan ran straight into the same brick wall confronting other Arctic demilitarization proposals. Because the Soviets have invested so much more in the Arctic region, they of necessity would concede the most in such a zone. If, though, the flexible exclusion line left out the Kola Peninsula and its massive military infrastructure, the zone would lose any real meaning. Newcombe also had to deal with ballistic-missile–carrying submarines, which she decided had to be allowed to operate under the ice because any ban would be difficult to verify. Notwithstanding the noble aim of this plan, the fundamental imbalance in the strategic importance placed on the Arctic by the Soviets against that placed by the Americans makes its acceptance almost impossible to imagine.

Taking this limitation into consideration, New Zealander Owen Wilkes later proposed a more restrained 'Circum-Arctic Demilitarized Zone' where there would be a total ban on the presence and transit of nuclear weapons.[16] Wilkes' zone, shown in the accompanying map, comprised most of the north of Canada, Greenland, and Iceland but excluded all of the mainland Soviet Union and most of Alaska. His proposal would ban the passage of superpower ships in the zone and also prohibit the stationing of any installations which contribute to nuclear-war fighting. While Wilkes's aim was to establish a barrier between the two superpowers, his proposed zone is fatally skewed to include virtually all Western territory tied to NATO but few, if any, sensitive Soviet installations. For NATO this would mean abandoning all its nuclear installations and options in the Arctic while leaving the more massive Soviet infrastructure intact, although marginally restricted. Neither NATO nor the United States could be expected to favour such a one-sided proposal.

It is just this asymmetry of interests which has also stymied all attempts to create a nuclear-weapons-free zone in Scandinavia. First promoted more than a quarter of a century ago, it is recently gaining prominent attention from the Kremlin. It was in 1963 that former Finnish president Urho Kekkonen first suggested that the development of nuclear weapons and delivery vehicles should be prohibited in Norway, Denmark, Sweden, and Finland. While the Soviets would be allowed to

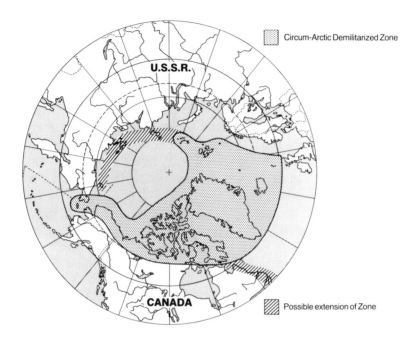

Owen Wilkes's 1984 Arctic proposal

continue using the Arctic Ocean for submarine transits, there would be limitations placed on the number of installations and warning systems in the Soviet regions directly adjacent to Scandinavia. In order to have any meaning, it has always been agreed that such a zone would require guarantees from both superpowers. For the past two decades, the Soviets have been ardent supporters of its realization, for it would effectively 'de-nuclearize' an area bordering directly on the Soviet heartland. Almost one-third of Soviet territory is closer to the Nordic countries than to other masses. Another advantage to the Soviets is that such a zone would effectively de-couple Norway and Denmark from NATO, denying the Alliance the option of moving nuclear weapons there in times of crisis. While both Norway and Denmark have been the permanent deployment of nuclear weapons and foreign troops on their soil, they have, as NATO members, accepted that such weapons might be rushed there in a crisis. Both Sweden and Finland, as essentially neutralist countries, are already nuclear-free by choice.

To NATO, Norway's position as watchdog over the Norwegian Sea is critical. The development of the Kola Peninsula into one of the planet's most densely militarized zones, directly adjacent to Scandinavia, has also heightened Western concerns about this flank. Consequently, NATO and in particular the United States have been most reluctant to essentially 'neutralize' Scandinavia, gaining nothing in return and in fact adding to the security of the Soviet military complex.

Realizing these objections would continue, the Soviets went on the offensive in late 1986.[17] The Kremlin announced that medium-ranged rockets targeted on Scandinavia and other NATO countries had been withdrawn from the Kola, and that heavy reductions had been made in rocket forces in the Baltic/Leningrad area. The Soviets timed their announcement to coincide with a rising tide of support for some type of nuclear-free zone, particularly in Norway. Norwegian prime minister Gro Bruntland, a long-time supporter of such a zone, had called for an intergovernmental committee to study an 'action plan' for its creation.[18] While there is still some doubt as to the extent of the Soviet withdrawals, there is no doubt the moves were intended to counter the traditional NATO objections. Sweden has already said that while it supports the creation of a nuclear-weapons-free zone, the Soviet Union must eliminate its nuclear arsenal in the region for the zone to have any meaning. While the Soviets have already expressed willingness to limit military and naval manoeuvres in both the Baltic and the Arctic, there is no chance of the Kola being dismantled. Nor does there appear to be any indication the United States has dropped any of its objections to the plan. Yet the proposal is far from dead. Its appeal to individual Scandinavians is growing despite many misgivings about the Soviet monolith, a virtual stone's throw away.

What is most encouraging about the Scandinavian proposal is that the Soviets are even prepared to make concessions to achieve it. For Canada, this may provide one of the best openings to join with its circumpolar neighbours in a limited CANDI (Canada, Norway, Denmark, [Greenland], and Iceland) Nuclear Weapons Free Zone. Norwegian defence minister John Holst wrote in 1984 that a 'possible countervailing option to a neutralist retreat could be a reactivation of a northern arch involving close cooperation between Canada, Norway, Denmark (Greenland) and Iceland.'[19] Taking up Franklyn Griffiths' idea that close scientific cooperation is one route to arms control, Holst argued this circumpolar constellation is a natural one since all its states are paying more attention to the Arctic. Earlier, Canadians Robert Reford and Rod Buyers had proposed an Arctic-wide nuclear-weapons-free zone covering roughly the same area.[20] Since all members of the CANDI constellation are also members of NATO, the same objections of one-sidedness would be inevitable from both NATO and the United States. The Americans, with their vital base at Keflavik in Iceland and their integrated defence relationship with Canada, stand to lose the most.

However, the first agreement need not be a full-blown nuclear-weapons-free zone. The CANDI group begins with the fact all its members have banned the permanent stationing of nuclear weapons on their soil. Various building blocks could be added one by one. For example, all countries in the group could declare submarine 'keep-out' zones, similar to the one recommended before for Canada. The group could then issue a joint declaration that the submarines of both superpowers would not be allowed regular transit through the group's combined territorial waters. Sweden is already going to some lengths to monitor Soviet intruders and Norway is just as wary. While exceptions would have to be made for transits through international waterways that overlap with territorial waters, such as the Kattegat and Skagerrak near Denmark, such a declaration in conjunction with East Bloc concessions would be a good start.

Second, the group could declare it supports the Anti-Ballistic Missile Treaty and will not allow any testing or deployment of missile defence systems that violate that treaty. Realistically, only Canada or Greenland would likely be involved in such testing, but a declaration would represent an open and public statement of intentions. It would also buttress Canadian resolve, if and when the United States comes asking for such testing. Third, the group could aim to sign as many scientific and research treaties among themselves as a measure of goodwill and circumpolar co-operation and as a route to a more generalized nuclear-weapons-free zone.

For now, however, certain rights seem non-negotiable to the United States, in the absence of Soviet concessions. While the Soviets' 1986 promise to remove medium-ranged rockets targeted on Scandinavia was a promising start, it is likely not enough. There will have to be more. It is difficult to imagine the United States unilaterally giving up the right for its planes and vessels to pay an occasional visit to most countries in the arc. Nor is the United States likely to abandon its Icelandic base.

Furthermore, Canada is too vital in defence of the u.s. heartland for the United States to lose all its nuclear options. The same reservations apply to NATO and Norway. None the less, the whole area of ballistic-missile-carrying submarines – their numbers and restrictions on areas where they can travel – is one worth studying. Compromises may also be achieved, with Soviet concessions, on severely limiting and eventually banning the number of installations in the CANDI countries capable of being used as auxiliary bases in the storing or launching of nuclear weapons. Similarly, an agreement by the Soviets to de-nuclearize most of the Warsaw Pact countries and limit its nuclear options is the type of *quid pro quo* that makes a comprehensive CANDI nuclear-weapons-free zone feasible.

As with more limited proposals, there are probably not enough elements in the Arctic alone to make an Arctic-only comprehensive arms-control proposal viable. In order to garner the necessary support from the United States, East Bloc concessions in other parts of the world would likely be necessary. With the recent period of 'glasnost' (openness) in Gorbachev's Soviet Union and the Soviets' apparent willingness to negotiate on the Scandinavian proposal, Canada should actively study options within the CANDI arc. At this point, it offers the best prospects for progress.

Finally, as part of its bargaining stance, Canada should also be prepared at the appropriate time to stop the testing of the cruise missile over its territory. There's a certain cruel irony that Canada is aiding in the testing of a weapon that in Soviet hands most directly threatens Canadian territory. By helping the United States test the guidance system of the missile over northern tundra, Canada in effect is encouraging the Soviets to do precisely the same thing to keep in step. When the testing agreement was first signed in 1983, Canada stipulated that it should not in any way be contrary to the arms-control objectives of Canada. Since then, the United States has deliberately violated the SALT II Treaty by modifying B-52 bombers to permit them to carry cruise missiles in excess of the treaty limits.[21] As argued before, the banning or limitation of air-launched cruise missiles has to be one of the first priorities on Canada's arms-control agenda. For the United States to ignore treaty limitations on a weapons system so critical to Canada can hardly be in Canada's best interests. For us to continue to be party to this testing sends a very definite message to the Soviets that Canada accepts such breaches and potentially encourages them to further their cruise-missile technology.

In conclusion, the most important step is for us to set our arms-control priorities and realize we *do* have specific concerns in the strategic arena which do not always coincide with those of the United States. If we continue to let the United States do our talking for us we do a disservice to those concerns. While many Arctic-specific plans have languished unnoticed, there do appear to be possibilities for success in limiting cruise missiles, restricting submarine activities in the Arctic, or forging some type of limited nuclear-weapons–free zone among the CANDI arc. Never again should it be said that we have not developed any disarmament policy of our own.[22] The stakes are just too high for that kind of apathy to continue.

FOREIGN POLICY

16

A circumpolar foreign policy

In July 1986 in the small outpost of Kotzebue on the western tip of Alaska, the 'Commonwealth of the North' held its fourth assembly. Unknown and virtually unpublicized south of 60 degrees latitude, this international assembly brought together delegates from the United States, Greenland, and Canada. No translation facilities were required since all participants shared the same Inuit language, spread among a smattering of dialects. As with Canada's two other Commonwealth membership – British and French – resolutions were hammered out on matters of mutual concern, in this case on everything from pollution to peace. And, the participants talked again of reaching out to include 'brothers and sisters' from the eastern Soviet Union, who so far have been denied the right to attend the triennial assemblies.[2]

All the participants, of course, were Inuit and the name of the Commonwealth is the Inuit Circumpolar Conference. Founded in 1977, this unique and innovative group is Canada's principal multilateral link with its circumpolar neighbours. The drive behind it, however, didn't come from Ottawa. In fact, the federal government until recently had been most reluctant even to support it financially. Instead, the idea sprang from the Inuit themselves, who perceived that the central government was indifferent to the needs of their region. To them, the conference is a 'meeting of Inuit minds' where members share ideas on various matters. Here is how Canadian elder Mark Gordon describes it: 'The Inuit Circumpolar Conference can make policies, but the job is to formulate and to put together the thinking in the three different countries who are now the players ... Then after we have formulated an overall policy ourselves, we go and convince our respective governments of the need for

Canadian delegates at Kotzebue General Assembly. Elders are seated at the front; Mary Simon, elected president at the assembly, is fourth from the left at the table (Photo by Alootook Ipellie courtesy Inuit Circumpolar Conference)

the policy and we use the lobbying forces with our respective countries ... so we have a coherent Arctic policy.'[3]

For a country that has always sought membership in international groupings, it is surprising if not downright negligent that in the Arctic, where it could be a power, Canada has done precious little. It has invested much effort and money on the 'North-South' dialogue between the rich and poor countries of the world. Yet, it has made virtually no effort to start any 'North-North' dialogue. Instead, the Inuit have led the way. As did polar explorers who learned from the Inuit the ways of survival in the North, we can learn from them on how to make friends in the Arctic. If Canada is to have any meaningful domestic northern policy, it must complement it by reaching out with more conviction and resolve to its circumpolar neighbours. In defence, arms control, sovereignty, or pollution control, there is greater protection and security in joint action. As the final piece in an integrated new policy for the North, Canada should find out what others living in a similar environment have accomplished and learned. It is simply time our foreign policy reflected Canada as an Arctic nation.

No one in Canadian officialdom is opposed to more ties in the circumpolar region. No one is much interested either. This point was driven home particularly forcefully when external affairs minister Joe Clark brought down the latest government green paper on external affairs in 1985. In a brave introduction on page one, the document speaks of Canada as an Arctic nation and 'ourselves as special because of it.'[4] Then, amazingly, the Arctic is never mentioned again. Later, after a special Senate-Commons joint committee recommended an expanded outreach to the circumpolar countries, the government's response reconfirmed the apathy in two-and-one-half brief pages.[5] The report began promisingly with talk of a coherent policy dealing with sovereignty, security, the use of the Northwest Passage, and expanded circumpolar links. Then, with a banality that sometimes seems within the exclusive domain of the public service, it concludes this way: 'Consistency between these foreign policy components and the government's domestic Arctic policy objectives is necessary to ensure the development of a truly coherent Arctic policy.'[6] One can only wonder what this means.

Part of the reason for 'Arctic apathy' within external affairs stems from a perception that the Arctic is not a separate region worthy of policy development. Unlike the Scandinavian countries where all foreign ministries have separate divisions dealing solely with Arctic affairs, Canada has none. In fact, much of the northern external relations are left to the minister of Indian affairs and northern development, who obviously is bound by the limits of his authority. This relative indifference is not confined to external affairs. It is reconfirmed by the structure of the entire federal bureaucracy, which reflects to a large extent past Canadian practice of dealing with the Arctic on an issue-by-issue basis. That means the defence department handles security, transport deals with the Coast Guard, external affairs is responsible for sovereignty matters, energy handles offshore exploration in conjunction with northern affairs, and northern foreign policy drops somewhere in between. According to Peter Burnet, executive director of the Canadian Arctic Resources Committee, this means: 'Because everything in the north is issue by issue, there is no one in government who can tell us whether or not it would be in Canada's interest to seek membership in the Nordic Council, to open an embassy in Reykjavik to find out how they are able to sustain their population in comparable environmental conditions, what lessons there are to be learned there.'[7] The point is a good one. If Ottawa is to develop a northern dimension to its foreign policy, then there must be people working on it full time. There are separate divisions with full-time staff working on the Caribbean, South-east Asia, and the African sub-continent – but no division for the Arctic. A separate branch dedicated to this purpose is the very minimum required. While it would do little to overcome the 'issue-by-issues' mentality, it would at least focus bureaucratic attention on the region.

For Canada to start believing in the Arctic as a region worthy of interest, we have to first shed our Mercator mind-set and begin thinking of ourselves as a circumpolar country. In the past, the fact that almost one-third of the country lies north of the Arctic Circle has not been reason enough. Yet there are pressing and immediate issues that, of geographic consequence, affect Canada, Norway, Sweden, Finland, Iceland, Greenland, the Soviet Union, and the United States. All of these nations, for example, have had to adjust to the rising militarization of the Arctic. They all have varying degrees of interest in Arctic arms-control proposals. They are all learning to cope with northern pollution, and they are all grappling with the technology required for commercial navigation and commercial exploitation of Arctic resources.

Admittedly, there have been certain factors working against treating the Arctic as an integrated region. The fact that two of its members are the same superpowers who are confronting each other over and under the Arctic ice tends to accentuate the East-West division. Furthermore, the Soviets have no Warsaw Pact allies in the Arctic while four of the region's members belong to NATO. The East-West stand-off explains in part why the Soviets have had a predilection to deal with its circumpolar neighbours on a bilateral basis. They have, for example, a very intricate relationship with Finland reflecting their geostrategic position one to each other. The Soviets' longstanding sharing of the Svalbard Islands with Norway is another example of one-to-one relationships. Yet by the same token, the Soviets, admittedly out of self-interest, seem anxious to deal with Scandinavia as a whole for some type of nuclear-free zone and are prepared to make some concessions to get it. This pattern suggests that, for the most part, security and defence matters have tended to divide the circumpolar region.

Canada, though, has also tended to follow the same pattern, dealing with most circumpolar issues on a bilateral basis in reaction to problems as they arise. Oil and gas exploration issues have been negotiated separately with either the United States or Denmark (Greenland). Salmon-fishing problems off Greenland were handled in the same way. So too was a marine environmental conservation regime for Baffin Bay and the Davis Strait.[8] In the security field, Canada has dealt almost exclusively with the United States through NORAD on the defence of North America. NATO is probably the sole forum in which Arctic strategic affairs are handled on a multilateral and somewhat integrated basis.

Despite this pattern of dealing with issues on a bilateral basis, there is some evidence it is beginning to weaken as the relative importance of non-security issues - pollution, resource extraction, Arctic navigation, and natural wildlife protection - continues to grow. To University of Toronto professor Franklyn Griffiths 'this is a pattern, which if I was to make a guess, is going to continue and which for obvious reasons Canada has every interest in furthering.'[9] Several examples of multilateral co-operation come to mind. During the Law of the Sea negotiations, for example, the circumpolar countries were in relative agreement - the United States excepted - over the special 'arctic clause' that gives coastal states wider scope to pass anti-pollution laws. In 1970, the circumpolar countries got together in the Polar Bear Treaty, which seeks to protect the species. In 1977, the United States, Canada, the Soviet Union, and France agreed to co-ordinate search-and-rescue operations through the use of meteorological satellites in what is called the SARSAT program. Even the superpowers managed to forget their security rivalry long enough to sign an agreement on fishing and wildlife management in the Bering Sea, where their collective geography brings them within fifty kilometres of each other.

To lessen superpower tensions in the Arctic while enhancing the chances for some arms-control agreement, Canada has every reason to encourage this multilateral trend, if not become its chief proponent. Our geography alone makes us a power in the region. Why not become a leader in pushing for more multilateral agreements? As an avowed advocate of arms control, why not stop insisting any Arctic arms-control proposal is impossible and start bringing the superpowers together on non-security issues? As a firm believer in multilateral groupings, why not foster one right on our northern doorstep? Or perhaps consider joining the Scandinavians' Nordic Council as an observer? Surely such an approach is a franker and more realistic reflection of our limited ability to do much about the superpower confrontation in the Arctic. It is certainly much cheaper than arming ourselves to the teeth on our northern border. It also helps us to come to grips with ourselves as an Arctic nation, something which has been a long time coming. By any standard, there is nothing to lose but much to gain from such a strategy.

Arctic research is an excellent place to begin. From a purely selfish viewpoint, Canada has much to learn from the Finns about ice-breakers, from the Norwegians about fish conservation, from the Soviets about Arctic navigation, and from Greenlanders about self-government. Nor does the list have to be restrictive. Britain, for example, through its Scott Polar Institute has always had a fascination with Arctic affairs. So too have the Danes and West Germans. Canada should take up the idea of former Indian affairs minister David Crombie and set up a polar institute for the sharing of information.[10] The Soviets, in particular, should be encouraged to take part. One recent encouraging sign was their two-year renewal of a program of exchanges on Arctic sciences with Canada.[11] The program, first signed in 1984, covers everything from Arctic petroleum research to environmental studies, Arctic construction, ethnography, and education. To centre such exchanges in a new polar institute is but a small step. Needless to say, the United States should be just as involved and with such an institute located in Canada, its participation is almost assured.

Satellite technology provides another prospect for circumpolar cooperation. The precedents are already in place. Under the RADARSAT program, for example, Canada, the United States, and the United Kingdom are about to join in a system under which a satellite carrying a modified radar pod would snap continuous pictures of the earth's surface. The system works night or day, rain or snow. For circumpolar countries wishing to follow the navigation of ships, to monitor for any ecological disasters, or simply to obtain more data on natural resources within their boundaries, this information would be invaluable. It is a system designed for peaceful purposes although as with any satellite, there are always some possible military applications. For example, the synthetic-aperture radar aboard RADARSAT is so powerful it will be capable of picking up objects the size of large cars. That means surfaced submarines or warships plying the seas would also be clearly visible. Under RADARSAT, Canada can sell the data and we should try to involve our circumpolar neighbours in the project.[12]

Another natural for the North is the search and rescue satellite system or SARSAT. Along with France and Canada, this joint venture also brought the superpowers together in a worthwhile purpose. SARSAT involves the use of meteorological satellites with repeaters working in conjunction with ground terminals, which have been developed in Canada. Here again the data can be sold as well as the technology for the terminals. Since search and rescue is a particular concern in the Arctic, it is another possibility for circumpolar co-operation.[13]

A third area for multilateral agreement is in ecological protection. There is little doubt the commercial development of Arctic petrocarbons will begin; the only question remaining is its timing. With increased nuclear-submarine traffic in the Arctic comes the added risk of nuclear accident. In both instances, Canadians have an overriding interest in negotiating pacts which set down exactly how such a disaster would be handled. The chaos and recriminations following the crash landing of the Soviet Cosmos satellite near Yellowknife provided some insight into the difficulties coping with an unforeseen northern disaster. While there aren't likely to be too many more crashing satellites, an ecological disaster is a distinct possibility and one that all circumpolar countries have a stake in minimizing. Something as basic as a step-by-step outline of how such events would be handled is surely a wise and inexpensive beginning.

Nor should the list stop there. While in some cases it may be too restrictive to negotiate Arctic-only ecological agreements, as in the case of air pollution where much of the pollutants emanate from non-Arctic countries, there are enough other Arctic-only issues to warrant joint action. This is an area were Canada has not only some natural interest and expertise but also a chance to be a forerunner. Laval professor Paul Painchaud is particularly eloquent on this point:

As we know, environmental problems know no boundaries or ideologies. In fact, like a certain number of other countries, Canada's geopolitical situation is such that it should consider both short-term and long-term environmental threats to be priority. Our country borders on three different oceans ... and in the Arctic the environment is extremely fragile ... Canada has the technology needed to become a greater environmental power, to articulate around this priority a certain number of other activities and to really play a role of leadership in international affairs.[14]

Here again there is a precedent on which to build. In 1983 Canada and Denmark signed a framework agreement for marine-environmental co-operation in the Davis Strait and Baffin Bay area. That agreement sets out a basis on which Canada and Greenland can develop procedures to handle pollution prevention, clean-up, and navigation in the waters between them. In this case, instead of waiting for disaster to strike, both countries exhibited some laudable foresight.

This agreement also reflects the common-sense point that on some issues, bilateral pacts may be necessary, especially when neighbours are involved. Thus agreements for environmental protection in either the Beaufort Sea or Baffin Bay are really matters for Canada to straighten out with the United States or Denmark (Greenland). Others, such as the scientific agreement renewed between Canada and the Soviet Union, may only have been possible through bilateral negotiation. The relatively small budgets of some of the Arctic states may also make participation in some of these joint projects impossible. For example, Franklyn Griffiths's proposal that Canada and the Soviet Union join in studying a drifting ice station which recently calved off Ellesmere Island,[15] may only be within the fiscal potential of these two countries.

When it comes to neighbours, Canadians often forget we have a second one, Greenland, lying off our eastern shores, one with whom we share a common waterway almost two thousand kilometres long. Iceland, too, is not that far away. Yet compared to the degree to which we are preoccupied with our more immediate southern neighbour, Greenland and Iceland barely enter most Canadians' consciousness. That has been the pattern except for a brief moment at the turn of the century when Canada secretly tried to acquire Greenland for itself.[16] However, former prime minister Wilfrid Laurier's efforts came to naught. During the early stages of the Second World War, Canada took full military responsibility for Iceland, under the strong urging of the British. But the then prime minister Mackenzie King flatly refused to let the Canadian forces stay. Iceland has always felt a special affinity for Canada because the largest emigrant group ever to leave Iceland did so at the turn of the century, settling principally in Manitoba. It is estimated there are up to forty thousand people of Icelandic descent now living in Canada.

To date Canada has done little to foster special ties with either neighbour. This attitude, along with fears of supertankers carrying Canadian crude in the North, has certainly make some Greenlanders wary. Most Greenlanders, in the words of the permanent head of the Greenland Home Rule Office, Lars Vesterbirk, 'just take for granted that Canada isn't much interested in us.'[17] If Canada is to change this, it will have to change its perception of its neighbours and what it can do. Whereas the scope for traditional foreign assistance is narrow, Canada could tailor its contribution to be more political, cultural, and social. Both Iceland and Greenland are heavily dependent on u.s. forces and bases for protection and may well see in Canada a perfect countervailing force. As veteran circumpolar observer Nils Orvik says: 'We must come across to our eastern neighbours in a way that makes them feel that we trust them and that they can trust us. Not the least in times of crisis, they will need somebody they can talk to on equal terms, who recognizes values that are not measured by size of population or gross national product. Canada is in a unique position to fill this need.'[18] A first step will have to be to start paying attention to our neighbours' concerns. That hasn't been the case in the past. Greenlanders, for example, are very conscious of the pollution threat. When Panarctic's Bent Horn project, involving the use of supertankers, was under government review, some Greenlanders protested to Ottawa. Yet when the final approval was given by the Canadian government, there wasn't even a mention of Greenland's concerns, let alone an attempt to assuage them. As Canadian Inuit advisor Peter Jull says: 'Shipping oil through the iceberg-strewn waters off Greenland's west coast is probably the most provocative act a Canadian government could perform towards Greenlanders at the present time.'[19] Although Canada and Denmark have signed that 1983 pollution framework agreement, it seems a reservoir of ill-will still exists.

Under its current arrangement with Denmark, Greenland is responsible for most internal matters although defence and foreign-policy rights still reside in Copenhagen. However, Greenland's 'Home Rule' is evolving quickly and it may be that some form of limited independence may result in the not too distant future. Within this context, Greenland is reaching out for foreign contact and several European countries are in the process of establishing consulates with Denmark's approval. Through our ambassador in Denmark, Canada had been pressing to do the same, and in fact, the joint committee studying Canada's foreign policy recommended it be done.[20] However, the government replied in the negative: 'the opening of a consulate is not considered cost effective at this time.'[21] As the Arctic opens up, it will become increasingly important if not essential for Canada to be able to co-operate with Greenland. A 'listening post' in Nuuk, the capital, similar to the one maintained during the Second World War is the barest minimum required. At some point, Canada will have to come to grips with the fact that it does have a second neighbour.

The final area for circumpolar co-operation is culture and here the Inuit have already laid the foundations. Through the Inuit Circumpolar Conference the ties have been cemented and the bonds formed. As mentioned before, Ottawa was initially most reluctant to support this effort. There are still fears that the conference, with its nuclear-free-zone resolutions and land-claims declarations, has intruded too far into the foreign policy domain of the federal government. However, the conference has probably done more to improve relations between Greenland and Canada than anything Canada has initiated since the Second World War. It has also acted as a stimulus for a small but growing trade between the two countries. As part of Canada's northern outreach, it is a noble beginning and any bureaucratic worries should be more than offset by the value of such links. The conference deserves full support, both moral and financial.

But the cultural outreach should not stop there. If, for example, Robertson Davies is right and Canadian writing is 'more like' Scandinavian writing than any other, American and British included, then there is great potential for expanded cultural ties. The same may well apply in other cultural areas. While there have been limited link-ups with Scandinavia in the cultural field, there is great scope for widening them. Here again, we may learn a valuable lesson from the Inuit.

In conclusion, there is much Canada can do to reach out to its circumpolar neighbours. What has been lacking is the will, not the issues. No one is suggesting a northern component of Canada's external policy should dominate this country's foreign relations. Yet to ignore the Arctic is to deny our geography. For us to become more involved would complement domestic policy as the Arctic opens up. In the final analysis, it *is* in Canada's interests to pursue more circumpolar links. The Inuit have already shown us how worthwhile and easy it can be.

17

Conclusion

As a group of parliamentarians studying Canada's foreign policy did a cross-country tour in 1986, they were repeatedly surprised at one issue which kept on cropping up. It was 'the North.' In the words of group co-chairman MP Tom Hockin, 'the message was "do something". The people we heard from weren't clear on what they wanted; but they *didn't* want the status quo.'[1] Hockin reported that Canadians' concerns about the North percolated through on many issues. Not surprisingly, though, concern often turned to passion whenever the discussion turned to Arctic sovereignty, security, peace, or arms control. Admittedly, the tour took place with the reverberations of the *Polar Sea*'s unauthorized passage still ricocheting in Canadian souls. Yet another member of the group, Senator Jerry Grafstein, felt the collective concern was somehow different than that once-every-decade phenomenon of the past when Canadians suddenly tuned in to the North. 'I had a sense that with Star Wars and the growing military interest in the North, the concern we picked up was more than a knee-jerk response to the *Polar Sea*. Canadians want something done.[2]

In the past, that collective clamour to 'do something' has usually prompted some government response. Following the highly publicized transit of the *Manhattan* through the Northwest Passage, for example, Ottawa rushed in with new anti-pollution laws and a widening of our territorial limits. After the *Polar Sea*'s passage, the government similarly announced, with great fanfare, stepped-up sovereignty patrols and plans for a new ice-breaker.[3] In each case,, once the furore died down, Ottawa's resolve died too. While the pollution laws were put in place, the means to enforce them never materialized. Similarly, the increased sovereignty patrols and Arctic exercises were planned but then later quietly postponed for 'budgetary reasons.'[4] Even the ice-breaker has had a tortuous journey taking more than eighteen months just to break through to the first contract stage.[5] Each time the pattern has been the same: the resolve appears firm at the outset but then quietly dissipates when it is time to sign the cheque. Politicians, most recently Joe Clark[6] and Perrin Beatty[7], are fond of saying Canada *can* afford its Arctic. The record, however, tells an entirely different tale. In the past, we've been able to survive our indifference. But the situation now is different. The Arctic challenges to our sovereignty, our resources, the environment, and our security and peace call out for immediate attention. The issues raised won't go away, but Canada must first break out of its previous habit of pigeon holing Arctic issues. The temptation to settle for a 'quick fix' is acute when political tempers run high. But the Arctic has suffered too long from a succession of quick fixes. What is needed is some perspective and an *integrated* policy that takes a longer-ranged view of the region.

Take, for example, the discussions between the United States and Canada over sovereignty rights to the Northwest Passage. As previously outlined, Canada wants its full sovereignty claim to the passage acknowledged by the United States. The Americans seem inclined to sign an agreement to that effect but are very wary of setting a bad precedent. Furthermore, they are anxious that their warships have full access to all Canadian Arctic waters. Yet the way Prime Minister Mulroney was talking in mid-1987, Canada might be prepared to accept a straight *quid pro quo* deal. That is, if the United States recognizes our sovereignty, in return we will guarantee their warships total access. When specifically pressed on this, Mulroney told a u.s. interviewer: 'As a member of NATO and as a member of NORAD, where we share common responsibilities for the defence of this continent, we would look with favor, obviously, on arrangements that would facilitate and expand those agreements. You can draw some pretty fundamental conclusions from that.'[8]

At first glance, the rationale for such an agreement makes some sense. Canadian sovereignty would be recognized by the only power to seriously question it. Canadian security would be enhanced and Ottawa might be able to win some guarantees for notification of when and how often u.s. warships enter our waters. We already know their subs are there. Finally, as members of NATO and NORAD, Canada would be playing a responsible alliance role while having to pay financially very little for it.

Under closer scrutiny, however, such an agreement looks to be another in the long tradition of 'quick fixes.' First, an accord with the United States on sovereignty would have absolutely no bearing on any other country. The true legal status of the Northwest Passage would remain unresolved; so either Japan or the Soviet Union could proceed to use the passage as the Americans have in the past. Second, under the guise of settling the sovereignty issue, Canada would be giving *carte blanche* to the Pentagon to ply our waters at will. That is a major step in the integration of the combined defence of North America, and before implementation needs a much fuller debate and discussion. Even though the United States has viewed the passage as an international waterway, Mulroney has assured Canadians that 'procedures' are already in place which allow Canada to know when U.S. subs enter our waters.[9] However, not too many officials, including former defence ministers Danson[10] and Macdonald,[11] really believe we are being told all the time. That's just not how the U.S. Navy operates. One might well ask then how a new agreement would make any difference?

This is not to suggest U.S. ships be totally banned. Canada has no means to do that even if it wanted to. Furthermore, we gain protection from the U.S. defence umbrella. However, there should be procedures laid down specifying when U.S. warships can come into our waters. A look at the map shows U.S. subs can just as easily reach the Arctic Ocean without passing through Canadian internal waters.

By signalling to the world and more particularly the Soviet Union that the Americans can freely use our Arctic waters, we would simply be placing our stamp of approval on the growing militarization of our North. That can hardly be in Canada's best interests. The most the Canadian military can predict is that the Soviets *may* use our waters, but there has not been a single verified Soviet sighting yet.[12] However, the repeated presence of U.S. subs in our waters may well prompt the Soviets to probe and explore there. That, in turn increases the risk of accident or unforeseen confrontation.

A further complication would be the message we would be sending the United States on continental defence. By virtually handing over defence of Canadian Arctic waters to the United States, we could be making it much more difficult for ourselves down the road to say 'no' to Star Wars – if and when the United States wanted to use Canadian soil. If Canada wants to keep its options open, this would hardly be the advisable course of action. Finally, granting the United States unrestricted rights of access to our waters takes away in one fell swoop a potentially key bargaining chip in any Arctic arms-control discussions. If Canada thinks it has a vested interest in maintaining the Arctic as it is, then arms control is a better answer. Allowing u.s. warships to roam through our waters at will is hardly the best way to achieve it. As an aside, there is also something unseemly about Canada having to 'negotiate' sovereignty over territory it considers its own. This does not mean Canada and the United States should not talk; but to bargain warship access for something we already think is ours strikes a rather dissonant chord.

This type of analysis underscores the need for more of an *integrated* approach. Canadians want to 'do something' about the Arctic. They are also increasingly worried about keeping the peace and concerned about the new weaponry that would fly over Canada in the event of a nuclear attack. The ideal policy then is one that addresses both concerns. At the outset, it was stated this book is a plan for action, as well as a call for Arctic action. While specific recommendations have been spelled out in each of the sections, it is worthwhile summarizing some of them as part of a new manifesto for the Arctic.

Turning first to sovereignty, we must be prepared to make our presence felt over the Northwest Passage. To this end we should:

– pursue Inuit land claims settlements which recognize a longstanding Inuit use of the waters of the passage,
– recruit and train the Inuit to do oceanographic and ice research in the passage,
– upgrade and publicize the operations of the 640-strong Arctic Rangers,
– station at least one Aurora long-range patrol aircraft in the Arctic,
– consider increasing the number of Auroras for sovereignty patrols,
– place reconnaissance pods on all CF-18s stationed in the North to help with sovereignty patrol,
– provide some military capacity to ice-breakers which will carry the front-line role of patrolling the passage,
– enter into negotiations with the United States over use of the passage but do not give away unlimited warship access to Canadian

waters as the price for a deal.
- failing to reach an agreement, wait and see while continuing to upgrade our presence on the waterway,
- implement a program of pilotage fees and upgraded navigation services to control all commercial traffic in the passage,
- build the Polar 8 ice-breaker, and
- establish a 'passage headquarters' as a centre for weather, ice-conditions information and surveillance, perhaps at Qausuittuq.

In the security field, certain other steps should be taken to help the military in its sovereignty role and to keep the level of militarization of the Arctic as low as possible. To these ends, we should:
- declare a 'keep-out' zone in the Arctic archipelago in which the submarines of either superpower would not be allowed to enter. (Such a zone could not be created until Canada has an adequate surveillance system of its own in which it can verify that the zone is being observed.)
- consider mining the entrances to the zone if practice shows it is not being observed,
- install an underwater radar network at all entrances to the passage and other major entry points to the Arctic archipelago,
- deploy more CF-18s to the Arctic for use in air defence and to preclude the use of any U.S. F-15s over Canadian soil,
- invest in an independent satellite system, designed for peacetime use, which gives a greater surveillance capacity, and
- investigate and acquire submarines capable of operating under ice for extended periods, which would also give Canada the capacity to deny entry to intruders into its waters.

Canadians should also be concerned about our territory becoming a staging ground for components of Star Wars and about NORAD, which could become the 'eyes and ears' for a space defence system. To prevent this, we should:
- create a new Canada–United States Defence Board which has senior political representatives on it and which oversees the functioning of the entire continental defence arrangement,
- seek to reinclude a clause in the NORAD agreement banning any contravention of the Anti-Ballistic Missile Treaty as soon as possible,
- state unequivocally that Canadian soil will not be used for testing of

any Star-Wars-related systems,
- state the Anti-Ballistic Missile Treaty should not be interpreted loosely to allow for such testing,
- stay within NORAD so long as no unacceptable Star Wars plan goes ahead,
- stay in all NORAD and Canada–United States joint defence planning studies, including SDA 2000, until a final decision on Star Wars is made, and
- push ahead with our own Star Wars 'insurance policy'; that is development of an independent surveillance system, so that we have a choice to say 'no' to Star Wars if the need arises.

In order to pay for these changes and to take into consideration the changed strategic environment, Canada must reassess its total commitment to NATO. To this end, we should:
- stay in NATO, but
- close down our two bases in southern West Germany,
- bring the Air Squadron of CF-18s back home,
- develop a rapid-deployment force, specializing in cold-weather fighting to be stationed in Schleswig-Holstein and to be on call for deployment in Norway, Denmark, or the northern front, and
- revise our NATO naval role with more emphasis on fast sovereignty-patrol and anti-submarine vessels.

As part of a new Arctic policy, Canada must also be prepared to develop its own perspective on arms control, particularly in the North. Therefore, we should:
- develop our own expertise and arms-control proposals, particularly for weapons such as submarines and cruise missiles, which most directly affect Canada,
- create the office of national-security advisor within the office of the prime minister,
- beef up the staff in external affairs working on disarmament proposals,
- hire a lobbyist to work on arms control in Washington,
- try to work out with our circumpolar neighbours some form of nuclear-weapons-free zone, and
- at the appropriate time, stop the testing of the cruise missile until the United States confines itself to the limits of the SALT II Treaty. The goal should be the end of such testing altogether.

As a final element in this new integrated approach to the Arctic, Canada should also design an Arctic element to its foreign policy. To this end, we should:

- support the Canadian Inuit in their membership in the Inuit Circumpolar Conference,
- set up a separate division in external affairs to deal with the circumpolar world,
- develop as many multilateral agreements with our circumpolar neighbours on satellites, pollution, or Arctic studies as is feasible,
- set up a polar institute in Canada to which all eight circumpolar countries would be invited,
- establish some diplomatic representation in Greenland, and
- increase the cultural links between Canada and Scandinavia.

At the outset it was argued that the age of the Arctic is coming. From whatever perspective you look, the evidence is overwhelming. This book has underlined the need for a new approach and offered a new plan of action. The destiny of the Arctic, after all, should be ours to determine. Let us make sure it does not get taken out of our hands.

List of full transits of Northwest Passage

Year	Ship	Captain	Country	Route & Remarks
1903–6	*Gjoa*	R. Amundsen	Norway	Explorer: took Route 3 westbound
1940–2	*St Roch*	H. Larsen	Canada	RCMP schooner: went eastbound via Route 3
1944	*St Roch*	H. Larsen	Canada	RCMP schooner: took Route 1 westbound
1954	CCGS *Labrador*	O. Robertson	Canada	First Coast Guard deep-draught ship to take Route 1 westbound
1957	USCG *Storis*	H. Wood	U.S.	First passage by a squadron of
	USCG *Bramble*	H. Carter	U.S.	Coast Guard ships: took Route 3
	USCG *Spar*	C. Crewing	U.S.	eastbound
1958	USN *Nautilus*	W. Anderson	U.S.	First submarine to do underwater transit (Beaufort Sea)
1960	USS *Seadragon*	G.S. Steele	U.S.	U.S. sub: took Route 2 westbound
1962	USS *Skate*	J. Calvert	U.S.	U.S. sub: took Route 2 westbound
1967	CCGS *John MacDonald*	P. Fournier	Canada	Coast-guard cutter: took Route 4 westbound
1969	*Manhattan*	R. Stuart	U.S.	Largest ship ever to cross taking Route 2, then Route 1
	CCGS *John MacDonald*	P. Fournier	Canada	Escorted *Manhattan* through Route 2, then Route 1 westbound
	USCG *Northwind*	J. McCann	U.S.	Ice-breaker: sent to help *Manhattan*
	USCG *Staten Island*	E. Walsh	U.S.	Ice-breaker: sent to help *Manhattan*
1970	CSS *Baffin*	P. Brick	Canada	Survey ships: took Route 1
	CSS *Hudson*	D. Butler	Canada	westbound
1975	*Pandora*	R. Dickinson	Canada	Survey ships: took Route 7
	Theta	K. Maro		eastbound
	CCGS *Skidegate*	P. Kalis	Canada	Ice-breaker: took Route 4 eastbound

	CCGS *John Macdonald*	G. Yarn	Canada	Ice-breaker: took Route 4 westbound to aid ships
1976	CCGS *J.E. Bernier*	P. Pelland	Canada	Ice-breaker: took Route 4 eastbound
	Canmar Explorer II	E. Harvey	Canada	Drill ship: took Route 4 westbound
1976–8	*J.E. Bernier II*	R. Bouvier	Canada	First yacht to cross, taking Route 4 westbound
1977	*Willilaw*	W. de Roos	Holland	Yacht: took Route 3 westbound
1978	CCGS *Pierre Radisson*	P. Toomey	Canada	Ice-breaker: took Route 1 eastbound
	CCGS *John MacDonald*	G. Yarn	Canada	Ice-breaker: took Route 1 westbound to help Dome in drilling
	CCGS *John MacDonald*	S. Goodyear	Canada	Ice-breaker: took Route 1 eastbound
	CCGS *Louis St Laurent*	G. Burdock	Canada	Ice-breaker: took Route 1 westbound
	MV *Canmar Kigoriak*	C. Cunningham	Canada	Ice-breaker: took Route 1 westbound
1980	CCGS *J.E. Bernier*	E. Chasse	Canada	Ice-breaker: took Route 3 eastbound
	Pandora II	R. Jones	Canada	Survey ship: took Route 3 eastbound
1981	CSS *Hudson*	F. Mauger	Canada	Survey ship: took Route 4 eastbound
	Mermaid	K. Horie	Japan	Yacht: took routes 3 and 4 westbound
	Morgan Stanley	R. Fiennes	Canada	Boston whaler: took Route 3 eastbound
1983	*Arctic Shiko*	J. Dool	Canada	Tug: took Route 4 eastbound
	Polar Circle	J.A. Strand	Canada	Survey ship: took Route 3 eastbound
1984	*Linbad Explorer*	H. Nilsson	Sweden	First passenger cruise ship to take routes 3 and 5 westbound
1985	USCG *Polar Sea*	J. Howell	U.S.	Coast-Guard vessel: took Route 1 westbound
	Arctic Helios	R. Huckfield	Canada	Supply ship: took Route 4 westbound
	Arctic Mallik	C. Eckford	Canada	Supply vessel: took Route 4 eastbound
	CCGS *John MacDonald*	G. Barry	Canada	Ice-breaker: took Route 4 westbound
	World Discoverer	H. Aye	U.S.	Passenger cruise ship: took routes 3 and 6 eastbound
1986	*Kalvik*	S. Schenk	Canada	Ice-breaking trials: took Route 1 eastbound

Source: *The Canadian Coast Guard, Northern Branch* (Ottawa: Department of Transport, 1987)

Notes

CHAPTER 1: The age of the Arctic

1 *The Observer*, 30 November 1986
2 This phrase was used by Peter Jull, *Proceedings of the Special Joint Committee of the Senate and the House of Commons on Canada's International Relations*, no. 25, 12 November 1985 (Ottawa: Supply and Services), p. 16 (hereinafter referred to as the *Special Joint Committee on Canada's International Relations*).
3 The Arctic Waters Pollution Prevention Act, *RSC*, chapt. 2 (suppl.)
4 This was the declaration of straight baselines around the Arctic archipelago, *Debates, House of Commons*, vol. 5 (1985), pp. 6462–4.
5 *Toronto Star*, 7 April 1987
6 *Toronto Star*, 6 April 1987
7 *International Herald Tribune*, 14 March 1987
8 Interview with General Paul Manson, Chief of the Defence Staff of Canada, 22 September 1986
9 *Globe and Mail*, 8 December 1986
10 *Globe and Mail*, 10 December 1986
11 *Toronto Star*, 18 March 1985
12 *Toronto Star*, 7 April 1987

CHAPTER 2: Canada: victim of a Mercator mind-set

1 George Lindsey, *Special Joint Committee on Canada's International Relations*, no. 49, 13 March 1986, p. 4
2 A circumpolar nation is generally defined as one with territory above the

Arctic Circle. Iceland, just south of the Circle, is usually included.

3 *Canadian Representatives Abroad* (Ottawa: Department of External Affairs), November 1986

4 *Canadian Press*, 13 March 1987

5 *Canadian Press*, 20 March 1987

6 *Competitiveness and Security: Directions for Canada's International Relations* (Ottawa: Supply and Services, 1985), p. 1

7 Paul Painchaud, *Special Joint Committee on Canada's International Relations*, no. 49, 13 March 1986, p. 40

8 Interview with Dr Franklyn Griffiths, 16 July 1986

9 *Independence and Internationalism* (Ottawa: Supply and Services, 1986), pp. 127–36 and cover

10 *Report of Senate Sub-Committee on National Defence: Canada's Maritime Defence* (Ottawa: Supply and Services, May 1983), p. 1

11 Ibid., pp. 48–9

12 Manson interview, 22 September 1986

13 *Debates, House of Commons*, vol. 5, 1985, p. 6462

14 *Estimates of the Government of Canada 1986–87: National Defence* (Ottawa: Supply and Services, 1986), p. 41

15 Ibid., p. 65

16 *Challenge and Commitment: A Defence Policy for Canada* (Ottawa: National Defence, June 1987), pp. 60–2 (hereinafter referred to as *Challenge and Commitment*).

17 *Report of the Senate Sub-Committee on National Defence: Manpower in Canada's Armed Forces* (Ottawa: Supply and Services, January 1982), p. 18

18 *Defence in the 70s: White Paper on Defence* (Ottawa: Information Canada, August 1971), pp. 1–5

19 *Globe and Mail*, 15 December 1986

20 Ibid.

21 Ibid.

22 As quoted in *The Northern Front* (Toronto: CBC Transcripts, 1985), p. 35

23 *Special Joint Committee on Canada's International Relations*, no. 49, 13 March 1986, p. 14

24 *The Northern Front*, p. 23

25 Interview with Paul Hellyer, 8 July 1986

26 *The Northern Front*, pp. 35–6

27 Paul Painchaud, *Special Joint Committee on Canada's International Relations*, no. 49, 13 March 1986, p. 42

28 Interview with senior Pentagon official, 17 April 1986
29 For example, see Martin Shadwick and Michael Slack, 'National Defence," *The Canadian Strategic Review: 1984* (Toronto: Canadian Institute of Strategic Studies, 1985), pp. 123-50
30 As quoted in Sandra Gwyn, 'Over Home,' *Saturday Night*, January 1987, p. 100
31 Ibid.

CHAPTER 3: Staking a human claim

1 This is the story as recounted by John Amagoalik in *Special Joint Committee on Canada's International Relations*, no. 60, 23 April 1986, pp. 80-2.
2 Ibid.
3 Ibid.
4 The group has organized itself with the name of 'Internal Exiles' and at the time of publishing it was seeking $10 million in 'damages' from the federal government.
5 Reports in both the *Toronto Star* and *Globe and Mail* for the week starting 8 December 1986 stated a few questions were asked but then the matter was dropped.
6 *Challenge and Commitment*, pp. 23-4
7 For an authoritative discussion of legal tests for sovereignty see Gordon W. Smith, 'Sovereignty in the North: The Canadian Aspect of an International Problem,' in *The Arctic Frontier*, edited by R. St. J. Macdonald (Toronto: University of Toronto Press, 1966), pp. 194-255.
8 For a discussion of law on glaciers and shelf ice see S.M. Olenicoff, 'Territorial Waters in the Arctic: The Soviet Position,' *A Rand Paper*, No. R-907-ARPA (Santa Monica: Rand Corp., July 1972), pp. 4-8.
9 Ibid., p. 8
10 For a good general discussion of background to transfer see Smith, 'Sovereignty in the North,' p. 203.
11 Ibid., pp. 203-4.
12 *Dominion Order in Council*, P.C. No. 1839, 23 September 1882
13 *Dominion Order in Council*, P.C. No. 2460, 2 October 1895
14 *Statutes of Canada*, 61 Vict., c.6, 13 June 1898
15 *Canadian Arctic Islands: Canadian Expeditions 1922-23-24-25-26* (Ottawa: Department of the Interior, 1927)
16 *Debates, House of Commons*, vol. IV (10 June 1925), pp. 4069, 4084
17 Smith, 'Sovereignty in the North,' pp. 216-21

18 V.L. Lakhtin, 'Rights over the Arctic,' as quoted in S.M. Olenicoff, 'Territorial Waters in the Arctic,' p. 4

19 *Debates, House of Commons*, vol. VII (3 August 1956), p. 6955

20 Smith, 'Sovereignty in the North,' p. 225

21 *Debates, House of Commons*, vol. V (10 September 1985), pp. 6462-4

22 Permanent Court of International Justice, 'Legal Status of Eastern Greenland' Series A/B, Fascicule No. 53, 5 April 1933

23 For a discussion of the patrol see H.C. Bach and Jorgen Taagholt, *Greenland and the Arctic Region* (Copenhagen: Information and Welfare Service of the Danish Defence, 1982), pp. 74-7.

24 Donat Pharand, *The Northwest Passage: Arctic Straits*, part of series on International Straits of the World (Boston: Martinus Nijhoff Publishers, 1984), p. 151

25 *Defence 85* (Ottawa: Department of Defence, 1986), p. 79

26 *Special Joint Committee on Canada's International Relations*, no. 25, 11 December 1985

27 *Proceedings of the Standing Commons Committee on External Affairs and National Defence*, No. 38, 10 October 1985 (Ottawa: Supply and Services Canada), p. 18. [Hereinafter referred to as *Standing Committee on National defence*.]

28 *Report of the Senate Sub-Committee on National Defence: Canada's Maritime Defence* (Ottawa: Supply and Services Canada, May 1983), p. xii

29 *Debates, House of Commons*, vol. V (10 September 1985), p. 6462

30 International Court of Justice Reports 1951, *The Fisheries Case* (United Kingdom *v* Norway), 18 December 1951, p. 152

31 John Amagoalik, *Special Joint Committee on Canada's International Relations*, pp. 75-6

32 Ibid., p. 69

33 Ibid., p. 48

34 Interview with Christian Jensen, permanent under-secretary for Ministry of Greenland, Copenhagen, 11 November 1986

CHAPTER 4: The Northwest Passage

1 Confirmation of this fact came from U.S. ambassador to Canada Thomas Niles in *Toronto Star*, 22 November 1985.

2 Formal notification was given by the United States to Canada in May 1985 through the Permanent Joint Board of Defence.

3 *Toronto Star*, 3 August 1985
4 *Toronto Star*, 7 August 1985
5 *Toronto Star*, 7 August 1985
6 *Toronto Star*, 2 August 1985
7 Canadian Hydrographic Service, *Sailing Directions: Arctic Canada*, Vol. I
  (1982), Vol. II (1985), Vol. III (1986) (Ottawa)
8 *Sailing Directions*, Vol. II, p. 51
9 Pharand, *The Northwest Passage*, pp. 20–1
10 For useful discussion of intricacies of law see ibid., pp. 88–98.
11 Film clip of Trudeau speech in Gwynne Dyer, *Defence of Canada*, shown
   on CBC TV 17 March 1986. Transcript available from CBC Toronto.
12 *International Court of Justice Reports 1949*, The Corfu Channel Case
   (United Kingdom *v* Albania), 9 April 1949, p. 1.
13 Ibid., p. 29.
14 Pharand, *The Northwest Passage*, p. 94
15 For complete list see Appendix.
16 Pharand, *The Northwest Passage*, p. 53
17 *Toronto Star*, 10 August 1985
18 *Toronto Star*, 10 August 1985
19 *Globe and Mail*, 8 December 1986
20 *Toronto Star*, 20 July 1985
21 *Globe and Mail*, 17 December 1986
22 *Debates, House of Commons*, vol. I (1963), pp. 621–3
23 *Debates, House of Commons*, vol. VI (1970), p. 5626
24 As quoted in Pharand, *The Northwest Passage*, p. 88
25 *Statement* from Bureau of Legal Affairs (Ottawa: Queen's Printer),
   December 1973
26 *Debates, House of Commons*, vol. I (1976), p. 675
27 *Debates, House of Commons*, vol. VI (1970), p. 5626
28 *Debates, House of Commons*, vol. V (1985), pp. 6462–4
29 Ibid., p. 6462
30 Ibid.
31 Ibid., p. 6263
32 Ibid., p. 6462

CHAPTER 5: Arctic gushers

1 *Toronto Star*, 9 July 1986, and *Saturday Night*, January 1987

2 *Canadian Petroleum Association Review*, November 1986, p. 8
3 Ibid.
4 *International Herald Tribune*, 14 March 1987
5 *Toronto Star*, 20 January 1987
6 For a comparative analysis, see *Petroleum Review*, May 1985, p. 42.
7 *The Arctic Marine Transportation Research and Development Plan*, Vol. I:
   Report, second edition, April 1986 (Ottawa: Sypher Consultants, August
   1985)
8 *Beaufort Sea Hydrocarbon Production and Transportation Proposal: Report
   of the Environmental Assessment Panel*, July 1984 (Ottawa: Supply and
   Services), p. 34
9 Ibid., pp. 27–9
10 Ibid., p. 34
11 Department of Indian and Northern Affairs, *The North* (Ottawa: Supply
    and Services, 1985), p. 32
12 Ibid., p. 34
13 Interview with Lars Vesterbirk, Permanent Head of Greenland Home Rule
    Office, 11 November 1986
14 *The Arctic Marine Transportation Research and Development Plan*, p. II: 9

CHAPTER 6: Time to plant the flag

1 It took seventeen months after the initial announcement for the federal
   government to decide it would allow one west-coast firm to bid on the
   project. At the last word, the contract had still not been let.
2 Interview with Canada's Chief of Defence Staff General Paul Manson, 22
   September 1986
3 For good discussion of duties of Coast Guard, RCMP, and Navy in the Arctic see W. Harriet Critchley, 'Canadian Military Requirements for Security in the Arctic,' a paper prepared for York University Conference on
   Sovereignty, Security and the Arctic, 9 May 1986.
4 Interview with Norwegian Defence Minister Johan Holst, 21 September
   1986
5 *Special Joint Committee on Canada's International Relations*, no. 25, 12
   November 1985, p. 26
6 Ibid., p. 13
7 Vesterbirk interview, 11 November 1986
8 Figures cited in *Report of Senate Subcommittee on National Defence: Cana-*

da's *Maritime Defence* (Ottawa: Supply and Services Canada, May 1983), p. 36
9 Address given to Canadian Aeronautics and Space Institute, 30 May 1984
10 *Report of Senate Subcommittee on Maritime Defence*, p. 52
11 *Globe and Mail*, 12 December 1986
12 *Canadian Press*, 27 May 1987
13 Ibid.
14 Interview with senior Pentagon official in Washington on basis any quotes attributed to 'senior official,' 17 April 1986
15 Interview with Mike MccGwire of Brookings Institute, 18 April 1986
16 Interview with Canadian general on 'no quote basis'
17 *Toronto Star*, 25 November 1985
18 *Senate Subcommittee on National Defence*, no. 39, 3 March 1983, p. 13
19 *Standing Committee on National Defence*, no. 53, 15 November 1985, pp. 4–24
20 *Challenge and Commitment*, pp. 51–5
21 Ibid., pp. 23–4
22 Statement of Canadian Centre for Arms Control, *Canadian Press*, 30 April 1987
23 *Guardian*, 4 May 1987

CHAPTER 7: Canada's Arctic: the new military frontier

1 As quoted in R.J. Sutherland, 'The Strategic Significance of the Canadian Arctic,' in R. St. J. Macdonald, ed., *The Arctic Frontier* (Toronto: University of Toronto Press, 1966), pp. 256–78
2 Interview with General Manson, 22 September 1986
3 Interview with William Arkin, 17 April 1986
4 For thorough discussion of submarines, missile ranges, and maps, see W. Harriet Critchley, 'Polar Deployment of Soviet Submarines,' in *International Journal*, XXXIX, autumn 1984, pp. 828–65, and International Institute for Strategic Studies, *The Military Balance 1986–1987* (London: Autumn 1986), p. 231 plus map
5 International Institute for Strategic Studies, *The Military Balance 1986–1987*, p. 36
6 Ibid., p. 19
7 Ibid., p. 41
8 *Los Angeles Times*, 14 June 1985

9 Ibid.

10 Ibid.

11 Ibid.

12 Interview with Don Kerr in London, 10 February 1987

13 Manson interview, 22 September 1986

14 Interview with Mike MccGwire, 18 April 1986

15 Arkin interview, 17 April 1986

16 Kerr interview, 10 February 1987

17 General Robert Herres, *Standing Committee on National Defence*, no. 54, 12 November 1985, p. 10

18 Albert Legault, *Special Joint Committee on Canada's International Relations*, no. 49, 13 March 1986, p. 27

19 Vesterbirk interview, 11 November 1986

20 Canadian Hydrographic Service, *Sailing Directions*, Vol. ɪɪ p. 179

21 *Standing Committee on National Defence*, no. 52, 6 December 1985, p. 13

22 *Globe and Mail*, 12 December 1986

23 *Special Joint Committee on Canada's International Relations*, no. 21, 20 November 1985, p. 41

24 International Institute, *The Military Balance 1986–1987*, pp. 36–43

25 Ibid., and General Herres, *Standing Committee on National Defence*, pp. 12–13

26 *Toronto Star*, 6 December 1986

27 *Globe and Mail*, 8 December 1986

28 Pharand, *The Northwest Passage*, pp. 50–2

29 Bill Keller, 'The Navy's Brash Leader,' *New York Times Magazine*, 15 December 1985, pp. 31–3

30 Arkin interview, 17 April 1986

31 Senior Pentagon official interview, 17 April 1986

32 International Institute, *The Military Balance 1986–1987*, p. 37

33 Ibid.

34 General Herres, *Standing Committee on National Defence*, no. 49, 13 March 1986, pp. 10–11

35 Ibid., p. 11

CHAPTER 8: NORAD: security at what price?

1 For a good overview of capabilities of Cheyenne Mountain see Michael

Ganley, 'NORAD Makes a Comeback as Soviet Strategic Threat Grows,' *Armed Forces Journal International*, January 1986 pp. 56–62.

2 For a more detailed explanation see General James Hartinger, 'The Resurgence of Strategic Defense,' *Defense 82*, June 1982, pp. 30–3

3 David Cox, *Canada and NORAD 1958–73: A Cautionary Perspective*, Aurora Papers no. 1, Canadian Centre for Arms Control and Disarmament, Ottawa, 1982, p. 4

4 As quoted in Hartinger, 'The Resurgence of Strategic Defense,' p. 56

5 Confirmation of this number came from General Robert Herres, current NORAD commander, in *Standing Committee on National Defence*, no. 54, 12 November 1985, p. 10

6 Hartinger, 'The Resurgence of Strategic Defense,' p. 31

7 Herres, *Standing Committee on National Defence*, p. 15

8 *Joint U.S.–Canada Defence Study 1979* (Ottawa: Supply and Services, 1980)

9 Herres, *Standing Committee on National Defence*, p. 13

10 Eric Neilsen, *Standing Committee on National Defence*, no. 56, 13 December 1985, p. 23

11 General Herres, 'Brief to the Standing Commons Committee on External Affairs and National Defence,' 11 December 1985, pp. 19–20

12 Several officials, including former cabinet minister Alvin Hamilton, have publicly complained of having to get prior approval from the United States even to land at these bases. Hamilton recalls his experience in *The Northern Front*, pp. 9–10.

13 *Standing Committee on National Defence*, no. 28, 16 September 1985, p. 8

14 Beattie Clay and K.R. Greenaway, 'Opening Up Canada's North,' *Northern Perspectives*, vol. 14, no. 4, September 1986

15 Canadian Press interview, 11 September 1986

16 Major-General Larry Ashley, *Standing Committee on National Defence*, no. 52, 6 December 1985, p. 28

17 Ibid.

18 Herres, *Standing Committee on National Defence*, p. 27

19 Presidential Directive 59 (PD-59), the White House, July 1980

20 'Brief to Standing Committee on National Defence,' no. 41, 31 October 1985, p. 5

21 Harriet Critchley, *Standing Committee on National Defence*, no. 41, 31 October 1985, p. 22

22 John Anderson, *Standing Committee on National Defence*, no. 52, 6 December 1985, p. 4
23 For example, see Govier and Colign, 'Brief to the Standing Committee on National Defence,' no. 41, 31 October 1985
24 *Special Joint Committee on Canada's International Relations*, no. 37, 29 January 1986, p. 18
25 'Brief to Standing Commons Committee on External Affairs and National Defence,' 3 December 1985, p. 11
26 *Standing Committee on National Defence*, p. 36
27 Arkin interview, 17 April 1986
28 *Standing Committee on National Defence*, p. 15
29 Ibid., pp. 18–19
30 Interview with Donald Macdonald, 24 June 1986
31 *Standing Committee on National Defence*, no. 37, 10 October 1985, p. 7

CHAPTER 9: Continental defence: a new approach

1 Full details given in Arkin interview, 17 April 1986
2 *Toronto Star*, June 10, 1985
3 *Toronto Star*, June 11, 1985
4 *Globe and Mail*, June 12, 1985
5 Ibid.
6 Joe Clark, *Standing Committee on National Defence*, no. 51, 4 December 1985, p. 25
7 *Toronto Star*, June 13, 1985
8 Ibid., p. 15
9 Arkin brief, p. 4
10 Ogdensburg Agreement, 18 August 1940
11 As quoted in *Standing Committee on National Defence*, no. 32A, 2 October 1985, p. 4
12 *Standing Committee on National Defence*, no. 37, 9 October 1985, p. 26
13 Albert Legault, *Special Joint Committee on Canada's International Relations*, no. 49, 13 March 1986, p. 32
14 Interview with Franklyn Griffiths, 16 July 1986
15 *1977 Military Posture Statement of the U.S. Joint Chiefs of Staff*, also found in Arkin brief, p. 13
16 John Hamre, 'Continental Air Defence, United States Security Policy and Canada–U.S. Defence Relations,' in G.R. Lindsey *Aerospace Defence:*

Canada's Future Role (Toronto: Wellesley Papers, September 1985), p. 25
17 See, for example, Govier and Colign Brief, p. 3
18 Interview with Barney Danson, 24 July 1986
19 *Standing Committee on National Defence*, no. 37, 9 October 1985, p. 26
20 Interview with George Ignatieff, 25 March 1985, and interview with John Halstead, 10 April 1986
21 Halstead interview, 10 April 1986
22 Ibid.
23 Nils Orvik, 'Northern Development Northern Security,' Centre for International Relations, Queen's University, *Northern Studies Series*, no. 1–83, 1983
24 Danson interview, 24 July 1986
25 Interview with Jean-Jacques Blais, 18 June 1986
26 Ibid.
27 John Anderson, *Standing Committee on National Defence*, no. 32, 2 October 1985, p. 34
28 Blais interview, 18 June 1986
29 'Trends in Continental Defence: A Canadian Perspective,' Occasional Paper of the Canadian Institute for International Peace and Security, no. 2, December 1986, Ottawa, p. 45
30 Interview with Admiral R.H. Falls, 23 May 1986
31 'Trends in Continental Defence,' p. 46
32 *Globe and Mail*, 12 March 1987
33 See *L.A. Times*, 20 June 1985
34 *Report of Senate Subcommittee on National Defence: Canada's Maritime Defence*, p. 51
35 *Fourth Report of the Standing Commons Committee on External Affairs and National Defence* (Ottawa: Supply and Services, 1986), p. 28
36 Herres, *Standing Committee on National Defence*, p. 23
37 Dr David Low, *Standing Committee on National Defence*, no. 55, 12 December 1985, p. 9
38 Ibid., p. 20
39 *Standing Committee on National Defence*, no. 53, 10 December 1985, p. 19
40 *Report of Senate Subcommittee on National Defence: Canada's Territorial Air Defence* (Ottawa: Supply and Services, Jan.
41 *Challenge and Commitment*, pp. 52–5
42 *Globe and Mail*, 5 June 1987, plus interview with Don Kerr, 8 June 1987

43 *Challenge and Commitment*, p. 52
44 *Canadian Press*, 30 April 1987
45 Kerr interview, 8 June 1987
46 Ibid.
47 *Globe and Mail*, 12 March 1987
48 *Challenge and Commitment*, p. 52
49 Kerr interview, 8 June 1987

CHAPTER 10: Star Wars and Canada

1 *Toronto Star*, 18 March 1985
2 Ibid.
3 As quoted in Lawrence S. Hagen, 'For Better or Worse: Altered States in Canada–U.S. Defence Relations,' a paper of the Canadian Centre for Arms Control and Disarmament, October 1985, p. 5
4 Interview with John Pike, 19 November 1985
5 For a good overview of initial Star Wars theory, see *The New York Times*, a six-part series entitled 'Weapons in Space,' 3–8 March 1985
6 *International Herald Tribune*, 12 February 1987
7 John Pike, 'The Strategic Defense Initiative and Canada,' a paper of the Federation of American Scientists, 17 March 1986
8 Ibid., pp. 3–4
9 Ibid., pp. 7–8
10 Ibid, pp. 6–7
11 Arkin interview, 17 April 1986
12 Danson interview, 24 July 1986
13 As quoted in Lt. Col. Richard Cammarote, "Defensive Watch,' *Air Force Magazine*, February 1985, p. 64
14 *Special Joint Committee on Canada's International Relations*, no. 49, 13 March 1986, p. 4
15 *Globe and Mail*, 7 March 1985
16 Richard Perle, 'The Strategic Defense Initiative: Addressing Some Misconceptions,' *Journal of International Affairs*, summer 1986, p. 26
17 Arkin interview, 17 April 1986
18 *Toronto Star*, 12 June 1986
19 *Toronto Star*, 12 June 1986
20 *International Herald Tribune*, 11 March 1987
21 John Anderson, *Standing Committee on National Defence*, no. 52, 6 December 1985, p. 10

22 *International Herald Tribune*, 3 March 1987
23 Douglas Ross, 'Canada, The Arctic and SDI: The Case for Early disengagement from Integrated Defence,' a paper presented to York University Conference on 'Sovereignty, Security and the Arctic,' 8 May 1986, p. 9

CHAPTER 11: West Germany: the key to the club

1 John Holmes, *Standing Committee on National Defence*, no. 37, 10 October 1985, p. 33
2 As quoted in R.B. Byers and Michael Slack, 'National Defence,' *The Canadian Strategic Review 1982*, ed. by R.B. Byers (Toronto: Canadian Institute of Strategic Studies, 1982), p. 73
3 Address of Chief of the Defence Staff to the 48th Annual Meeting of the Conference of Defence Associations, 11 January 1985, p. 28
4 Budget of the Government of Canada 1987–88
5 For a brief summary of classic position see John Anderson, *Standing Committee on National Defence*, no. 30, 1 October 1985, pp. 20–2
6 *Defence in the 70s: White Paper on Defence*, pp.1–5
7 Interview with senior diplomat on a non-attribution basis
8 *The Military Balance 1986–1987*, p. 67
9 Ibid., p. 28
10 For a full breakdown see William Arkin and Richard Fieldhouse, *Nuclear Battlefields* (Cambridge: Ballinger Publishing Co., 1985), pp. 101–19
11 *The Military Balance 1986–1987*, p. 208
12 *International Herald Tribune*, 12 November 1986
13 Hellyer interview, 8 July 1986
14 *The Military Balance 1986–1987*, p. 225
15 Hellyer interview, 8 July 1986
16 Macdonald interview, 24 June 1986
17 *National Defence News Release*: AFN: 32/86, 12 June 1986
18 Byers and Slack, 'National Defence,' p. 77
19 *Senate Committee Report on National Defence: Canada's Maritime Defence*, p. 2
20 *Jane's Fighting Ships 1984–85*, p. 133
21 For a general discussion of naval requirements see *Senate Committee Report on National Defence: Canada's Maritime Defence*, pp. 1–21
22 Ibid., pp. 34–6
23 Ibid., p. 35

CHAPTER 12: Norway and Denmark: the 'Hong Kong commitments'

1 Briefing given to reporters in Narvik 20 September 1986
2 Manson interview, 22 September 1986
3 Ibid.
4 *Challenge and Commitment*, pp. 59–63
5 See for example, Nils Orvik, 'Northern Development Northern Security'
6 Manson interview, 22 September 1986
7 Danson interview, 24 July 1986
8 *Challenge and Commitment*, pp. 62–3
9 MccGwire interview, 18 April 1986
10 *Washington Post*, 29 December 1983
11 *Investigating Kola* (London: Brassey's Defence Publishers Ltd, 1987). Passage quoted is a translation from Norwegian.
12 *Senate Committee Report on National Defence: Canada's Maritime Defence*, pp. 41–6
13 See map showing ice-free route in chapter 7
14 For discussion of Denmark's role see Flemming Nielsen, AMF – NATO's crisis Force (Copenhagen: Information and Welfare Services of the Danish Defence, 1982)
15 Interview with senior Danish defence officials on basis of no direct quotes, 7 November 1986
16 For details see Nielsen, 'AMF – NATO's Crisis Force,' pp. 12–37
17 Interviews with Danson, Macdonald, Hellyer, and Blais
18 *Senate Report on National Defence: Manpower in Canada's Armed Forces*, p. 18
19 Ibid.
20 Manson interview, 22 September 1986
21 Ibid.
22 Macdonald interview, 24 June 1986
23 Manson interview, 22 September 1986
24 Interview with senior Danish defence official on a non-attribution basis, 7 November 1986
25 Interview with Norwegian Defence Minister Johan Holst, 21 September 1986
26 Ibid.

CHAPTER 13: One role in Europe or out

1 It is called the 'Canadian-U.S. Regional Planning Group' (CUSRPG) and confirmation of its inactivity came in interviews with NATO Ambassadors George Ignatieff, John Halstead, and the current ambassador, Gordon Smith.
2 As quoted in Gwynne Dyer, *Defence of Canada*, 17 March 1986
3 *Toronto Star*, 26 May 1986 (Gallup Poll)
4 See, for example, Gwynne Dyer, *Defence of Canada*
5 *Toronto Star*, 13 April 1986
6 *The Military Balance* (Sweden) p. 85 and (Switzerland) p. 86
7 As quoted in Gwynne Dyer, *Defence of Canada*, 17 March 1986
8 Interview with Denis Healey, 22 October 1985
9 Halstead interview, 10 April 1986
10 'A Plan to Reshape NATO,' *Time*, 5 March 1983
11 *New York Times*, 15 February 1986
12 *Standing Committee on National Defence*, no. 25, 10 October 1985, p. 25
13 Interviews with Halstead and Ignatieff
14 John Holmes, *Standing Committee on National Defence*, p. 25
15 Interview with Cynthia Cannizzo, 23 December 1985
16 *Senate Committee Report on National Defence: Canada's Maritime Defence*, p. 44
17 Ibid., p. 56
18 Ibid., p. 44
19 Healey interview, 22 October 1985
20 Interview with Phillipe Moreau-Desfarges, 21 November 1986
21 Interview with George Carver, 17 April 1986
22 Interview with senior Pentagon official, 17 April 1986

CHAPTER 14: The Arctic and arms control

1 For a good discussion of the history of arms-control proposals see Ronald Purver, 'Arms Control Options in the Arctic,' a paper presented to the York University Conference on 'Sovereignty, Security and the Arctic,' Toronto, May 9, 1986
2 *Standing Committee on National Defence*, no. 56, 13 December 1985, p. 26
3 Interview with Ambassador Gordon Smith, 4 November 1986

4 *Special Joint Committee on Canada's International Relations*, no. 37, 29 January 1986, p. 7

5 For fuller discussion see R.J. Sutherland, 'The Strategic Significance of the Canadian Arctic,' in *The Arctic Frontier*, ed. R. St. J. Macdonald (Toronto: University of Toronto Press, 1966), pp. 275-6

6 As quoted in Purvey, 'Arms Control Options in the Arctic,' p. 2

7 For good discussion of how treaty works now see 'Coexisting Coldly,' *The Sunday Times Magazine*, 26 October 1986, pp. 29-39

8 Alexander Rich and Aleksandr P. Vinogradov, 'Arctic Disarmament,' *Bulletin of the Atomic Scientists*, no. 20, November 1964, pp. 21-5

9 The Antarctic Treaty of 1959

10 William Arkin and Richard Fieldhouse, *Nuclear Battlefields* (Cambridge: Ballinger Publishing Co., 1985), pp. 172-4

11 Franklyn Griffiths, *A Northern Foreign Policy*, Wellesley Papers 7 (Toronto: Canadian Institute of International Affairs, 1979)

12 Ronald Purver, *Arms Control in the North*, National Security Series May 1981 (Kingston: Queen's Centre for International Relations, 1981)

13 Interview with Ron Purver, 23 May 1986

14 For example see Douglas Ross, *Special Joint Committee on Canada's International Relations*, no 27, 18 December 1985, pp. 29-30

15 Interview with Mike MccGwire, 18 April 1986

16 Ronald Purver, 'Arms Control Options in the Arctic,' p. 35

17 *The Military Balance 1986-1987*, pp. 19 and 39

18 For a good analysis of the 1985 discussions see David Cox, 'The Strategic Proposal on Strategic Arms Reductions,' a paper of the Canadian Institute for International Peace and Security, Ottawa, 28 October 1985

19 Purver interview, 23 May 1986

20 *Globe and Mail*, 6 June 1986

CHAPTER 15: The CANDI arc: a nuclear-weapons-free zone for Canada?

1 *Toronto Star*, 15 March 1986

2 The NDP has always favoured a non-nuclear role and at its November 1986 convention the federal Liberal party passed a resolution favouring a nuclear-weapons-free zone.

3 The policy was first announced in 1978 and 1985 the last Genie nuclear missile was removed

4 See discussion above in chapter 9

5 Canada, Department of External Affairs, *Statements and Speeches*, 78/7, 26 May 1978, p. 2
6 These definitions have been the basis for discussion for all United Nations Special Sessions on Disarmament.
7 Interview with senior Pentagon official, 17 April 1986
8 *New York Times*, 16 February 1986
9 *New York Times* 16 March 1986
10 *Special Joint Committee on Canada's International Relations*, no. 49, 13 March 1986, p. 32
11 *International Herald Tribune*, 12 February 1987
12 *The Times*, 17 June 1987
13 Resolution of the first Inuit Circumpolar Conference (1977)
14 'In Self-Defence,' *Maclean's*, 21 April 1980
15 'A Proposal for a nuclear-free zone in the Arctic,' *Peace Research*, vol. 12 (October 1980)
16 'Proposal for a Circum-Arctic Demilitarized Zone (CADZ),' working paper for Project Ploughshares (October 1984)
17 *International Herald Tribune*, 15 November 1986
18 Ibid.
19 *A Nuclear Weapon Free Zone in the Nordic Area: Conditions and Options – a Norwegian View* (Oslo: Norwegian Institute of International Affairs, June 1983), pp. 233–43
20 'Our seat at the table: a Canadian menu for arms control,' *International Journal* 36 (Summer 1981), pp. 663–4
21 *Toronto Star*, 8 November 1986
22 *A Seat at the Table: The Struggle for Disarmament* (Toronto: Clark Irwin, 1972), p. 9

CHAPTER 16: A circumpolar foreign policy

1 This expression was used by Mark Gordon to describe the triennial assembly in an interview published by *Canadian Press*, 16 July 1986
2 Invitations have been sent to the Soviet Union but so far have not been acknowledged.
3 *Special Joint Committee on Canada's International Relations*, no. 25, 12 November 1985, p. 19
4 *Competitiveness and Security: Directions for Canada's International Relations* (Ottawa: Supply and Services, 1985), p. 1

5 *Canada's International Relations: Response of the Government of Canada to the Report of the Special Joint Committee* (Ottawa: External Affairs, December 1986), pp. 85–87
6 Ibid., p. 85
7 *Special Joint Committee on Canada's International Relations*, no. 60, 23 April 1986, p. 43
8 A framework agreement signed in 1983
9 Griffiths interview, 16 July 1986
10 *Toronto Star*, 17 March 1986
11 *Canadian Press*, 11 March 1987
12 For background on this project see Dr David Low, *Standing Committee on National Defence*, no. 55, 12 December 1985, pp. 19–21
13 For some background on SARSAT, see Dr Derek Schofield, *Standing Committee on National Defence*, no. 36, 10 September 1985, pp. 27–9
14 *Special Joint Committee on Canada's International Relations*, no. 49, 13 March 1986, p. 42
15 Ibid., p. 17
16 See Stanley Ing, 'Greenland Home Rule and Canada,' *International Perspectives*, Jan/Feb. 1984, p. 24
17 Vesterbirk interview, 11 November 1986
18 Nils Orvik, 'Northern Development Northern Security,' pp. 176–7
19 'Greenland's Home Rule and Arctic Sovereignty: A Case Study,' a paper presented to York University Conference on 'Sovereignty, Security and the Arctic,' Toronto, 8 May 1986, p. 3
20 *Independence and Internationalism*, p. 130
21 *Canada's International Relations: Response of the Government of Canada*, p. 86

CHAPTER 17: Conclusion

1 Interview with Tom Hockin, 9 April 1986
2 Interview with Jerry Grafstein, 9 April 1986
3 See chapter 4 for details.
4 *Canadian Press*, 18 February 1987
5 *Canadian Press*, 31 March 1987
6 *Toronto Star*, 15 September 1985
7 *Globe and Mail*, 12 March 1987
8 *Toronto Star*, 7 April 1987

9 *Toronto Star*, 12 December 1987
10 Interview with Danson, 24 July 1986
11 Interview with Macdonald, 24 June 1986
12 See chapter 7 for details

Index